To my mother
Alice Cook Park
R.C.P.

To the memory of my mother
Joy Cecelia Johnson McFarland
D.D.M.

*

Computer–Aided Exercises on Civil Procedure

Fifth Edition

By

Roger C. Park
James Edgar Hervey Chair of Litigation
University of California, Hastings College of the Law

Douglas D. McFarland
Professor of Law
Hamline University

THOMSON

WEST

Mat #40264999

COPYRIGHT © 1974–1976, 1983 ROGER PARK
COPYRIGHT © 1991, 1995 WEST PUBLISHING CO.
© 2004 West, a Thomson business
    610 Opperman Drive
    P.O. Box 64526
    St. Paul, MN 55164–0526
    1–800–328–9352

Printed in the United States of America
ISBN 0–314–15418–3

TEXT IS PRINTED ON 10% POST CONSUMER RECYCLED PAPER

PREFACE

This fifth edition carries forward the philosophy and structure of the four earlier editions. The book is not a comprehensive treatise on the subject of civil procedure, yet it provides a mixture of expository text, cases, and self-testing questions in nearly all of the major areas of the subject. This edition features a substantial new exercise on joinder devices and supplemental jurisdiction. Other exercises have been substantially revised. The individual exercises also are reorganized and expanded so that they follow a more standardized pattern: expository text on the topic area, workbook questions, and introduction to the computer-aided exercise(s).

This book, and the accompanying computer exercises available through the Center for Computer-Assisted Legal Instruction (CALI),[1] are intended to provide a challenging educational experience. For each exercise, students should read the text in this book and answer the questions before accessing the rest of the exercise on their computer.

Professors choosing to assign only some of the exercises—or students looking for additional work only in certain areas of the subject—may especially want to consider Exercise Two: Jurisdiction; Exercise Three: Pleading a Complaint; Exercise Five: Motions to Dismiss and Waiver under Federal Rule 12; Exercise Eight: Summary Judgment; and Exercise Eleven: Preclusion. New Exercise Six: Joinder and Supplemental Jurisdiction may prove worthy to join this list. Additionally, Exercise One: Holding and Dicta in the Context of a Diversity Case is an excellent introduction to legal method.

The first two editions of this book, by Roger Park, included Exercises One (Holding and Dicta in the Context of a Diversity Case), Two (Jurisdiction), Three (Pleading a Complaint), Four (Demurrers and Judgments on the Pleadings), Five (Motions to Dismiss and Waiver Under Rule 12), Nine (Judgment as a Matter of Law), and Ten (Evidence for Civil Procedure Students). For the last three editions of

---

[1]The Center for Computer-Assisted Legal Instruction (CALI) provides computer-aided lessons in a broad range of legal subjects to its nearly 200 member law schools and their students. These lessons are available on the CALI website [   ] and on CDs distributed to the law schools annually. As of the writing of this fifth edition in 2004, the CALI library contains over 400 lessons, including 17 in civil procedure. The school's reference librarian or computer services manager should be able to provide assistance on access to these lessons. The user can also write or call CALI at 565 West Adams Street, Chicago, IL 60661, telephone: 312.906.5307, fax: 312.906.5338, Email: jmayer@cali.org.

V

this book, Douglas McFarland has edited the above exercises and added Exercises Six (Joinder and Supplemental Jurisdiction), Seven (Discovery), Eight (Summary Judgment), and Eleven (Preclusion). Accordingly, the book has become more comprehensive, expanding from seven to eleven exercises. Of course, each new edition incorporates changes and updates in procedural law.

All of the information necessary to prepare for a computer exercise is contained in this book. Reference to additional materials may be useful, but is not necessary. Each exercise can be assigned separately. No exercise is a prerequisite for another. In fact, students will find the expository material and workbook questions in each exercise independently valuable even without completing the computer-aided exercise for that chapter. The exercises are valuable either to provide additional understanding and self-testing of subjects discussed in class or as primary substitutes for areas not covered in depth in class.

In general, the computer-aided exercises follow a non-linear branching format. They seek to present challenges and questions instead of rote learning or leading students through an error-free educational experience. Although the exercises eventually evaluate student answers, they sometimes eschew immediate feedback in favor of development of a line of questions. The ideal is creation of a classroom-like Socratic dialogue. For a description of general goals and educational theory of the exercises, see Roger C. Park & Russell Burris, *Computer-Aided Instruction in Law: Theories, Techniques, and Trepidations*, 1978 AM.B.FOUND.RES.J. 1. This book and accompanying computer exercises cannot reproduce the spontaneity and flexibility of the live classroom, but they can be a useful supplement. They require an active learning process in which students respond to questions dozens of times during each hour of instruction, and receive prompt evaluation of their answers.

Another benefit of computer-aided instruction is its "individualized" nature. Law professors and students should not take this literally, however. Surveys administered at several law schools indicate that an overwhelming majority of students believe that the exercises are more valuable when done in pairs or threes instead of alone. Students who do the exercises with a partner are more likely to consider their responses carefully and to enjoy the experience. They also have lively discussions about what their response should be and why the computer responded as it did.

As with previous editions, we continue to welcome and solicit comments from professors and students about the book and the computer exercises.

ROGER C. PARK
DOUGLAS D. MCFARLAND

October, 2004

TABLE OF CONTENTS

ESTIMATED TIME AT THE COMPUTER

The following is an estimate of the amount of time that should be allowed for completion of the computer portion of each of the exercises that we have written. Additional exercises on civil procedure distributed by CALI, but not written by us, are included as an aid to users. The amount of time will, of course, differ from student to student. These estimates assume two students will be taking the exercise together and they will discuss the computer's questions and responses. The first two exercises should if possible be completed in one sitting because the answers to initial questions affect the computer's responses to later questions. Other exercises may be done in segments—the computer will ask students where they want to recommence.

Exercise One: Holding and Dicta in the Context of a Diversity Case
    CALI CIV 05: Analysis of a Diversity Jurisdiction Case   1.5 hours

Exercise Two: Jurisdiction
    CALI CIV 03: Jurisdiction and Venue   2 hours
    CALI CIV 19: Jurisdiction over the Person

Exercise Three: Pleading a Complaint
    CALI CIV 01: Drafting a Complaint   2 hours

Exercise Four: Demurrers and Judgments on the Pleadings
    CALI CIV 02: Demurrers and Judgments on the Pleadings   1 hour

Computer–Aided Exercises on Civil Procedure

*

EXERCISE ONE

Holding and Dicta in the Context of a Diversity Case

I. OF *STARE DECISIS*, HOLDING, AND DICTA

A. The Law of Stare Decisis

When presented with a case that requires decision on a controlling issue of first impression, a court may look to history, custom, logic, morals, public policy, and justice considerations as guides to decision. When presented with a case that presents a controlling issue the court has already decided in a previous case, the court may look to its previous decision alone. Once a legal question has been decided by a court, the court will follow its decision in subsequent cases presenting the same legal question. That is the legal doctrine known by its Latin name *stare decisis*,[1] or simply as following precedent.

Stare decisis requires that after a ruling on a question of law necessary to decision in a case, the ruling becomes a binding authority in that court and lower courts[2] in future cases in which the same question of law is presented for decision. The court will be bound by its earlier decision simply because it is an earlier decision, even though the court may believe a different result would be better.

1. The complete Latin phrase "*stare decisis et non quieta movere*" is translated "stand by precedents and not disturb settled points."

2. The earlier decision binds lower courts in the same judicial system, e.g., a decision of the Supreme Court of the United States binds later decisions in federal courts of appeal and district courts. The decision does not bind courts in other judicial systems, such as state courts, although it will be persuasive authority.

Certainly important public policies support application of the doctrine of *stare decisis* instead of *de novo* decision of *every* case. The doctrine recognizes that law should provide certainty and definiteness both so that judges decide on principle instead of what may appear to be personal whims and so that lawyers can predict the result of future cases. People structure their actions in reliance on the law. The law treats people equally. The courts are able to dispose of cases with efficiency. Even when a court decides to change the law, it will do so only after extended consideration of the prior decision, which helps to ensure that the new law is sound. The Supreme Court has expressed these policies in the following words:

> The doctrine of *stare decisis* imposes a severe burden on the litigant who asks us to disavow one of our precedents. For that doctrine not only plays an important role in orderly adjudication; it also serves the broader societal interests in evenhanded, consistent, and predictable application of legal rules. When rights have been created or modified in reliance on established rules of law, the arguments against their change have special force.[3]

The doctrine of *stare decisis* is not as dominating as it might thus far appear. First, it applies only when the facts of the second case are sufficiently similar to the facts of the precedent case that the second court decides the cases should be treated alike. Oftentimes, the second court will reject the binding effect of the first decision by distinguishing the case on the facts. Second, *stare decisis* does not apply to everything a court might write in a judicial opinion. It applies only to the actual, narrow "holding" of the earlier case. The concept of holding is loosely synonymous with the *ratio decidendi* of the opinion, i.e., the reason the court gives for its result (although a careful reader of an opinion might decide the reason the court gives for its decision is not the actual holding of the case). A comment the court might express during the course of the opinion that does not control the actual result is known as a dictum; the plural of such comments is dicta. The *stare decisis*, or binding effect, of the decision applies only to the holding, or *ratio decidendi*, and not to any dicta the court might have seen fit to mention along the way. A sound statement of this is the following:

> [N]ot every statement made in a judicial decision is an authoritative source to be followed in a later case presenting a similar situation. Only those statements in an earlier decision which may be said to constitute the *ratio decidendi* of that

---

3. Thomas v. Washington Gas Light Co., 448 U.S. 261, 272, 100 S.Ct. 2647, 2656, 65 L.Ed.2d 757, 767 (1980).

case are held to be binding, as a matter of general principle, in subsequent cases. Propositions not partaking of the character of *ratio decidendi* may be disregarded by the judge deciding the later case. Such nonauthoritative statements are usually referred to as *dicta* or (if they are quite unessential for the determination of the points at issue) *obiter dicta*.[4]

The holding of a case is binding. Dicta may be disregarded. Clearly, judges and lawyers must be able to separate the holding from a dictum. Developing that ability to analyze and dissect court opinions is one of the most important tasks for a law student in the first year of law school. The remainder of this exercise assists in that task.

B. The Concepts of Holding and Dictum

We begin with a hypothetical court opinion. Suppose that plaintiff [P] brings a tort suit in federal district court under diversity of citizenship jurisdiction. The governing statute, 28 U.S.C. § 1332(a), requires that the "matter in controversy" must exceed $75,000. P in the complaint asks for $85,000 in compensatory damages. Defendant [D] moves under Federal Rule of Civil Procedure 12(b)(1) to dismiss on the ground that P will be unable to convince the jury to award more than $75,000. The district judge denies the motion, writing "The face of the complaint controls the amount in controversy." The opinion also notes "Interest and costs cannot be added." Finally, the judge ruminates about the increasing federal caseload and concludes "The attorney for any plaintiff who files an inadequate amount diversity claim should be subject to Federal Rule 11 sanctions."

These three statements are treated differently. Lawyers would describe the statement about the face of the complaint as the holding, or the *ratio decidendi*, of the case. The other two statements would be classified as dicta; the last statement about Rule 11, since it is far from the holding of the case—and indeed would be relevant only had the decision been for D instead of for P— might be called an obiter dictum.

Sometime later another federal judge is presented with a similar case. This court distinguishes P's case on its facts and rules that the face of the complaint does not control when to a legal certainty plaintiff's recovery cannot exceed $75,000. Then another federal court interprets P's case to apply only to pleading in good faith, and not to a situation where plaintiff has in bad faith claimed

4. EDGAR BODENHEIMER, JURISPRUDENCE: THE PHILOSOPHY AND METHOD OF THE LAW 432 (Rev. ed. 1974).

in excess of $75,000. Still another federal court rules that interest can be considered when it is the basis of the claim, such as interest on a loan.

All of these cases add qualifications to the rule announced in P's case without rejecting it on its facts. Does this mean that a lawyer who reads the holding of the case as "The face of the complaint controls the amount in controversy" is wrong?

We answer no, because that is an accurate statement of the decision of the court on the facts of the case before it. Lawyers describe the court's statement about the face of the complaint as holding rather than dictum, even though recognizing that the holding may be qualified in a subsequent case arising in a different factual context. In that subsequent case, the lawyer will wish to state the holding of the first case broadly or narrowly, depending on which interpretation will favor the lawyer's client.[5]

Some other scholars might answer yes. Because of the expanding and contracting nature of judicial precedent, one scholar has asserted that every statement of a rule of law in a judicial opinion is "mere dictum."[6] Another has argued that the holding of a case should be determined from the material facts relied on by the court, not by the rules of law set forth in its opinion.[7] Another

5. Karl Llewellyn describes the process of extending and narrowing precedent and advises students as follows:

> Applying this two-faced doctrine of precedent to your work in a case class you get, it seems to me, some such result as this: You read each case from the angle of its *maximum* value as a precedent, at least from the angle of its maximum value as a precedent *of the first water*. You will recall that I recommended taking down the ratio decidendi in substantially the court's own words. You see now what I had in mind. Contrariwise, you will also read each case for its *minimum* value as a precedent, to set against the maximum. In doing this you have your eyes out for the narrow issue in the case, the narrower the better. The first question is, how much can this case fairly be made to stand for by a later court to whom the precedent is welcome? You may well add—though this will be slightly flawed authority—the dicta which appear to have been well considered. The second question is, how much is there in this case that cannot be got around, even by a later court that wishes to avoid it?

Karl N. Llewellyn, The Bramble Bush 69 (1951).

6. The determination of similarity or difference is the function of each judge. Where caselaw is considered and there is no statute, he is not bound by the statement of the rule of law made by the prior judge even in that controlling case. The statement is mere dictum, and this means that the judge in the present case may find irrelevant the existence or absence of facts which prior judges find important.

Edward H. Levi, An Introduction to Legal Reasoning 2–3 (1964).

7. *See* Arthur L. Goodhart, *Determining the Ratio Decidendi of a Case,* 40 Yale L.J. 161, 182 (1930).

has said that the true rule of a case is not what the court said, but what a later court will say the case held.[8]

These views are possibly misleading. Statements of rules of law in an opinion are not mere epiphenomena—not mere bothersome noise that accompanies the business of hammering out facts and a decision. The rule of law stated in P's case tells us what facts the court thought important. The court found jurisdiction over P's case because the complaint demanded a recovery exceeding $75,000, not because the facts pleaded could be recast into a federal question, even though such a suggestion might appear in the court's opinion. A subsequent court looking at the case would scrutinize the facts and language relating to the jurisdictional amount, not the facts and language relating to a possible federal question. And the rule that "The face of the complaint controls the amount in controversy" might be overruled, modified, distinguished, or refined, but it cannot be ignored with a clear conscience.

The court's statement about the face of the complaint is better described as holding, not dictum, even though we may recognize that any broad statement of holding may be qualified in a subsequent case arising in a somewhat different factual context.

The term holding, as used in this exercise, is not meant to describe a rule of law that will never be qualified or refined in subsequent cases. Rather, holding is used to describe the result reached by the court on the facts of the case before it. Such rules are not immune from subsequent modification, but they are at least partly free from the infirmities of dicta. Rules stated in dicta have diminished significance because they concern matters that probably were not briefed or argued, and so were not carefully considered by the court. Also, the judges of the court are familiar with the uses of precedent and the conventions of the legal profession, so they normally will not expect dicta to be given the same respect as holding. In fact, some of the judges who signed on to the opinion might have disagreed with its dicta, but refrained from explaining their position because of an expectation that the dicta would be lightly treated.

This exercise proceeds on the assumption that a lawyer will distinguish holding from dicta in a fashion that permits a statement of a general rule of law to be characterized as holding. At the same time, you should recognize that whether a rule is a holding or a dictum is only one of many considerations taken into account by

---

8. "[T]he distinction [is] between the ratio decidendi, the court's own version of the rule of the case, and the *true* rule of the case, to wit, what *it will be made to stand for by another later court*." KARL N. LLEWELLYN, THE BRAMBLE BUSH 52 (1951).

subsequent courts in deciding on the weight and scope to be given to the rule. A subsequent court may give full precedential weight to a welcome dictum of an earlier opinion, or, because a broadly stated holding shares some of the infirmities of a dictum, a subsequent court may properly narrow it in factually distinguishable cases.

The following paragraphs set forth definitions of the terms holding and dictum. These definitions are consistent with usage in ordinary discourse among lawyers. You should bear in mind, however, that no set of definitions could possibly embrace all of the different meanings that have been given to these concepts by courts, lawyers, and scholars.

1. A Holding Is a Rule of Law Applied by the Court to the Case Before It

a. The rule must have been *applied* by the court. That is, the rule must have been applicable to the facts before the court, and the rule must apparently have influenced the court in reaching its result. If a rule meets these requirements, it is holding even if the court would probably have reached the same result had it declined to accept the rule, and even if the same result could have been reached by framing a more narrow rule.

Examples:

(1) An appellate opinion reverses a jury verdict for plaintiff on the ground that the jury instructions were erroneous. The rule stated in the case is holding, even though the court suggests that, had it declined to accept the defendant's argument on the instructions, it would have reversed the verdict anyway on the ground that the evidence was insufficient to support the verdict.[9]

(2) A wife confesses in confidence to her husband that she committed a crime. At trial of the wife, the husband refuses to testify about the confession. He is held in contempt. The appellate court reverses, declaring that "No one may be compelled to testify against a spouse in any criminal proceeding." The broadly-stated principle is holding, even though the same result could have been reached by adopting a narrower rule that excluded compelled testimony only about confidential communications.

b. The rule of law need not have been *stated* by the court. All cases have holdings, but in some cases the court does not attempt to state any general rule of law.

9. *Cf.* Henry Friendly, *In Praise of Erie-and of the New Federal Common Law,* 39 N.Y.U.L.REV. 383, 385–86 (1964) ("A court's stated and, on its view, necessary basis for deciding does not become dictum because a critic would have decided on another basis").

Example:

An appellate opinion reviewing a defendant's verdict in a personal injury case begins with a three-page statement of facts pointing out that the defendant's lawyer brought improper evidence to the jury's attention, made an inflammatory closing argument, and engaged in other inappropriate conduct throughout the trial. After its statement of facts, the court closes its opinion by stating simply "In the circumstances of this case, the defense counsel's conduct was so reprehensible that we feel compelled to reverse." A lawyer attempting to summarize the holding of this case in a meaningful fashion would have to generalize; no particular passage from the court's opinion could be quoted as the holding.

2. A Rule of Law Stated in an Opinion is Dictum if the Rule Is Not Applicable to the Facts Before the Court

Example:

In a slander case, the court upholds a verdict against a prosecutor who made untrue statements about a criminal defendant at a press conference. The court opines that the prosecutor's statements would have been privileged had they been made during the course of courtroom proceedings instead of at a press conference. The court's statement about courtroom privilege is dictum, since it does not apply to the facts of the case before it.

3. A Rule of Law Stated in an Opinion Is Dictum if the Rule Does Not Contribute Support to the Result Reached by the Court

a. This requirement means that an opinion's statement of legal doctrine must not only apply to the facts but also support the result. The holding *must follow the result* in the case. This requirement is often expressed by saying that the holding must be "necessary" to the result, but that seems to be too strict a statement of the requirement, since a person could always conceive of a way in which the court could have reached the same result on another ground or endorsed a narrower rule of decision; no rule of law stated in an opinion is absolutely necessary to the result.[10] The definition set forth here adopts a more permissive test based upon whether the stated rule "supports" the result. It thus sweeps into its category of holding broad statements of law that some lawyers would characterize as dicta on grounds that the statements were not necessary to the result.[11]

10. Literal adherence to the necessity principle would lead to the position espoused by Professor Edward Levi in n. 6, *supra*, that all statements of rules of law in an opinion are dicta.

11. Under this holding-dictum distinction, by designating a statement of a rule of law as holding, one is merely suggesting that it is entitled to the weight accorded

Examples:

(1) An appellate opinion in one paragraph reverses the trial court for failure to grant plaintiff the proper number of peremptory challenges. The opinion then continues for several pages to analyze the tort doctrine of proximate cause "since this case will have to be retried," and concludes that the trial court's application of proximate cause was correct. The holding of the case cannot pertain to proximate cause because the case was reversed, and the result of the proximate cause discussion would have produced an affirmance. The holding lies in the ruling on peremptory challenges.

(2) In a libel case, a jury returns a verdict against a newspaper that had printed an untrue story about a movie star. The trial judge had instructed the jury that since movie stars are public figures, news stories about them are conditionally privileged; therefore, the movie star would recover damages only by establishing that the newspaper either knew the story was false or acted with reckless disregard of whether the story was true or false.

The appellate court agrees with the instruction that stories about movie stars are conditionally privileged, yet it affirms the judgment against the newspaper on grounds that the movie star produced sufficient evidence to justify a verdict that the newspaper knew that the story was false.

The appellate court's statement that stories about movie stars are conditionally privileged is dictum; although applicable to the facts before the court, the statement does not support the result reached. (Had the court reversed on grounds that the evidence was insufficient, the court's statement about privilege may have been holding instead of dictum.)

b. When a court states more than one ground for its decision, each may be a holding of the court, so long as each contributes support to the result. This is so even though any one of the grounds relied on independently would support the result. Holdings of this nature are often called "alternative holdings."

Example:

Plaintiff sues the state, claiming benefits provided by state statute for persons who served in the war in Iraq. Plaintiff had enlisted in the Army during the war and served at Fort Benning, Georgia, for five weeks before receiving a medical discharge. The trial judge grants a defense motion for summary judgment, and the appellate court affirms, stating that

a proposition that was probably argued before the court and given careful consideration by the court. Designation as holding does not mean that all of the particulars of the stated rule will be followed as binding precedent. Even lower courts, which lack the power to overrule the prior decision, may nevertheless narrow it or distinguish it. The broader the holding, the more likely this narrowing will take place. Whether a statement is holding or dictum is only one of many considerations that subsequent courts will take into account in determining what precedential message to draw from it.

plaintiff is ineligible for benefits (1) because the statute applies only to persons who serve their entire enlistment period, and (2) because the statute applies only to persons actually stationed in Iraq. Both of the rulings are holdings of the court.

C. Stating the Holding of a Case in Class

A question asking you for the holding of a case requests the precedential message. To prepare a satisfactory answer, a student must discard irrelevant facts, separate holding from dicta, and decide what issues were framed for decision in the procedural posture of the case. Then you must summarize the essence of the case. If you cannot do these things, you probably do not really understand the case. Certainly the holding cannot be extemporized on the spot in class: it must be carefully crafted, probably in a case brief, ahead of time.

The following guidelines may be helpful in formulating the holding of a case:

1. Formulate a rule that would be helpful to a lawyer *who has not read the case* and wants to know what the case holds. "The court held that the plaintiff was entitled to damages" is useless. It is not a summary of any rule of law established by the case. It is merely a statement of the procedural result. Even the length of the supposed holding gives away its inadequacy. A holding will seldom be so short; it must contain enough detail so that a person who has not read the case can understand the rule of law the case establishes as a precedent.

2. State the holding that is most relevant to the purpose for which the case is being studied. A case may have multiple holdings. Suppose that a case has been appealed because plaintiff claims the trial judge denied a valid jurisdictional defense, denied an amendment to the complaint, excluded admissible evidence, and erroneously instructed on the law of products liability. Any of these grounds would be sufficient for reversal. When the appellate court determines there was no error, it will necessarily have produced a holding on each one of these issues.

When asked to state the holding of a case, you are expected to choose from among these holdings the one that is most germane to the topic being studied. For example, if you are studying jurisdiction, then you should state the court's holding on jurisdiction.

3. State the holding at a level of generality that is useful for the purpose for which the case is being studied.

Your goal is to state the holding at a high level of generality so that the precedent can be applied to other cases. At the same time, the holding can be no broader than the rule of law established by the case. Finding the right level of generality/specificity is a skill learned over time. Beginning students often state holdings at such a high level of generality that they fail to show how the case has contributed to the body of precedent being studied.

Examples:

(1) Suppose that the general law governing personal jurisdiction over a defendant served by a long-arm statute is that the defendant must have minimum contacts so that maintenance of the suit in the state does not offend traditional notions of fair play and substantial justice. This was the holding of a famous Supreme Court decision in 1945.[12] Since that year, thousands of cases have mentioned the minimum contacts language. Your casebook contains a series of cases interpreting this rule. Undoubtedly almost every case contains somewhere in the opinion this language about minimum contacts. Although this rule is one of the holdings of these cases, stating the holding at such a high level of generality is pointless. You do not advance the inquiry at all. You should state a holding that adds some additional content to the basic rule. In a case that applies the language to specific facts, for example, the holding might be "A defendant seller who solicits and purposefully enters a single contract for goods to be shipped into the state has sufficient minimum contacts to support personal jurisdiction by the state over it in an action to collect damages when the goods shipped into the state are defective." One can be no more general without losing the rule of law established by the holding.

(2) In your first torts class, you read a case in which defendant playfully slaps plaintiff lightly across the face. The appellate court affirms a verdict for plaintiff for the intentional tort of battery. To say the holding is "A battery is an intentional touching of the person that is harmful or offensive" is worth little. It merely restates the law that has existed for hundreds of years prior to this case. Instead the holding should center on what this case adds to the law. It might be "A playful slap to the face is sufficient to establish an offensive touching of the person as an element of a battery."

Although beginning law students tend to err on the side of excessive generality, they also can state a holding at a level that is too specific for the purpose for which the case is being studied. One way of stating a holding is to recite all of the relevant facts and then describe the result that the court reached on those facts; a holding so narrowly tied to the facts of the case will not usually be a useful study aid. You should remember that your first-year

12. International Shoe Co. v. Washington, 326 U.S. 310, 66 S.Ct. 154, 90 L.Ed. 95 (1945).

courses are survey courses, covering vast areas of doctrine in a short period. Your statement of a holding should be general enough to contribute to a broad doctrinal framework. To achieve a general statement, you must necessarily omit some possibly relevant facts.

4. Use the court's own language from the opinion when possible.

In your attempt to state a holding at a useful level of generality, you may find language you can quote directly from the opinion. Sometimes the court will write "our holding today is" or "we decide the issue of." You may be able simply to lift an entire sentence as your holding, but be careful. Some such statements in opinions precede excellent holdings; others precede language no more valuable than "whether the case should be reversed." Even when the court does not provide such an obvious guide to its holding, you will often be able to—and should—seize on a sentence, phrase, or key words from the opinion that build your holding.

You should construct your holding entirely from your own language only when you conclude that none of the court's phrasing adequately captures its holding. You will be unable to lift language from the opinion in a surprisingly large number of cases.

II. WRITTEN EXERCISE: STATING THE HOLDING OF A CASE

You are attending your first civil procedure class. You have been given an advance assignment to read and brief *Louisville & Nashville R.R. v. Mottley,* 211 U.S. 149, 29 S.Ct. 42, 53 L.Ed. 126 (1908). This case is in a section of your casebook entitled "The General Definition of Federal Question Jurisdiction."

Read the following opinion with an eye to stating the holding. At the end of the opinion, you will be asked to state the holding. You will also be asked to evaluate seven possible statements of the holding.

LOUISVILLE & NASHVILLE RAILROAD CO. v. MOTTLEY
Supreme Court of the United States, 1908.
211 U.S. 149, 29 S.Ct. 42, 53 L.Ed. 126.

The appellees (husband and wife), being residents and citizens of Kentucky, brought this suit in equity in the Circuit Court of the United States for the Western District of Kentucky against the appellant, a railroad company and a citizen of the same State. The object of the suit was to compel the specific performance of the following contract:

"Louisville, Ky., Oct. 2nd, 1871."

"The Louisville & Nashville Railroad Company in consideration that E.L. Mottley and wife, Annie E. Mottley, have this day released Company from all damages or claims for damages for injuries received by them on the 7th of September, 1871, in consequence of a collision of trains on the railroad of said Company at Randolph's Station, Jefferson County, Kentucky, hereby agrees to issue free passes on said Railroad and branches now existing or to exist, to said E.L. & Annie E. Mottley for the remainder of the present year, and thereafter to renew said passes annually during the lives of said Mottley and wife or either of them."

The bill alleged that in September, 1871, plaintiffs, while passengers upon the defendant railroad, were injured by the defendant's negligence, and released their respective claims for damages in consideration of the agreement for transportation during their lives, expressed in the contract. It is alleged that the contract was performed by the defendant up to January 1, 1907, when the defendant declined to renew the passes. The bill then alleges that the refusal to comply with the contract was based solely upon that part of the act of Congress of June 29, 1906 (34 Stat. at L. 584, Chap. 3591, U.S.Comp.Stat.Supp.1907, p. 892), which forbids the giving of free passes or free transportation. The bill further alleges: First, that the act of Congress referred to does not prohibit the giving of passes under the circumstances of this case; and, second, that, if the law is to be construed as prohibiting such passes, it is in conflict with the 5th Amendment of the Constitution, because it deprives the plaintiffs of their property without due process of law. The defendant demurred to the bill. The judge of the circuit court overruled the demurrer, entered a decree for the relief prayed for, and the defendant appealed directly to this court....

MR. JUSTICE MOODY, after making the foregoing statement, delivered the opinion of the court.

Two questions of law were raised by the demurrer to the bill, were brought here by appeal, and have been argued before us. They are, first, whether that part of the act of Congress of June 29, 1906 (34 Stat. at L. 584, Chap. 3591, U.S.Comp.Stat.Supp.1907, p. 892), which forbids the giving of free passes or the collection of any different compensation for transportation of passengers than that specified in the tariff filed, makes it unlawful to perform a contract for transportation of persons who, in good faith, before the passage of the act, had accepted such contract in satisfaction of a valid cause of action against the railroad; and, second, whether the statute, if it should be construed to render such a contract unlawful, is in violation of the 5th Amendment of the Constitution of the United States. We do not deem it necessary, however, to consider either of these questions, because, in our opinion, the court below was without jurisdiction of the cause. Neither party had questioned that jurisdiction, but it is the duty of this court to see to it that the jurisdiction of the circuit court, which is defined and limited by statute, is not exceeded. This duty we have frequently performed of our own motion. [Citations omitted.]

There was no diversity of citizenship, and it is not and cannot be suggested that there was any ground of jurisdiction, except that the case was a "suit . . . arising under the Constitution or laws of the United States." Act of August 13, 1888, L. 866, 25 Stat. 433, 434. It is the settled interpretation of these words, as used in this statute, conferring jurisdiction, that a suit arises under the Constitution and laws of the United States only when the plaintiff's statement of his own cause of action shows that it is based upon those laws or that Constitution. It is not enough that the plaintiff alleges some anticipated defense to his cause of action, and asserts that the defense is invalidated by some provision of the Constitution of the United States. Although such allegations show that very likely, in the course of the litigation, a question under the Constitution would arise, they do not show that the suit, that is, the plaintiff's original cause of action, arises under the Constitution. . . . [I]n Boston & M. Consol. Copper & S. Min. Co. v. Montana Ore Purchasing Co., 188 U.S. 632, 47 L.Ed. 626, 23 Sup.Ct.Rep. 434, the plaintiff brought suit in the circuit court of the United States for the conversion of copper ore and for an injunction against its continuance. The plaintiff then alleged, for the purpose of showing jurisdiction, in substance, that the defendant would set up in defense certain laws of the United States. The cause was held to be beyond the jurisdiction of the circuit court, the court saying, by Mr. Justice Peckham (pp. 638, 639):

"It would be wholly unnecessary and improper, in order to prove complainant's cause of action, to go into any matters of defense which the defendants might possibly set up, and then attempt to reply to such defense, and thus, if possible, to show that a Federal question might or probably would arise in the course of the trial of the case. To allege such defense and then make an answer to it before the defendant has the opportunity to itself plead or prove its own defense is inconsis-

13

tent with any known rule of pleading, so far as we are aware, and is improper.

"The rule is a reasonable and just one that the complainant in the first instance shall be confined to a statement of its cause of action, leaving to the defendant to set up in his answer what his defense is, and, if anything more than a denial of complainant's cause of action, imposing upon the defendant the burden of proving such defense.

"Conforming itself to that rule, the complainant would not, in the assertion of proof of its cause of action, bring up a single Federal question. The presentation of its cause of action would not show that it was one arising under the Constitution or laws of the United States.

"The only way in which it might be claimed that a Federal question was presented would be in the complainant's statement of what the defense of defendants would be, and complainant's answer to such defense. Under these circumstances the case is brought within the rule laid down in Tennessee v. Union & Planters' Bank, *supra*. That case has been cited and approved many times since. . . ."

It is ordered that

the Judgment be reversed and the case remitted to the Circuit Court with instructions to dismiss the suit for want of jurisdiction.

You anticipate that in class the professor will ask "What is the holding of *Mottley*?" Of course your answer must be prepared ahead of time in your brief. State here your wording of the holding in *Mottley*.

_____

_____

_____

_____

Some mistakes in stating a holding are common. See whether any of the "Common Mistakes" listed below apply to your statement of the holding.

COMMON MISTAKES IN STATING A HOLDING

1. Inaccurately describing a rule of law applied by the court.

2. Stating a dictum instead of holding.

3. Stating a rule of law that is one of the holdings of the case, but not the holding most relevant to the purpose for which the case has been read.

4. Stating a rule of law in terms too general to be useful for the purpose for which the case has been read.

5. Stating a rule of law in terms too specific to be useful for the purpose for which the case has been read.

6. Stating the result of the case instead of stating a rule of law.

Now that you have stated your own formulation of the holding in *Mottley,* assume that the professor asks the same question to eight of your classmates. Consider each of the following answers and decide whether it would be satisfactory, or whether it is flawed by one of the above Common Mistakes in Stating a Holding. After making your own evaluations, you can then compare your answers with the authors' evaluations that follow.

ANSWER 1. Where there is no diversity of citizenship or other basis for federal jurisdiction, a federal court should dismiss the case before it.

Is this a satisfactory statement of the holding? Circle yes or no.

If no, why not? Answer with a number from the Common Mistakes in Stating a Holding. _____

ANSWER 2. The Supreme Court may consider an issue of subject matter jurisdiction on its own motion, even if the parties did not raise the issue below.

Is this a satisfactory statement of the holding? Circle yes or no.

If no, why not? Answer with a number from the Common Mistakes in Stating a Holding. _____

ANSWER 3. In a bill demanding specific performance of a contract, allegations that the defendant has based its refusal to perform the contract upon federal law are superfluous.

Is this a satisfactory statement of the holding? Circle yes or no.

If no, why not? Answer with a number from the Common Mistakes in Stating a Holding. _____

ANSWER 4. Plaintiffs asking for specific performance of a contract cannot create federal question jurisdiction by alleging in the complaint that the defendant has relied on a privilege created by federal law in refusing to perform the contract.

Is this a satisfactory statement of the holding? Circle yes or no.

If no, why not? Answer with a number from the Common Mistakes in Stating a Holding. _____

ANSWER 5. Federal question jurisdiction does not exist when the federal issue appears in the plaintiff's complaint only as an anticipated defense.

Is this a satisfactory statement of the holding? Circle yes or no.

If no, why not? Answer with a number or numbers from the Common Mistakes in Stating a Holding. _____

ANSWER 6. A federal question is presented to the court if the pleadings of the parties show that the case will involve an important issue of federal law.

Is this a satisfactory statement of the holding? Circle yes or no.

If no, why not? Answer with a number from the Common Mistakes in Stating a Holding. _____

ANSWER 7. This case must be dismissed for lack of jurisdiction.

Is this a satisfactory statement of the holding? Circle yes or no.

If no, why not? Answer with a number from the Common Mistakes in Stating a Holding. _____

ANSWER 8. No diversity of citizenship exists between two plaintiffs and a defendant who are all citizens of the same state.

Is this a satisfactory statement of the holding? Circle yes or no.

If no, why not? Answer with a number from the Common Mistakes in Stating a Holding. _____

AUTHORS' EVALUATION OF THE STATEMENTS OF THE *MOTTLEY* HOLDING

1. Where there is no diversity of citizenship or other basis for federal jurisdiction, a federal court should dismiss the case before it.

This statement is not satisfactory for reason 4. The statement is accurate and relevant to the purpose for which the case is being studied, but the statement is so general that it does not usefully describe the precedent established by the case. More specificity is needed.

2. The Supreme Court may consider an issue of subject matter jurisdiction on its own motion, even if the parties did not raise the issue below.

This statement is not satisfactory for reason 3. This rule is certainly *one* of the holdings of the case. If a lawyer were arguing a case presenting the issue whether a defense of subject matter jurisdiction had been waived, this statement could properly be described as the holding of the case. On the other hand, the student should never ignore the casebook Table of Contents. The editors' placement of *Mottley* in "The General Definition of Federal Question Jurisdiction" suggests that the case has been assigned because of its definition of federal question jurisdiction, not because of its holding on the waiver issue. Therefore, one might argue that the waiver rule is not the holding because it is not the rule of law most relevant to the purpose for which the case has been read.

3. In a bill demanding specific performance of a contract, allegations that the defendant has based its refusal to perform the contract upon federal law are superfluous.

This statement is not satisfactory for reason 3. This rule is one of the holdings of the case, but it is not the holding most relevant to the purpose for which the case has been assigned. The placement of *Mottley* in the casebook shows that it is meant to be read for its holding about the nature of federal question jurisdiction, not for its holding about superfluity in pleading.

4. Plaintiffs asking for specific performance of a contract cannot create federal question jurisdiction by alleging in the complaint that the defendant has relied on a privilege created by federal law in refusing to perform a contract.

This statement is not satisfactory for reason 5. Even though a reasonable argument can be made that this statement of the holding is satisfactory, the statement is probably too specific to be useful for the purpose for which the case has been read. This might be an appropriate statement of the holding if the case were being studied for a more narrow purpose—for example, by a lawyer doing research for an appellate argument in a contract case in which the plaintiff sought to base federal jurisdiction upon allegations that the defendant had relied upon federal law in failing to perform its promise. The placement of this case in the casebook indicates that it is meant to convey a general rule about federal question jurisdiction rather than a specific rule for contract cases. The holding should be stated with greater generality, so that it applies to cases other than contract cases.

5. Federal question jurisdiction does not exist when the federal issue appears in the plaintiff's complaint only as an anticipated defense.

This is a good statement of the holding. It formulates the relevant holding of the case at the appropriate level of generality. Of course, this statement is not a magic form of words. Other similar formulations would also be acceptable, *e.g.,* "There is no federal question jurisdiction if the facts that give rise to the federal issue should have been pleaded by the defendant instead of the plaintiff," or "There is no federal question jurisdiction unless the facts giving rise to a federal issue are made to appear, without inserting superfluous language, in the plaintiff's initial pleading."

6. *A federal question is presented to the court if the pleadings of the parties show that the case will involve an important issue of federal law.*

This statement is not satisfactory for reason 1. It is an inaccurate statement of the doctrine of *Mottley.* The opinion states there is no federal question jurisdiction unless the facts giving rise to the federal issue appear, without inserting superfluous language, in the plaintiff's complaint. The fact that defendant's answer reveals the existence of an important federal issue will not suffice to create federal question jurisdiction.

7. *This case must be dismissed for lack of jurisdiction.*

This statement is not satisfactory for reason 6. It merely describes the result reached, not a rule of law established by the case.

8. *No diversity of citizenship exists between two plaintiffs and a defendant who are all citizens of the same state.*

This statement is not satisfactory for reason 2. While the court did note there was no diversity of citizenship, the case clearly is decided on the issue of federal question jurisdiction. The discussion of diversity jurisdiction is a dictum.

III. COMPUTER–AIDED EXERCISE: BAKER v. KECK

This written material and the accompanying computer-aided exercise, CALI CIV 05: Analysis of a Diversity Case, explore the nature of holding and dictum in the context of an opinion on diversity of citizenship jurisdiction. The computer will require you to distinguish holding and dicta so that you can state the holding of *Baker v. Keck,* an opinion that appears following this introductory note. The computer will also ask you other questions to analyze the meaning of passages in the opinion.

Take this exercise with you to the computer terminal, as questions will ask you to refer to the *Baker v. Keck* opinion.

You are a new associate working for a law firm in the state of Fraser. One of the firm's partners asks you to do some research on a personal injury action the firm has brought on behalf of Pam Pedestrian against David Driver. Pedestrian's tort claim arises under state law, and the only plausible basis for federal jurisdiction is diversity of citizenship.

Your firm filed Pedestrian's suit in federal district court for Fraser. Driver moved under Federal Rule of Civil Procedure 12(b)(1) to dismiss for lack of subject matter jurisdiction; he asserts that both Pedestrian and Driver are citizens of the same state, Fraser, so there is no diversity of citizenship. The motion has been set for hearing next week and the partner wants to submit to the court a legal memorandum on the issue of diversity of citizenship. She tells you to work with the following set of facts, which have already been developed in the case file.

Pam Pedestrian is without question a citizen of Fraser. She suffered injuries that are serious enough to satisfy the $75,000 jurisdictional amount requirement.

David Driver is a law student, age 25, single, born and reared at his parents' home in Fraser. He graduated from college at Fraser State University, and is now a student at Coffman Law School in the state of Coffman. Driver is living in an apartment in Coffman while finishing the last half of his final year in law school. Driver's parents have continued to support him during his attendance at law school, and he has frequently returned to his parents' home during vacation periods. Driver recently accepted a full-time job with a law firm in a third state, Northrop.

In an affidavit submitted with the motion to dismiss, Driver swore to the following facts:

> I went to high school and college while living at home in Fraser. Two-and-a-half years ago I entered law school in Coffman. I have always had a definite intent to leave Coffman immediately after graduation. I voted in Coffman during the last election, but have never participated in politics here in any other way. I have never belonged to any organizations in Coffman or held a job here. I have now accepted a job with a law firm in Northrop. I received the offer by telephone after interviewing in Coffman; I have never been in Northrop. I am living in an apartment in Coffman while finishing my last year of law school. I intend never to come back to Coffman after I leave. During law school my parents have paid my expenses, and I have visited them during vacations at our family home in Fraser; however, I do not plan on going back to Fraser. I

19

have always wanted to go to a populous state like Northrop to practice.

You have started research for the memorandum that will be submitted to the trial court. You quickly found the relevant jurisdictional statute, 28 U.S.C. § 1332:

(a) The district courts shall have original jurisdiction of all civil actions where the matter in controversy exceeds the sum or value of $75,000, exclusive of interest and costs, and is between—

(1) citizens of different states * * *.

Initial research also revealed that in your federal district, consistent with all other districts, the following two propositions are generally accepted:

1. A United States citizen is also a citizen of the state in which that person is domiciled. [Both Pedestrian and Driver are United States citizens.]

2. A domicile once established endures until a new one is acquired. Consequently, Driver is still domiciled in Fraser unless he has acquired a new domicile in Coffman or Northrup.

Your research also discovered *Baker v. Keck,* 13 F.Supp. 486 (E.D. Ill.1936). Even though the opinion is today more than two-thirds of a century old, the legal principles it states remain good law. For the purposes of this computer-aided exercise, treat *Baker* as a recent case decided by the district judge who is assigned to your case.

The computer exercise will ask you to participate in a discussion with other associates in your law firm. Your associates will make assertions about *Baker,* and you will be asked to agree or disagree with them. Please study *Baker* carefully before going to the computer. The opinion is divided into sections, each of which is numbered. Some questions asked by the computer will refer to the sections by number. As part of your preparation, you should write out a statement of the holding of *Baker v. Keck.*

BAKER v. KECK

United States District Court, Eastern District of Illinois, 1936.
13 F.Supp. 486.

LINDLEY, DISTRICT JUDGE.

[§ 1]

Plaintiff has filed herein his suit against various individuals and the Progressive Miners of America charging a conspiracy, out of which grew certain events and in the course of which, it is averred, he was attacked by certain of the defendants and his arm shot off. This, it is said, resulted from a controversy between the United States Mine Workers and the Progressive Miners of America.

[§ 2]

Plaintiff avers that he is a citizen of the state of Oklahoma. Defendants filed a motion to dismiss, one ground of which is that plaintiff is not a citizen of the state of Oklahoma, but has a domicile in the state of Illinois, and that therefore there is no diversity of citizenship. To this motion plaintiff filed a response, with certain affidavits in support thereof.

[§ 3]

Upon presentation of the motion, the court set the issue of fact arising upon the averments of the complaint, the motion to dismiss, and the response thereto for hearing. A jury was waived. Affidavits were received and parol evidence offered.

[§ 4]

It appears that plaintiff formerly resided in Saline County, Ill., that he was not a member of United Mine Workers, but was in sympathy with their organization. The averment of the declaration is that he was attacked by members of, or sympathizers with, the Progressive Mine Workers of America. He was a farmer, owning about 100 acres of land. After his injury, he removed to the state of Oklahoma, taking with him his family and all of his household goods, except two beds and some other small items. His household furniture was carried to Oklahoma by truck, and the truckman was paid $100 for transportation. Near Ulan, Okl. he rented 20 acres and a house for $150 per year, and began occupancy thereof October, 1934. He testified that he had arrangements with another party and his own son, living with him, to cultivate the

[§ 5]

ground, but that farming conditions were not satisfactory, and that it was impossible, therefore, to produce a crop in 1935. He produced potatoes, sweet corn, and other garden products used in the living of the family. He had no horses or other livestock in Oklahoma. He was unable to do any extensive work himself because of the loss of his arm. In the summer of 1935 he leased for the year 1936 the same 20 acres and an additional 20 acres at a rental of $150.

[§ 6]

At the first opportunity to register as a qualified voter in Oklahoma after he went there, he complied with the statute in that respect and was duly registered. This was not until after he had been in the state for over a year, as, under the state statute, a qualified voter must have resided within the state for twelve months prior to registration. He has not voted, but he testified that the only election at which he could have voted after he registered was on a day when he had to be in Illinois to give attention to his lawsuit. He has returned to Illinois for short visits three or four times.

[§ 7]

He testified that he moved to Oklahoma for the purpose of residing there, with the intention of making it his home and that he still intends to reside there. He testified that the family started out to see if they could find a new location in 1934. Upon cross-examination it appeared that the funds for traveling and removal had been paid by the United Mine Workers or their representative; that he left his livestock on the Illinois farm, but no chickens; that he had about 60 chickens on his farm in Oklahoma; that, when he removed to Oklahoma, he rented his Illinois farm for a period of five years; that the tenant has recently defaulted upon the same.

[§ 8]

In the affidavits it appears that plaintiff's house in Illinois was completely destroyed by fire shortly after he left. It was not insured and was a total loss. Witnesses for the defense testified that he had told them that he intended to move back to Illinois after he got his case settled; that he had told one witness in 1935 that he was going to Oklahoma but did not know for how long. Plaintiff denies that he told these witnesses that he expected to return to Illinois as soon as his litigation was completed.

[§ 9]

I think it is a fair conclusion from all the evidence that at the time plaintiff removed to Oklahoma one of his motives was to create diversity of citizenship so that he might maintain a suit in the United States courts. But that conclusion is not of itself decisive of the question presented. There remains the further question of whether there was at the time this suit was begun an intention upon his part to become a citizen of Oklahoma. One may change his citizenship for the purpose of enabling himself to maintain a suit in the federal court, but the change must be an actual legal change made with the intention of bringing about actual citizenship in the state to which this removal is made.

[§ 10]

Citizenship and domicile are substantially synonymous. Residency and inhabitance are too often confused with the terms and have not the same significance. Citizenship implies more than residence. It carries with it the idea of identification with the state and a participation in its functions. As a citizen, one sustains social, political, and moral obligation to the state and possesses social and political rights under the Constitution and laws thereof. Harding v. Standard Oil Co. et al. (C.C.) 182 F. 421; Baldwin v. Franks, 120 U.S. 678, 7 S.Ct. 763, 32 L.Ed. 766; Scott v. Sandford, 19 How. 393, 476, 15 L.Ed. 691.

[§ 11]

Accordingly it is commonly held that the exercise of suffrage by a citizen of the United States is conclusive evidence of his citizenship. Foster on Federal Practice, vol. 1 (6th Ed.) p. 159, and cases there cited. Voting in a party primary and membership in a local political party are strong evidence of citizenship. Gaddie v. Mann (C.C.) 147 F. 955. The registration of a man as a voter and the assessment of a poll tax against him are likewise strong evidence of domicile or citizenship, though not conclusive. In re Sedgwick (D.C.) 223 F. 655.

[§ 12]

Change of domicile arises when there is a change of abode with the absence of any present intention not to reside permanently or indefinitely in the new abode. This is the holding of the Supreme Court in Gilbert v. David, 235 U.S. 561, 35 S.Ct. 164, 167, 59 L.Ed. 360, where the court said: "As Judge Story puts it in his work on 'Conflict of Laws' (7th Ed.) § 46, page 41, 'If a person has actually removed to another place, with an intention of remaining there for an indefinite time, and as a place of fixed present domicile, it is to be deemed his place of domicile, notwithstanding he may entertain a floating intention to return at some future period. The requisite animus is the present intention of permanent or indefinite residence in a given place or country, or, negatively expressed, the absence of any present intention of not residing there permanently or indefinitely.' "

[§ 13]

It will be observed that, if there is an intention to remain, even though it be for an indefinite time, but still with the intention of making the location a place of present domicile, this latter intention will control, even though the person entertains a floating intention to return at some indefinite future period. In this respect the court in Gilbert v. David, *supra,* further said: "Plaintiff may have had, and probably did have, some floating intention of returning to Michigan after the determination of certain litigation.... But, as we have seen, a floating intention of that kind was not enough to prevent the new place, under the circumstances shown, from becoming his domicile. It was his place of abode, which he had no present intention of changing; that is the essence of domicile."

[§ 14]

In discussing a similar situation, in McHaney v. Cunningham (D.C.) 4 F.(2d) 725, 726, the court said: "He says he always intended at some indefinite future time, ... to return to Arkansas to practice the legal profession; but, when he registered and voted in this state, he must have decided to give up that idea, for I cannot assume that he intended to commit a fraud upon its laws by claiming and exercising rights such as were given alone to a bona fide citizen. I take it, when these things were done, it was with the intention of identifying himself with the state in a political sense, which is the basis of citizenship." See, also, Reckling v. McKinstry (C.C.) 185 F. 842; Philadelphia & R. Ry. Co. v. Skerman (C.C.A.) 247 F. 269; Collins v. City of Ashland (D.C.) 112 F. 175.

[§ 15]

In Dale v. Irwin, 78 Ill. 170 (1875), the court said, referring to a statutory provision: "The legislature, by this section, sought to establish a criterion of residence, by declaring that a permanent abode shall be such criterion. Now, what is 'a permanent abode?' Must it be held to be an abode which the party does not intend to abandon at any future time? This, it seems to us, would be a definition too stringent for a country whose people and characteristics are ever on a change. No man in active life, in this State, can say, wherever he may be placed, this is and ever shall be my permanent abode. It would be safe to say a permanent abode, in the sense of the statute, means nothing more than a domicile, a home, which the party is at liberty to leave, as interest or whim may dictate, but without any present intention to change it."

[§ 16]

In Kreitz v. Behrensmeyer, 125 Ill. 141, 195, 17 N.E. 232, 8 Am.St.Rep. 349 (1888), the Court said: "A man may acquire a domicile ... if he be personally present in a place and select that as his home, even though he does not design to remain there always, but designs at the end of some time to remove and acquire another."

[§ 17]

The statement of the Restatement of the Law, Conflict of Laws, § 15, Domicil of Choice, is as follows:

"(1) A domicil of choice is a domicil acquired, through the exercise of his own will, by a person who is legally capable of changing his domicil.

[§ 18]

"(2) To acquire a domicil of choice, a person must establish a dwelling-place with the intention of making it his home.

[§ 19]

"(3) The fact of physical presence at a dwelling-place and the intention to make it a home must concur; if they do so, even for a moment, the change of domicil takes place."

[§ 20]

In Holt v. Hendee, 248 Ill. 288, 93 N.E. 749, 752, 21 Ann.Cas. 202, the court said: "The intention is not necessarily determined from the statements or declarations of the party but may be inferred from the surrounding circumstances, which may entirely disprove such statements or declarations. On the question of domicile less weight will be given to the party's declaration than to his acts."

[§ 21]

Though it must be confessed that the question is far from free of doubt, I conclude that, under the facts as they appear in the record, despite the fact that one of plaintiff's motives was the establishment of a citizenship so as to create jurisdiction in the federal court, there was at the time of his removal a fixed intention to become a citizen of the state of Oklahoma. He testified that he worked on a community project in that state without compensation. It appears that he registered as a voter; he thus became a participant in the political activities of the state. Such action is inconsistent with any conclusion other than that of citizenship, and, in view of his sworn testimony that it was his intention to reside in Oklahoma and to continue to do so, it follows that the elements constituting the status of citizenship existed.

25

[§ 22]

True, there is some evidence that he had said he might return to Illinois as soon as his case was settled. The language of the cases above indicates that such a floating intention is insufficient to bar citizenship, where active participation in the obligations and enjoyment of the rights of citizenship exist.

[§ 23]

Defendants contend that the fact that the cost of plaintiff's transportation and maintenance were paid by the United Mine Workers is of decisive weight upon this issue. I cannot agree. It seems to me immaterial what motives may have inspired the United Mine Workers to help him, and the court is not now concerned with their alleged charitable and philanthropic practices.

[§ 24]

I conclude, therefore, that plaintiff was at the time of the commencement of the suit, and is now, a citizen of the state of Oklahoma. The findings herein embraced will be adopted as findings of fact of the court and entered as such. It is ordered that the motion to dismiss because of lack of diversity of citizenship be, and the same is hereby, denied. An exception is allowed to defendants.

[§ 25]

If possible, in view of the expense involved in a trial upon the merits, it is desirable that a review of this decision be had before such trial.

———————

Write here your statement of the holding in *Baker v. Keck*.

_____

_____

_____

_____

_____

_____

You are now ready to do the computer-aided exercise, CALI CIV 05: Analysis of a Diversity Case.

EXERCISE TWO

Jurisdiction

I. THE LAW OF JURISDICTION

A. Types of Jurisdiction

Before suit can be brought in a given forum, the court must have "jurisdiction," the power to speak (diction) the law (juris). Jurisdiction is divided into three components: 1) subject matter jurisdiction, 2) personal jurisdiction, and 3) notice and opportunity to be heard. The court needs all three types of jurisdiction to proceed to adjudicate the lawsuit. In addition, venue must be properly laid: plaintiff must bring the suit in a proper district.

Subject matter jurisdiction is a question of authority of the court over the nature of the litigation, *i.e.,* the subject matter presented. The rules of subject matter jurisdiction ask whether the court has been given power to decide a certain type of legal controversy. In order to determine whether a federal court possesses subject matter jurisdiction, a lawyer will look to the Constitution of the United States and federal statutes; for a state court, the lawyer will look to the state constitution and state statutes.

Many state courts are given broad power to hear all types of cases. They are courts of general subject matter jurisdiction. Other courts are limited in the types of cases they may hear, and are courts of limited subject matter jurisdiction. The common limits are the type of claim or the amount claimed. For example, a state might have a court of general jurisdiction, plus a specific court to deal with probate law, another to deal with tax cases, and a third to deal with workers' compensation cases. In such a system, a suit on a contract brought in probate court would be dismissed for lack of subject matter jurisdiction. Another state might establish a small claims court to hear cases not exceeding an amount in controversy of $5,000. A case seeking in excess of $5,000, brought in that court, would be dismissed for lack of subject matter jurisdiction.

All federal courts—district courts, courts of appeals, and the Supreme Court of the United States—are courts of limited subject matter jurisdiction. The limits on federal jurisdiction are discussed in section I.B.2, *infra*.[1]

Because subject matter jurisdiction is conferred by constitution and statute, it cannot be conferred on a court by the parties. The parties can neither consent to nor waive subject matter jurisdiction. The federal court rule that subject matter jurisdiction may be challenged at any stage of the litigation [*see* Fed.R.Civ.P. 12(h)(3)] necessarily follows from this principle.

Personal jurisdiction refers to the court's power over the parties, or over the parties' property, in the case. Some writers prefer to call this type of jurisdiction basis jurisdiction, but the more common usage is personal jurisdiction, which as we use the term, includes power over both persons and things. Since a plaintiff who commences an action consents to the personal jurisdiction of the court, the question is power over defendants.

When the court possesses power over the person of the defendant, the court has *in personam* jurisdiction. The traditional method for a court to obtain power over the person of a defendant has always been service on that person within the boundaries of the state. The human or corporate defendant had to be "present" within the state for the court to be able to exercise power. As twentieth century advances in transportation and commerce made commercial activity far from home common, courts began to shift emphasis away from physical presence in the state to a consideration of whether the state was a convenient geographic location for the lawsuit. States enacted long-arm statutes to reach out beyond state boundaries to bring defendants into the state from afar. Even today, however, convenience has not become the sole consideration for jurisdiction; respect for the sovereignty of sister states is thought to require that a state refrain from exercising jurisdiction over a defendant who has insufficient "minimum contacts" with the forum state, even though the forum would be a convenient location for the lawsuit, as discussed in section I.C.1(d).

Personal jurisdiction is broader than in personam jurisdiction, since the court's power may be based not directly on the person of the defendant, but on the defendant through property owned.

1. Because federal courts have limited subject matter jurisdiction, a party seeking to enter federal court must specifically plead that jurisdiction. See the jurisdictional allegations in Exercise Three II.B.1.

When the purpose of the litigation is to determine rights in a piece of property, the *res,* located in the state, the action is an *in rem* proceeding. When the claim in the litigation is unrelated to the property, and the plaintiff seizes the res for the sole purpose of obtaining jurisdiction over the defendant within the state, the jurisdiction is *quasi in rem.* The court's power over the person of the defendant will extend only to the limits of the value of the defendant's interest in the seized property. *See* the discussion in section I.C.2.

Since personal jurisdiction means power over the person or the property of the defendant, defendant can confer it on the court by consent or waiver. A personal jurisdiction defense not raised by defendant at the first opportunity is waived [*see* Fed.R.Civ.P. 12(h)(1)]. This possibility of waiver is explored in detail in Exercise Five: Motions to Dismiss and Waiver Under Federal Rule 12.

Notice and opportunity to be heard form the third part of the jurisdictional triangle. The defendant must receive notice of the pending action and a meaningful opportunity to be heard in defense before defendant's property is taken. Due process requires no less. Notice is accomplished by service of a summons on the defendant, whether by personal service in hand, substituted service on another for the defendant, or constructive service of publication of the summons in a newspaper. Of these methods, the problematical one is service by publication, since that method may not be reasonably calculated to achieve actual notice to defendant.[2]

Note that personal service on a defendant out of state cannot raise an objection to notice: defendant certainly has received proper notice, even though the defendant might have a valid objection to personal jurisdiction. Finally, since notice may be received even through improper procedures, the defendant may consent to notice.

Opportunity to be heard problems arise in two situations. First, and rarely, defendant is given an inadequate time to respond to the complaint. Second, more commonly, property of the defendant is seized prior to judgment; defendant must receive a meaningful chance to defend the case before, or at least shortly after, the property is taken.[3]

2. *See* Mullane v. Central Hanover Bank & Trust Co., 339 U.S. 306, 315, 70 S.Ct. 652, 657, 94 L.Ed. 865, 874 (1950): "The means employed must be . . . reasonably certain to inform those affected."

3. *See* the discussion of the Supreme Court's series of pre-judgment seizure cases in JACK H. FRIEDENTHAL, MARY KAY KANE & ARTHUR R. MILLER, CIVIL PROCEDURE § 3.21 (3d ed. 1999).

Venue is not a jurisdictional requirement, yet it is closely associated with jurisdiction and the two are sometimes confused. The difference is that jurisdiction deals with the power of the court, while venue allocates judicial business among various courts that have jurisdictional power. Should one federal district court have subject matter jurisdiction over a case, all 94 federal district courts will have subject matter jurisdiction. Every one of them will be able to give proper notice. Perhaps even all of them will have personal jurisdiction over the defendant. Yet the federal venue statutes (*see* section I.E.2) will require that the case be brought only in a small number, or even only one, of those 94 districts. The rules of venue are designed to ensure that trials are conducted in a convenient place.

A case laying venue in the wrong federal district may be dismissed [Fed.R.Civ.P. 12(b)(3)] or may be transferred to a district "in which it could have been brought" [28 U.S.C. § 1406]. A defendant may also consent or waive objection to venue [Fed. R.Civ.P. 12(h)(1); *see* Exercise Five: Motions to Dismiss and Waiver Under Federal Rule 12].

B. Subject Matter Jurisdiction

1. *State Courts*

Even though state court systems do have courts of limited subject matter jurisdiction, every state has a state court of general subject matter jurisdiction that is able to hear all types of cases. That court may be called the superior court, the district court, the supreme court, the circuit court, or some other name. You may assume that all state courts mentioned in this exercise are courts of general jurisdiction.

2. *Federal Courts*

Since subject matter jurisdiction is dependent on the constitution and statutes that empower the court, we look first to the Judicial Article of the United States Constitution to determine what types of cases it permits federal courts to hear:

Section 2. The judicial power shall extend to all Cases, in Law and Equity, arising under this Constitution, the Laws of the United States, and Treaties made, or which shall be made, under their Authority;—to all Cases affecting Ambassadors, other public Ministers and Consuls;—to all Cases of admiralty and maritime Jurisdiction;—to controversies to which the United States shall be a Party;—to Controversies between two or more States;—between a State and Citizens of another State;—between Citizens of different States;—between Citizens of the same State claiming Lands under Grants of different States, and between a State, or the Citizens thereof, and foreign States, Citizens or Subjects.[4]

The two most commonly-used types of federal court subject matter jurisdiction are federal questions ["all Cases, in Law and Equity, arising under this Constitution, the laws of the United States, and Treaties made"] and diversity of citizenship ["between Citizens of different States"]. Even though the Constitution provides the federal judicial power "shall extend" over these two areas, Congress must pass legislation to vest such authority in the federal courts.[5]

a. Federal Question Jurisdiction

The statute implementing the Constitutional grant of power over federal questions reads as follows:

28 U.S.C. § 1331. Federal question

The district courts shall have original jurisdiction of all civil actions arising under the Constitution, laws, or treaties of the United States.

When a case arises under the Constitution, laws, or treaties of the United States, it presents a federal question. Even though the key words of the statute—"arising under"—are identical to the Constitution, the courts interpret the statute more narrowly than the Constitution. For example, the famous rule that a federal question must arise in the well-pleaded complaint and cannot arise in defense[6] is recognized as an interpretation of § 1331 but not of the Constitution.

4. U.S.Const. art. III, § 2.

5. While the matter is not free from doubt, the Supreme Court has often said that the judicial power of the United States—within the outer limits of the Constitution—is dependent on Congress, which may invest the inferior federal courts "with jurisdiction either limited, concurrent, or exclusive, and [withhold] jurisdiction from them in the exact degrees and character which to Congress may seem proper for the public good." *Sheldon v. Sill,* 49 U.S. (8 How.) 441, 12 L.Ed. 1147 (1850). Indeed, Congress did not grant the federal courts authority to hear federal question cases until 1875, and proposals to eliminate diversity jurisdiction are even today pending. *See* Charles A. Wright & Mary Kay Kane, The Law of Federal Courts §§ 10, 23 (6th ed. 2002).

6. Louisville & Nashville R.R. v. Mottley, 211 U.S. 149, 29 S.Ct. 42, 53 L.Ed. 126 (1908), reproduced in Exercise One at p. 11.

Despite the best efforts of some of the best judges of our national history—Chief Justice John Marshall, Justice Oliver Wendell Holmes, Justice Benjamin Cardozo, and Judge Henry Friendly among them—the phrase "arising under" has remained elusive. Perhaps the most widely accepted approach to a federal question issue today is the one offered many years ago by Justice Cardozo:

> If we follow the ascent far enough, countless claims of right can be discovered to have their source or their operative limits in the provisions of a federal statute or in the Constitution itself with its circumambient restrictions upon legislative power. To set bounds to the pursuit, the courts have formulated the distinction between controversies that are basic and those that are collateral, between disputes that are necessary and those that are merely possible. We shall be lost in a maze if we put that compass by.[7]

Suppose, for example, that an author assigns a copyright (issued under federal copyright law) to an entrepreneur in exchange for an agreement to share royalties on marketing of the composition. Some time later, the author sues for failure to pay royalties and seeks an accounting. Is this a federal question? No, said Judge Henry Friendly: the complaint presents a state law claim of breach of contract.[8]

At the ends of the continuum, cases can easily be classified as arising under federal law or arising under state law. Near the middle, the question of whether a case presents a federal question can be exceedingly difficult.[9]

b. Diversity Jurisdiction

Diversity cases involve citizens of different states. The statute implementing the Constitutional grant of power over diversity of citizenship cases reads as follows:

---

7. Gully v. First Nat. Bank in Meridian, 299 U.S. 109, 118, 57 S.Ct. 96, 100, 81 L.Ed. 70, 75 (1936).

8. [A]n action "arises under" the Copyright Act if and only if the complaint is for a remedy expressly granted by the Act, e.g., a suit for infringement ... or asserts a claim requiring construction of the Act ... or, at the very least and perhaps more doubtfully, presents a case where a distinctive policy of the Act requires that federal principles control the disposition of the claim.

T.B. Harms Co. v. Eliscu, 339 F.2d 823, 828 (2d Cir.1964).

9. Further discussion of federal questions is beyond the scope of this brief note. The topic is explored in depth in a course in federal jurisdiction. *See generally* CHARLES A. WRIGHT & MARY KAY KANE, THE LAW OF FEDERAL COURTS § 17 (6th ed. 2002).

28 U.S.C. § 1332. *Diversity of citizenship; amount in controversy; costs*

(a) The district courts shall have original jurisdiction of all civil actions where the matter in controversy exceeds the sum or value of $75,000, exclusive of interest and costs, and is between—

(1) citizens of different States;

(2) citizens of a State and citizens or subjects of a foreign state;

(3) citizens of different States and in which citizens or subjects of a foreign state are additional parties; and

(4) a foreign state, defined in section 1603(a) of this title, as plaintiff and citizens of a State or of different States.

For the purposes of this section, section 1335, and section 1441, an alien admitted to the United States for permanent residence shall be deemed a citizen of the State in which such alien is domiciled.

(b) Except when express provision therefor is otherwise made in a statute of the United States, where the plaintiff who files the case originally in the Federal courts is finally adjudged to be entitled to recover less than the sum or value of $75,000, computed without regard to any setoff or counter-claim to which the defendant may be adjudged to be entitled, and exclusive of interest and costs, the district court may deny costs to the plaintiff and, in addition, may impose costs on the plaintiff.

(c) For the purposes of this section and section 1441 of this title—

(1) a corporation shall be deemed a citizen of any State by which it has been incorporated and of the State where it has its principal place of business,[10] except that in

---

10. Because of this provision, a corporation is said to have dual citizenship: state(s) of incorporation *and* state "where it has its principal place of business." The statute does not define "principal place of business," although it requires a determination of only one such state.

Two lines of authority emerged in the federal courts. One line looked to the location of the executive offices or "nerve center" of the corporation as the principal place of business. The other line held that the principal place of business was the state in which the corporation carried on the bulk of its activity; this test worked especially well for corporations that manufactured goods from a single plant. Recent federal decisions have attempted to blend the two lines of authority into a "total activity" test, looking to the state where the largest share of corporate activity occurred. *See* Charles A. Wright & Mary Kay Kane, The Law of Federal Courts § 27, at 170 n. 34 (6th ed. 2002).

any direct action against the insurer of a policy or contract of liability insurance, whether incorporated or unincorporated, to which action the insured is not joined as a party-defendant, such insurer shall be deemed a citizen of the State of which the insured is a citizen, as well as of any State by which the insurer has been incorporated and of the State where it has its principal place of business; and

(2) the legal representative of the estate of a decedent shall be deemed to be a citizen only of the same State as the decedent, and the legal representative of an infant or incompetent shall be deemed to be a citizen only of the same State as the infant or incompetent.

(d) The word "States", as used in this section, includes the Territories, the District of Columbia, and the Commonwealth of Puerto Rico.

This statute clearly requires that for a federal court to have diversity jurisdiction, the case must satisfy two requirements: 1) diversity of citizenship of the parties and 2) an adequate jurisdictional amount.

1.   Determining Citizenship of the Parties. While 28 U.S.C. § 1332 states at least a partial test for determining the citizenship of a corporation, it offers no guidance for determining the citizenship of a natural person—or other entities such as partnerships or unions. The following two cases exemplify the law that federal courts have created to determine the citizenship of a natural person. Please read them carefully, as you will be called on to apply the principles announced in them, and you will also be asked questions specifically about the opinions, when you do the computer exercise.

BAKER v. KECK

United States District Court, Eastern District of Illinois, 1936.
13 F.Supp. 486.

[This opinion is reproduced in Exercise One: Holding and Dicta in the Context of a Diversity Case, at 20. Please reread *Baker v. Keck* as part of your preparation for this exercise. Remember that even though the opinion is old, it still states good law today and you should treat it as a recent decision.]

SCOGGINS v. POLLOCK

United States Court of Appeals, Eleventh Circuit, 1984.
727 F.2d 1025.

ALBERT J. HENDERSON, CIRCUIT JUDGE:

The issue presented by this case is whether the appellant, Kay Scoggins, was domiciled in South Carolina or Georgia at the time she filed this medical malpractice suit in the United States District Court for the Southern District of Georgia. Diversity of citizenship is alleged as the basis of federal jurisdiction pursuant to the provisions of 28 U.S.C. § 1332. All of the appellees-defendants are residents of Georgia. The district court concluded that Mrs. Scoggins was also a citizen of Georgia and dismissed the case for lack of subject matter jurisdiction. Finding that the district court was not clearly erroneous, we affirm.

Mrs. Scoggins and her husband lived in Washington, Georgia. He was a high school principal and Mrs. Scoggins worked as a media specialist in a grade school. As a result of Mr. Scoggins' sudden death in October, 1979, Mrs. Scoggins filed suit in October, 1981 against the doctors, clinic and hospital that treated him.

Mrs. Scoggins remained in Washington, Georgia for over a year after her husband's death. Rev. Robert Murphy, who counseled with her, stated that he advised her not to do anything for at least a year until she overcame her grief. Rev. Murphy Deposition at 13. Still, Mrs. Scoggins contended that she decided soon after her husband's death to leave Washington and start a new life somewhere else. Mrs. Scoggins Deposition at 131.

In January or February 1981 Mrs. Scoggins applied for admission to a one year Master in Librarianship program at the University of South Carolina. After her acceptance in mid-April, 1981, she notified her employer, Dr. Fred Dorminy, of her intent to resign her job in the Wilkes County school system. She rented an apartment in West Columbia, South Carolina and began her course of study in August, 1981. Later she accepted a job as a graduate assistant, a position open only to students. She neither sold nor rented her house in Washington, Georgia. She and her two children stayed there occasionally when they were in Washington. She claimed that she was holding on to the house until she graduated and found a permanent job and then would use the proceeds of the sale to purchase a new home. Mrs. Scoggins Deposition at 132–33.

The district court correctly noted that a change of domicile requires "[a] concurrent showing of (1) physical presence at the new location with (2) an intention to remain there indefinitely. . . ."

Opinion at 4. *Mas v. Perry,* 489 F.2d 1396, 1399 (5th Cir.), *cert. denied,* 419 U.S. 842, 95 S.Ct. 74, 42 L.Ed.2d 70 (1974); *Stine v. Moore,* 213 F.2d 446 (5th Cir.1954). The plaintiff bears the burden of proving her domicile by a preponderance of the evidence. *Vacca v. Meetze,* 499 F.Supp. 1089 (S.D.Ga.1980).

It is undisputed that Mrs. Scoggins was physically present in South Carolina when she filed this suit. She had rented an apartment, registered to vote, registered her car and obtained a South Carolina driver's license. After a summer vacation she apparently was in South Carolina full time once classes began. The second element of the test, her intent to remain in South Carolina indefinitely, however, presents a greater problem. The district court found that she initially went to South Carolina to undertake graduate studies and had not positively decided upon her residence after graduation. Citing 13 Wright, Miller & Cooper, *Federal Practice and Procedure* § 3613 (1975), the district court stated that out-of-state students are usually regarded only as temporary residents and "[i]t is therefore usually presumed that they retain their domicile at their former place of abode." Opinion at 10. Because Mrs. Scoggins lacked the requisite intent to remain in South Carolina and was still a Georgia domiciliary, the district court then dismissed the suit for lack of jurisdiction.

The district court's finding of domicile will not be disturbed unless clearly erroneous. *Combee v. Shell Oil Co.,* 615 F.2d 698 (5th Cir.1980). We conclude that, although there is some conflicting evidence, we are not "left with the 'definite and firm conviction that a mistake has been committed.'" *Inwood Laboratories v. Ives Laboratories,* 456 U.S. 844, 855, 102 S.Ct. 2182, 2189, 72 L.Ed.2d 606, 616 (1982) (*quoting United States v. United States Gypsum Co.,* 333 U.S. 364, 395, 68 S.Ct. 525, 542, 92 L.Ed. 746, 766 (1948)). There is sufficient evidence in the record to support the district court's finding.

Mrs. Scoggins clearly intended to leave Washington, Georgia, but her plans after that were more nebulous. Instead of consistently exhibiting an intent to remain in South Carolina, there were many indications that she considered moving to Florida or even returning to Georgia. Rev. Murphy stated that he discussed cities like Atlanta with Mrs. Scoggins and that "[s]he did name to me on more than one occasion that she was having thoughts of perhaps teaching in Florida." Rev. Murphy Deposition at 15. Further,

> she never indicated to me that she had made any plans to settle in South Carolina, nor did she say she didn't. The fact is, she didn't exclude Georgia really in her conversations to me.

Id. at 24. Dr. Dorminy, the county school superintendent in Wilkes County, testified by deposition that Mrs. Scoggins "indicated that when she finished her work at the University of South Carolina, that Florida was a possibility." Dorminy Deposition at 17. Dr. Dorminy additionally remarked that she told him she was unsure where she would go after graduation and she did not say anything to him suggesting that she considered South Carolina as her permanent home. *Id.* at 13, 17.

Mrs. Scoggins herself testified that her plans at the time were unsettled. "My intentions were to leave Georgia. I really didn't know where I was going, but I intended to leave Washington. I did not intend to live there any longer. I had options of where to go." Mrs. Scoggins Deposition at 160. Initially, it appears that she went to South Carolina solely to pursue her graduate studies. The University of South Carolina offered one of the few accredited programs in which she was interested. When asked when she decided to move to South Carolina, she replied "[a]fter I received my acceptance from the University of South Carolina." *Id.* at 134. Also,

> Q. The only reason you went was to go to school then—you didn't go to Columbia for any other reason, except to go to the University of South Carolina, is that correct?
>
> A. That's where I was accepted, so that's why I am in Columbia, South Carolina.

Id. at 158.

The former Fifth Circuit Court of Appeals considered this precise question in *Mas v. Perry,* 489 F.2d 1396 (5th Cir.), *cert. denied,* 419 U.S. 842, 95 S.Ct. 74, 42 L.Ed.2d 70 (1974). [Note: the Eleventh Circuit Court of Appeals adopts as precedents the decisions of the Fifth Circuit Court of Appeals issued prior to the division of that court into the Fifth and Eleventh Circuits in 1981.] Mr. and Mrs. Mas were graduate students at Louisiana State University and worked as graduate assistants. Mrs. Mas previously lived in Mississippi. The couple moved to Illinois but planned to return to Louisiana for Mr. Mas to complete his doctorate degree. They each sued their former landlord who was a Louisiana resident. He challenged diversity jurisdiction over Mrs. Mas' claim, alleging that Mrs. Mas also was domiciled in Louisiana. The court rejected this argument, stating:

> Mrs. Mas' Mississippi domicile was disturbed neither by her year in Louisiana prior to her marriage nor as a result of the time she and her husband spent at LSU after their marriage, since for both periods she was a graduate assistant at LSU. Though she testified that after her marriage she had

no intention of returning to her parents' home in Mississippi, Mrs. Mas did not effect a change of domicile since she and Mr. Mas were in Louisiana only as students and lacked the requisite intention to remain there.

Id. at 1400.

Mas is directly on point. Although Mrs. Scoggins may now intend to remain in South Carolina, we must look to the facts as of the date she filed this suit. She initially moved to South Carolina as a student. Even if she did not intend to return to Georgia, she was undecided about her future plans. Her domicile before she moved to South Carolina continued until she obtained a new one. Georgia remained Mrs. Scoggins' domicile for diversity purposes. We also note that the Court of Appeals for the Eighth Circuit, also in a medical malpractice case, dismissed the diversity suit of a student in Ohio against a Missouri doctor, holding that the student retained his Missouri domicile because he lacked the intent to remain in Ohio. *Holmes v. Sopuch*, 639 F.2d 431 (8th Cir.1981). The district court's finding that Mrs. Scoggins was a Georgia domiciliary is supported by the record and is not clearly erroneous.

Mrs. Scoggins also asserts that the district court abused its discretion by denying her motion to amend her complaint, purportedly to cure any jurisdictional defects. Such motions usually are granted liberally. Fed.R.Civ.P. 15(a). *See Dussouy v. Gulf Coast Investment Corp.*, 660 F.2d 594 (5th Cir.1981). Yet because the district court found there was no diversity jurisdiction, granting the motion would not have affected the outcome of the case.

For the foregoing reasons, the judgment of the district court dismissing the complaint for lack of jurisdiction is affirmed.

----

2. Determining the Amount in Controversy. The diversity jurisdictional statute, 28 U.S.C. § 1332, requires that the "matter in controversy exceeds the sum or value of $75,000, exclusive of interest and costs." This means diversity of citizenship alone is unavailing; the plaintiff must also be seeking to recover in excess of $75,000.

Since the first Congress, the diversity statute has required a minimum amount in controversy. The Judiciary Act of 1789 set that amount at $500. Congress raised the amount in 1887 to $2000; in 1911 to $3000; in 1958 to $10,000; in 1988 to $50,000, and again in 1996 to $75,000. In part, this jurisdictional amount has been raised in response to broader attempts to abolish diversity jurisdiction. In part, the amount has been raised as Congress attempts to set it "not so high as to convert the Federal courts into courts of big business nor so low as to fritter away their time in the trial of petty controversies."[11]

As might be expected, the courts have developed many rules for determining the amount in controversy. Probably the basic rule is that the good faith face of the complaint controls:

> The rule governing dismissal for want of jurisdiction in cases brought in the federal courts is that, unless the law gives a different rule, the sum claimed by the plaintiff controls if the claim is apparently made in good faith. It must appear to a legal certainty that the claim is really for less than the jurisdictional amount to justify dismissal.[12]

That general rule is sufficient for purposes of this exercise. This note does not develop rules that surround such questions as when plaintiff's claimed amount is not in good faith, how to value injunctive or declaratory relief, or when amounts sought in separate claims can be aggregated.[13]

c. Removal Jurisdiction

Removal jurisdiction is a question of federal subject matter jurisdiction. A defendant in an action filed by plaintiff in a state court may remove the case to federal court, if the federal court would have had original jurisdiction over it. Removal jurisdiction is a one-way street, state court to federal court; removal from federal court to state court does not exist. Also, the federal removal statute, 28 U.S.C. § 1441, allows removal by "the defendant or the defendants." This means a plaintiff cannot remove a case from state court to federal court, even when the defendant has asserted a counterclaim.

The basic statute governing removal reads as follows:

§ 1441. Actions removable generally

> (a) Except as otherwise expressly provided by Act of Congress, any civil action brought in a State court of which the district courts of the United States have original jurisdiction, may be removed by the defendant or the defendants, to the district court of the United States for the district and division embracing the place where such action is pending.

---

11. S. Rep. No. 1830, at 4 (1958), *reprinted in* 1958 U.S.C.C.A.N. 3099, 3101.

12. St. Paul Mercury Indem. Co. v. Red Cab Co., 303 U.S. 283, 288–89, 58 S. Ct. 586, 590, 82 L. Ed. 845, 848 (1938).

13. *See generally* Charles A. Wright & Mary Kay Kane, The Law of Federal Courts §§ 32–37 (6th ed. 2002).

For purposes of removal under this chapter, the citizenship of defendants sued under fictitious names shall be disregarded.

(b) Any civil action of which the district courts have original jurisdiction founded on a claim or right arising under the Constitution, treaties or laws of the United States shall be removable without regard to the citizenship or residence of the parties. Any other such action shall be removable only if none of the parties in interest properly joined and served as defendants is a citizen of the State in which such action is brought.

(c) Whenever a separate and independent claim or cause of action within the jurisdiction conferred by section 1331 of this title is joined with one or more otherwise nonremovable claims or causes of action, the entire case may be removed and the district court may determine all issues therein, or, in its discretion, may remand all matters in which State law predominates. * * *

As can be seen, the basic removal provision is § 1441(a). Removal is limited in diversity cases by § 1441(b). In addition to these primary provisions, § 1441(c) allows removal when the case includes a "separate and independent claim" based on federal question jurisdiction.[14] Most state procedures require some connection, such as being part of the same transaction or occurrence, between claims for them to be joined together in a complaint. The connection required to get the defendants together in *state* court is usually strong enough to prevent the claims from being separate enough for removal to *federal* court.

14. The separate and independent claim statute, § 1441(c), encompasses only federal question cases (§ 1331). Diversity cases, part removable and part not, must remain in state court. This treatment has changed several times over the years. Prior to the most recent amendment in 1990, § 1441(c) included both federal question and diversity cases. What constitutes a "separate and independent claim" was construed narrowly in *American Fire & Cas. Co. v. Finn*, 341 U.S. 6, 71 S.Ct. 534, 95 L.Ed. 702 (1951). Consequently, claims are rarely removable as "separate and independent."

As it is written today, § 1441(c) may well be unconstitutional. Because a "claim" is broadly construed to include an entire Constitutional case, which is essentially a single set of facts, a separate claim must be factually unrelated. Such an unrelated state law claim, while calling § 1441(c) into operation, would be beyond the scope of the Constitutional case allowed into federal court under supplemental jurisdiction under 28 U.S.C. § 1367 and indeed would exceed the judicial power allowed by Article III, § 2 of the Constitution. *See generally* 14C CHARLES A. WRIGHT, ARTHUR R. MILLER & EDWARD H. COOPER, FEDERAL PRACTICE AND PROCEDURE 3D § 3724 (1998).

Removal works in this fashion. Suppose a citizen of Connecticut sues a citizen of New York in Connecticut state court on a $150,000 personal injury claim arising from an accident that occurred in Connecticut. The Connecticut court, as a court of general subject matter jurisdiction, could try the case and render a valid judgment. On the other hand, § 1441 entitles the defendant to remove the case to federal court. Defendant could file a notice of removal in federal court within 30 days of "receipt by the defendant, through service or otherwise, of a copy of the initial pleading setting forth the claim for relief." 28 U.S.C. § 1446(b). Upon being notified of the removal, the state court "shall proceed no further" with the case. 28 U.S.C. § 1446(d). A plaintiff who believes the case has been removed improperly, *i.e.*, the federal court lacks subject matter jurisdiction, must bring a motion in the federal court to remand the case to state court. 28 U.S.C. § 1447(c).

The defendant's attorney might have any number of reasons, good or bad, to want to remove the case to federal court. The attorney might want to take advantage of federal discovery devices. The attorney might believe a federal judge or federal jury would be more favorable to the defendant. The attorney might simply be seeking an advantage if she has more experience in federal court than does plaintiff's attorney.

d. Supplemental Jurisdiction

Supplemental jurisdiction is discussed in Exercise Six: Joinder and Supplemental Jurisdiction.

C. Personal Jurisdiction

1. Rules of In Personam Jurisdiction

The following paragraphs describe four traditional grounds for jurisdiction over the person of the defendant—*in personam* jurisdiction—that have achieved general acceptance in American courts.

(a) *Consent.* A court has personal jurisdiction over a party who consents to the jurisdiction of the court. This consent may be express, as by an admission in open court; implied, as by driving on the roads of a state that has a statute deeming use of the state's roads to be a submission to jurisdiction; or even inadvertent, as by waiver of the defense for failure to raise it in the first response to the complaint [Fed.R.Civ.P. 12(h)(1). *See* Exercise Five: Motions to Dismiss and Waiver Under Federal Rule 12].

(b) *Domicile.* Courts can exercise personal jurisdiction over natural persons who are domiciled within the state even when they are temporarily absent. An analogous rule permits jurisdiction to be asserted over a corporation that is incorporated within the state or has its principal place of business there. Mostly this doctrine is part of the common law, but some states have embodied it in statute.

(c) *In-state Service.* Service on a natural person physically present within the territorial jurisdiction of a court secures personal jurisdiction over that defendant. Such "transient jurisdiction" was firmly established prior to *Pennoyer v. Neff*, 95 U.S. (5 Otto) 714, 24 L.Ed. 565 (1877), and remains good law today. This doctrine came under scholarly attack in the 1980s, but was reaffirmed in *Burnham v. Superior Court*, 495 U.S. 604, 110 S.Ct. 2105, 109 L.Ed.2d 631 (1990).

(d) *Contacts with the forum state.* After *Pennoyer*, absent consent or domicile, service on a defendant had to be within the boundaries of the forum state; service outside the state was unavailing. This rigid set of rules became more and more difficult to apply as the twentieth century produced a mobile society, interstate commerce, and corporate defendants. Courts could easily determine whether a natural person had been served within a state, but where was an incorporeal entity such as a corporation located? Under what circumstances was a corporation "present" or "doing business" in a state?

Finally, with its 1945 decision in *International Shoe Co. v. Washington*,[15] the Supreme Court of the United States completely changed the landscape of in personam jurisdiction. *International Shoe* decided that the due process clause of the United States Constitution allowed service on a defendant outside the state, so long as the defendant "have certain minimum contacts with [the state] such that the maintenance of the suit does not offend 'traditional notions of fair play and substantial justice.' "[16] This language became known as the minimum contacts test.

While due process allowed service outside the state, it did not require or implement such service. States had to pass statutes to assert "long-arm" jurisdiction—reaching out to seize a defendant beyond the boundaries of the state. Today all 50 states have long-arm statutes.

When this basis for personal jurisdiction is employed, the court must follow a two-step process. First, the defendant's act(s) must fall within the ambit of the long-arm statute. That is a question of

15. 326 U.S. 310, 66 S.Ct. 154, 90 L.Ed. 95 (1945).

16. *Id.* at 316, 66 S.Ct. at 158, 90 L.Ed. at 102.

statutory interpretation. Second, the exercise of jurisdiction under the long-arm statute must comply with the constitutional requirements of due process (the minimum contacts test). Only when both steps are satisfied may the court exercise jurisdiction.

(1) The state long-arm statutes. Over the years since *International Shoe*, states have enacted two primary types of long-arm statutes. The first type might be called enumerated acts statutes, in which the statute enumerates a list of actions by the defendant that will allow the state to assert jurisdiction over it. The court must decide whether the statute reaches the actions of the defendant. When the statute does not reach the defendant, the court need not consider due process. The second type might be called limits of due process statutes, which simply assert jurisdiction over any action of defendant and cast the entire decision of the appropriateness of jurisdiction on the minimum contacts test. We will discuss both types of long-arm statutes briefly.

The first state to enact a long-arm statute was Illinois in 1959. The drafters of the Illinois statute created an enumerated acts statute, listing four specific actions within the state's boundaries that would bring a nonresident defendant within the jurisdiction of the state: "transaction of any business," "commission of a tortious act," "ownership, use, or possession of any real estate," or "contracting to insure." Because Illinois was the first long-arm statute, its language was borrowed, at least in part, by a majority of American states.

Each state drafted its enumerated acts long-arm statute with different provisions, so we reproduce only one example. Uniform Interstate and International Procedure Act § 1.03 was promulgated for adoption by the states by the National Conference of Commissioners on Uniform State Laws in 1962, and it was adopted in many states:

(a) A court may exercise personal jurisdiction over a person, who acts directly or by an agent, as to a [cause of action] [claim for relief] arising from the person's

(1) transacting any business in this state;

(2) contracting to supply services or things in this state;

(3) causing tortious injury by an act or omission in this state;

(4) causing tortious injury in this state by an act or omission outside this state if he regularly does or solicits business, or engages in any other persistent course of conduct, or derives substantial revenue from goods used or consumed or services rendered, in this state; [or]

(5) having an interest in, using, or possessing real property in this state [; or

(6) contracting to insure any person, property, or risk located within this state at the time of contracting].

(b) When jurisdiction over a person is based solely upon this Section, only a [cause of action] [claim for relief] arising from acts enumerated in this Section may be asserted against him.[17]

Today, a large majority of American states have enumerated acts long-arm statutes. The situation is complicated, however, by a development in the law that began in Illinois in 1957. The state supreme court, in interpreting the nation's first long-arm statute, inserted a dictum into its opinion that the statute had a purpose to assert jurisdiction over nonresidents to the full extent permitted by the due process clause.[18] Even though Illinois continued to interpret its long-arm statute in a limited fashion, many other states' courts seized on that dictum and held that their limited, enumerated acts long-arm statutes were intended to, and so did, extend to the full limits of due process. Thus, by judicial decision, those courts converted their state statutes from enumerated acts statutes into limits of due process statutes.[19] Even though such interpretation of

17.   The categories of the Uniform Interstate and International Procedure Act can be seen as designed to confer personal jurisdiction over nonresidents in situations in which the state has a legitimate interest in adjudicating the action and is likely to be a fair and convenient location for the lawsuit. For example, consider § 1.03(a)(3), conferring jurisdiction over a person who causes tortious injury by an act or omission in the state. This provision would apply in a case in which a civil action is brought against a nonresident who had allegedly committed assault and battery within the state. The state has a legitimate interest in keeping peace within its boundaries. Moreover, it is likely to be a convenient place to try the action, since the witnesses to the incident and to any resultant injury are likely to be located within the state.

The justification for jurisdiction is weaker in the situation covered by § 1.03(a)(4), which deals with injury caused within the state by a tort committed outside the state. This provision would apply to a defendant that manufactured a product outside the state and shipped it into the state, where it caused injury. The evidence concerning alleged negligent manufacture of the product is likely to be located outside of the state. On the other hand, evidence relating to the plaintiff's injury is likely to be located in the state; the state has a legitimate interest in insuring that products within its borders are safe; and the requirement that the defendant have engaged in a persistent course of conduct in the state means that the defendant has had contacts with the state and should have been able to foresee the possibility of being sued there.

18.   Nelson v. Miller, 11 Ill. 2d 378, 389, 143 N.E.2d 673, 679 (1957).

19.   *See* Douglas D. McFarland, *Dictum Run Wild: How Long-arm Statutes Extended to the Limits of Due Process*, 84 Boston U. L. Rev. 491 (2004). This article concludes that today eighteen states have enumerated acts statutes that are interpreted by their limited language, twelve states have enumerated acts statutes that are interpreted to extend to the limits of due process, nine states have enumerated

detailed statutory language is highly questionable, it induced the withdrawal of Uniform Interstate and International Procedure Act § 1.03 in 1977 as "obsolete."

The second common type of long-arm statute is the limits of due process statute, which plainly asserts the power of the state over all actions of nonresident defendants that the due process clause, through the minimum contacts test, will allow. The first state to enact such a statute was Rhode Island in 1960. It hewed closely to the *International Shoe* language by passing a long-arm statute that reached nonresidents "that shall have the necessary minimum contacts with the state of Rhode Island." California extended this approach to the ultimate limit in 1969 by passing a statute that reads only "A court of this state may exercise jurisdiction on any basis not inconsistent with the Constitution of this state or of the United States."

To summarize, state long-arm jurisdiction requires the court to consider two steps: the long-arm statute and the due process clause (minimum contacts test). A state with an enumerated acts long-arm statute must first determine whether defendant's act is encompassed within the language of the statute, and can proceed to the second step only after an affirmative answer. A state that has a limits of due process long-arm statute, or that has interpreted its enumerated acts statute to reach the limits of due process, can proceed directly to the second step.

(2) Constitutional limits on in personam jurisdiction (the minimum contacts test). The long-arm statutes of the states can reach only so far as the Constitution allows. The constitutional limits of long-arm jurisdiction are found in the due process clause.

International Shoe established the test of due process to require that defendant has "certain minimum contacts with [the state] such that the maintenance of the suit does not offend 'traditional notions of fair play and substantial justice.' "[20] Later cases have interpreted, developed, and expanded this test. One early case emphasized that these minimum contacts with the state must be voluntary, or in other words, the defendant must "purposely avail" itself of the laws of the forum state.[21] Another decision apparently bifurcated the test into a minimum contacts part and a fair play and substantial justice part. In evaluating the latter portion of the test, the court can consider such things as the

acts statutes that have an additional limits of due process clause, and eleven states have limits of due process statutes.

20. 326 U.S. at 316, 66 S.Ct. at 158, 90 L.Ed. at 102.

21. Hanson v. Denckla, 357 U.S. 235, 253, 78 S.Ct. 1228, 1240, 2 L.Ed.2d 1283, 1298 (1958).

burden on the defendant, the plaintiff's interest, the forum state's interest, the interstate judicial system's interest, and the shared policy interests of the several states.[22]

Accordingly, a state court may not exercise jurisdiction over a nonresident defendant unless (1) the defendant has had minimum contacts with the state, (2) those contacts were voluntary, and (3) the state is a fair and convenient location for the lawsuit. When the defendant has had no contact with the state, then the state may not assert jurisdiction even if it is a convenient forum for the litigation.

The requirement of voluntary contact between the defendant and the state does not mean that the defendant need be physically present within the state. For example, a corporation that regularly ships its products into the forum state will likely be considered to have made voluntary contact even if none of its agents have ever been in the state. Still, the contact with the state must be purposeful. When a retailer sold an allegedly defectively designed automobile to a consumer in New York, who then drove the auto to Oklahoma and had an accident there, jurisdiction was not allowed in Oklahoma even though the retailer could reasonably have foreseen that some of the cars it sold would be driven nationwide. The defendant did not purposefully direct its product/activities toward the forum state.[23] In the intermediate area between the two examples given, a good deal of uncertainty remains about the boundaries of the requirement of voluntary contact.

The other requirement, fair play and substantial justice, is one that invites courts to consider a number of convenience factors. One is the probable location of witnesses and evidence. For example, in an action involving injury allegedly caused by a defective product, the state in which the injury occurred is likely to be one in which much of the relevant evidence may be found. The witnesses to the accident, and perhaps to the diagnosis and treatment of the injury, are likely to be there. Physical evidence, such as the product itself, may also be located there.

The forum state's interest in hearing the lawsuit also has a bearing on whether it can exercise jurisdiction. For example, a state has a particular interest in regulating insurance companies, and hence may hear a suit involving a nonresident insurance company that insured one of its citizens, when perhaps the facts would not justify permitting jurisdiction over an ordinary corporate defen-

22. Burger King Corp. v. Rudzewicz, 471 U.S. 462, 476–77, 105 S.Ct. 2174, 2184, 85 L.Ed.2d 528, 543 (1985).

23. World–Wide Volkswagen Corp. v. Woodson, 444 U.S. 286, 100 S.Ct. 559, 62 L.Ed.2d 490 (1980).

dant.[24] Thus, businesses that are especially in need of regulation to protect the consumer (insurance, stock brokerage), or companies and individuals that engage in dangerous activities, are subject to broader jurisdiction than other businesses or individuals.

Another factor that courts will consider is the connection between the defendant's activity in the state and the claim asserted. The question is whether the claim against defendant arises out of its activities within the state. For example, a mail order company may ship a widget to plaintiff in the forum state. Plaintiff is injured when the widget proves defective. Plaintiff's claim arises from defendant's contact with the forum state, so this is sometimes called specific jurisdiction. In contrast, a mail order company may ship may widgets into the forum state, but plaintiff is injured when he is struck by one of the company's delivery vehicles in another state. Plaintiff's claim does not arise from defendant's contacts with the forum state, so this is sometimes called general jurisdiction. While due process permits general jurisdiction—power over a defendant based on a claim unrelated to defendant's contacts with the forum state—many courts are reluctant to assert general jurisdiction over a nonresident defendant and will require a strong showing of continuous and systematic contacts.[25] This judicial regard for relatedness between defendant's activity in the state and the claim may arise from concern about the foreseeability of the litigation; a defendant who sells a product within a state should be able to foresee that it might be haled into court to defend lawsuits there based upon that product.

One area of continuing controversy is jurisdiction over a company that puts a product into the stream of commerce, and the stream carries the product into a state where it causes injury. The Supreme Court has split on the issue.[26]

24. *See* McGee v. International Life Ins. Co., 355 U.S. 220, 78 S.Ct. 199, 2 L.Ed.2d 223 (1957).

25. The long-arm statutes of many states do not even reach a defendant that engaged in one activity in a state but opened a potential liability with another, unrelated activity out of state. For example, Uniform Interstate and International Procedure Act § 1.03(a), pp. 43–44, required that the claim arise from the person's acts in the state.

One example of a court reluctant to assert general jurisdiction can be found in Helicopteros Nacionales de Colombia, S.A. v. Hall, 466 U.S. 408, 104 S.Ct. 1868, 80 L.Ed.2d 404 (1984).

26. In Asahi Metal Industry Co. v. Superior Court, 480 U.S. 102, 107 S.Ct. 1026, 94 L.Ed.2d 92 (1987), the Court splintered on the stream of commerce theory. Four Justices concluded that the theory is not constitutionally acceptable because a defendant by merely putting a product into the stream of commerce does not purposefully direct its activities at a particular state. Four Justices disagreed and concluded that the stream of commerce theory is constitutionally valid, but con-

Another area of emerging controversy is assertion of jurisdiction over a defendant whose contact with the forum state is through the internet. While the Supreme Court has not addressed the issue, lower courts appear to be coalescing around a "sliding scale" test.[27] The test results in jurisdiction when the defendant's activity over the internet increases: a passive web site does not, and an active web site does, create jurisdiction.

A student of long-arm jurisdiction should note that from *International Shoe* in 1945 until 1980, the trend of the law of personal jurisdiction was decidedly expansionary. The courts appeared to be moving toward a test of pure fairness and convenience, and the long arms of the states became ever longer. After the 1980 decision in *World–Wide Volkswagen Corp. v. Woodson,*[28] the trend halted abruptly. The courts, following the lead of the Supreme Court, have become more wary of jurisdictional assertions, and today closely examine the facts of each individual case to decide whether the particular assertion of jurisdiction satisfies the requirements of due process.

2. Rules of In Rem Jurisdiction

(a) Types of in rem jurisdiction. Courts may exercise jurisdiction over defendants who own property located within the state. When the action is to determine rights to property, the action is *in rem.* An action to quiet title or an action to probate an estate are examples of in rem jurisdiction.

When the underlying claim is unrelated to the property, and the property is seized solely to establish jurisdiction in the state, the action is *quasi in rem.* The location of the property, whether real or personal, in the state, gives the state court power over the action. For example, plaintiff wishes to sue defendant for $100,000 damages incurred in an automobile accident. The accident happened in Florida, but plaintiff wishes to sue in his home state of Illinois. Defendant has never been to Illinois, so that state's courts cannot

---

curred in dismissal because jurisdiction over the defendant did not meet fair play and substantial justice. The ninth Justice decided that jurisdiction was not fair, but expressed an opinion that selling a large number of units annually into a state would amount to a purposeful availment. Consequently, four Justices rejected the stream of commerce theory while five accepted it, although the Court was unanimous for dismissal. Since *Asahi,* five new Justices have joined the Court, so the constitutional status of the stream of commerce is murky.

27. The test was created in Zippo Mfg. Co. v. Zippo Dot Com, Inc., 952 F.Supp. 1119 (W.D.Pa. 1997).

28. 444 U.S. 286, 100 S.Ct. 559, 62 L.Ed.2d 490 (1980).

assert in personam jurisdiction over her. Defendant's uncle dies and leaves her a boat docked in Lake Michigan (Chicago docks) worth $35,000. The Illinois court can seize the boat to establish quasi in rem jurisdiction. Should plaintiff prevail in the suit, he can enforce the judgment against the boat, and will have a remaining claim of $65,000 to assert against defendant in another state. Such an assertion of quasi in rem jurisdiction is, however, limited by a standard of reasonableness required by the United States Constitution, as discussed in the next section.

Both of these types of jurisdiction are well recognized by American courts. Recently, courts have sometimes grouped both of these types of jurisdiction together as in rem jurisdiction.

(b) Constitutional limits on in rem jurisdiction. For many years, the requirements of fairness and convenience that restrict the assertion of in personam jurisdiction were thought to have no application to in rem and quasi in rem jurisdiction. Under this traditional view, the presence of property within the state could, without more, serve as a sufficient basis for jurisdiction. Thus, if the defendant owned property within State A, that state could take quasi in rem jurisdiction over a case arising from a factually unrelated automobile accident in State B, even if none of the evidence or witnesses were to be found in State A and defendant had never set foot in State A. The theoretical basis for jurisdiction was the state's power over the property, which would be seized (actually or symbolically) at the commencement of the action. While many states refused jurisdiction in such circumstances, others used their constitutional power to assert such jurisdiction.

In 1977, the Supreme Court swept away the special status of in rem and quasi in rem jurisdiction, holding that all assertions of state-court jurisdiction must be evaluated according to the standard of reasonableness of the minimum contacts test.[29] Consequently, states may continue to classify jurisdiction as in rem or quasi in rem if they wish, but exercises of jurisdiction under those labels are not valid merely because of the existence of property in the state. A nonresident defendant, who is not served in the state, must also have minimum contacts with the state so it is a minimally fair and convenient location for the lawsuit.

3. Personal Jurisdiction of Federal Courts

Even though Congress could probably, within the bounds of the Constitution, provide for exercise of nationwide personal juris-

---

29. Shaffer v. Heitner, 433 U.S. 186, 97 S.Ct. 2569, 53 L.Ed.2d 683 (1977).

diction by federal courts, it has not chosen so to extend the federal judicial power. As a general rule, the process (and therefore the personal jurisdiction) of a federal district court may not extend beyond the boundaries of the state in which the court sits, absent a state long-arm statute. Fed.R.Civ.P. 4(k)(1)(A). The federal district courts also exercise in rem jurisdiction to the extent it is exercised in the state where the federal court sits, at least when personal jurisdiction in the district cannot otherwise be obtained with reasonable efforts. Fed.R.Civ.P. 4(n)(2). Accordingly, federal court personal jurisdiction is generally co-extensive with state court personal jurisdiction: a federal court sitting within a given state may exercise personal jurisdiction only when a court of that state could do so. A few expansions to this territorial limit have been made by the Federal Rules of Civil Procedure or by statute, but none of these is relevant here.

D. Notice and Opportunity to Be Heard

The requirement of notice and opportunity to be heard is a jurisdictional prerequisite, but is easily satisfied and uncommonly disputed. The brief discussion at p. 29 is sufficient for purposes of this exercise.

E. Venue

1. State Courts

While jurisdiction deals with the authority of a court to exercise judicial power, venue deals with the place where that power should be exercised. State venue provisions name a county or a few counties within the state where the suit may be brought. Venue statutes vary widely from state to state, so the individual state's statute must be consulted.

Typical bases for venue include where the plaintiff resides, where the defendant resides, where the plaintiff or the defendant does business, and where the claim arose. These statutes are written on an abstract assessment of which courts are likely to be convenient to one or both parties. The limiting effect of a venue statute is to preclude the plaintiff from bringing the action in certain counties within the state that are likely to be inconvenient, particularly to the defendant.

2. Federal Courts

As do state venue statutes, the general federal venue statute divides judicial business among the federal courts on a basis of predicted convenience to the parties.

28 U.S.C. § 1391: Venue generally

(a) A civil action wherein jurisdiction is founded only on diversity of citizenship may, except as otherwise provided by law, be brought only in (1) a judicial district where any defendant resides, if all defendants reside in the same State, (2) a judicial district in which a substantial part of the events or omissions giving rise to the claim occurred, or a substantial part of property that is the subject of the action is situated, or (3) a judicial district in which the defendants are subject to personal jurisdiction at the time the action is commenced, if there is no district in which the action may otherwise be brought.

(b) A civil action wherein jurisdiction is not founded solely on diversity of citizenship may, except as otherwise provided by law, be brought only in (1) a judicial district where any defendant resides, if all defendants reside in the same State, (2) a judicial district in which a substantial part of the events or omissions giving rise to the claim occurred, or a substantial part of property that is the subject of the action is situated, or (3) a judicial district in which any defendant may be found, if there is no district in which the action may otherwise be brought.

(c) For purposes of venue under this chapter, a defendant that is a corporation shall be deemed to reside in any judicial district in which it is subject to personal jurisdiction at the time the action is commenced. In a State which has more than one judicial district and in which a defendant that is a corporation is subject to personal jurisdiction at the time an action is commenced, such corporation shall be deemed to reside in any district in that State within which its contacts would be sufficient to subject it to personal jurisdiction if that district were a separate State, and, if there is no such district, the corporation shall be deemed to reside in the district within which it has the most significant contacts.

(d) An alien may be sued in any district. * * *

As can be seen, § 1391(a) governs venue in diversity cases, and § 1391(b) governs venue in all other—typically federal question—cases. Historically, these two subsections were substantially different. For example, at one time, the district where all plaintiffs resided was an appropriate venue in diversity cases, but not in other cases. With the most recent revision of the venue statute in 1990, the two provisions are largely identical, and thus mostly redundant. Congress could revisit the statute and meld the two sections, but as with many areas of judicial administration, simply has not got around to it.

Accordingly, 28 U.S.C. §§ 1391(a)(1) and (b)(1) in all cases allow venue to be laid in a district where a defendant resides so long as all defendants reside in the same state.[30] Of course, when plaintiff sues multiple defendants, and not all reside in the same state, this venue possibility is unavailable. When this venue choice is unavailable or when plaintiff so chooses, 28 U.S.C. §§ 1391(a)(2) and (b)(2) in all cases allow venue to be laid in a district where "a substantial part of the events or omissions giving rise to the claim occurred." This second option may be only one state, or it may include several states. At one time, the statutory language for this option provided "where the claim arose." This was properly interpreted to mean a single state, and it produced much litigation when the claim arose in activities covering multiple states. Congress amended the statute in 1990 so that every state in which a substantial part of the claim arose is a proper venue.

The third options in §§ 1391(a) and 1391(b) are alike in that both are fallback provisions. They are available only when "there is no other district in which the action may otherwise be brought." That means all defendants do not reside in the same state and a substantial part of the claim did not arise in any district. This situation will occur when the claim arose in a foreign country. Despite this similarity, each of the two provisions does differ. For diversity cases, § 1391(a)(3) venue is proper in any district where any defendant is "subject to personal jurisdiction at the time the action is commenced." For cases other than diversity, § 1391(b)(3) venue is proper in any district in which "any defendant may be found." These two differing phrases are probably the result of

---

30. The statute does not require all defendants reside in the same federal district. Many states include more than one federal district. All defendants must reside in the same state, not the same district.

Federal courts treat residence in the venue statute as identical to citizenship. *See* CHARLES A. WRIGHT & MARY KAY KANE, THE LAW OF FEDERAL COURTS § 42 (6th ed. 2002). Citizenship is determined by domicile. *See Scoggins v. Pollock*, at p. 35. You should therefore treat "where a defendant resides" as equivalent to the state of which the party is a citizen in this exercise.

legislative inadvertence in the Congressional drafting process.[31] Accordingly, a court will likely interpret either as requiring only that a court have personal jurisdiction over a defendant. On the other hand, the language of the two sections is different and could lead to differing interpretations. For example, § 1391(b)(3) requires a district where "defendant may be found." This could mean where a defendant is present for in-state service. In differing language, § 1391(a)(3) requires personal jurisdiction "at the time the action is commenced." This could mean venue does not exist at the time of commencement of an action,[32] even though defendant later enters the state and is served within the Fed.R.Civ.P 4(m) 120–day time limit for service following commencement.

The venue provisions over certain types of defendants or actions are broader. A corporation is deemed by § 1391(c) to reside in any district in which it is subject to personal jurisdiction, which will almost certainly broaden the proper venues under both § 1391(a)(1) and § 1391(b)(1). Venue in a suit against an alien may be laid in any district by 28 U.S.C. § 1391(d). In addition to the proper venues in § 1391, many federal statutes have individual venue provisions, *e.g.*, 28 U.S.C. § 1396 (internal revenue taxes); 28 U.S.C. § 1400 (patent or copyright laws). For this exercise, we will limit our consideration to the general federal venue statute, 28 U.S.C. § 1391.

When a plaintiff lays venue in a wrong federal district, the defendant may waive objection to venue, either intentionally or inadvertently [Fed.R.Civ.P. 12(h)(1). *See* Exercise Five: Motions to Dismiss and Waiver Under Federal Rule 12]. When the defendant does object to venue, the court may either dismiss under Fed. R.Civ.P. 12(b)(3) for improper venue or transfer the action pursuant to the authority of 28 U.S.C. § 1406(a) to a district "in which it could have been brought."

3. Forum Non Conveniens

Sometimes a state trial court may decline to hear a case even when jurisdiction and venue are proper. Under the doctrine of *forum non conveniens*, the court has discretion *to dismiss* an action if the forum is so inconvenient that justice requires the action be brought elsewhere. A state court can only retain the action or dismiss; it cannot transfer the action to another state.

31. *See* David D. Siegel, *Commentary on 1995 Revision of Subdivision (a), Clause (3)*, 28 U.S.C.A. § 1391, 13–14 (1993).

32. Fed.R.Civ.P 3: "A civil action is commenced by filing a complaint with the court."

A federal court has the additional option of transfer of the case to a more convenient federal district: "For the convenience of parties and witnesses, in the interest of justice, a district court may transfer any civil action to any other district or division where it might have been brought."[33] In deciding whether to grant transfer under § 1404, federal courts generally take into account the same factors as do state courts in ruling on *forum non conveniens* motions, including availability of evidence, possibility of view, location of the parties, and location of witnesses.

A federal court may also dismiss on *forum non conveniens* when the more convenient court is in a foreign country. In making its decision whether to retain the case or to dismiss and hence require plaintiff to recommence in the foreign court, the federal court will consider "private interest factors," including convenience to parties and witnesses, and "public interest factors," including familiarity with the governing law.[34]

33.   28 U.S.C. § 1404(a).

34.   Piper Aircraft Co. v. Reyno, 454 U.S. 235, 102 S.Ct. 252, 70 L.Ed.2d 419 (1981).

*

II. QUESTIONS ON JURISDICTION

Instructions. The questions are on the left-hand page, and the answers are on the right-hand page. Cover the right-hand page, write your answers to the questions in the spaces provided, and compare your answers to the suggested answers on the facing page. P represents plaintiff, and D represents defendant.

A. Subject Matter Jurisdiction

1. Original Jurisdiction

Q–1. P1, an individual, and P2, a corporation, file a joint complaint in state X's court of general jurisdiction against defendants D1, D2, and D3. The complaint alleges several counts: violation of federal civil rights law, breach of contract, wrongful interference with business, and trespass to land. Is there subject matter jurisdiction?

Your answer _____.

Note: The remaining questions in this section place the action in federal court.

Q–2. P enters a contract with D Mint to provide 1000 commemorative coins for a festival P is promoting. D Mint is later informed by a Treasury agent that the coin would be too close to U.S. currency, and D Mint refuses to perform the contract. P pleads breach of contract, and that the defense of violation of federal coinage laws is ineffective. Is this a federal question?

Your answer _____.

Q–3. P is employed by D Corporation, which operates nationally. On P's 50th birthday, a supervisor fires her because "we do not want people above a certain age working for us." P sues in federal court for breach of the employment contract. Is this a federal question?

Your answer _____.

Q–4. P purchases stock from D in reliance on representations that prove false. P sues D for violation of § 10(b) of the Securities Exchange Act of 1934, for violation of the state anti-fraud securities statute, and for common law fraud. Is this a federal question?

Your answer _____.

Q–5. P, a citizen of California, sues D, a citizen of Iowa. The damages sought exceed the jurisdictional amount required. Is there diversity jurisdiction?

Your answer _____.

Answer to Q–1. Yes. A court of general subject matter jurisdiction has power to hear cases involving all types of parties and all types of claims. There is no jurisdiction problem here, although there may be a joinder problem (depending on the state's joinder provisions).

The fact that one of the theories presents a federal question *may allow*, but does *not require*, the case to be brought in federal court. This would be an example of concurrent jurisdiction (although some federal questions, such as bankruptcy, are exclusive federal jurisdiction).

Answer to Q–2. No. A federal question cannot arise in defense. *See Louisville & Nashville R.R. v. Mottley*, 211 U.S. 149, 29 S.Ct. 42, 53 L.Ed. 126 (1908), reproduced in Exercise One at p. 11. This question presents a variation on the same theme; the federal question is raised in an anticipated defense, which the defendant may or may not choose to assert. The federal question must arise in the *well-pleaded* complaint.

Answer to Q–3. No. Although plaintiff would appear to be able to assert a claim under the federal Age Discrimination in Employment Act on these facts, she has not done so. She pleaded only breach of contract, a state law theory. As a general proposition, plaintiff is master of her own complaint. This case is not within 28 U.S.C. § 1331.

Answer to Q–4. Yes. P's claim arises under a federal statute, the Securities Exchange Act of 1934. P's other theories of recovery, the state statute and common law fraud, while state law theories, can also be heard in federal court under the doctrine of supplemental jurisdiction. *See* the discussion of 28 U.S.C. § 1367 in Exercise Six: Joinder and Supplemental Jurisdiction.

Answer to Q–5. Yes. Diversity jurisdiction exists because the suit is between citizens of different states, and the minimum amount in controversy is satisfied. 28 U.S.C. § 1332(a)(1).

Q–6. P, a citizen of France, sues D, a citizen of Iowa, for damages exceeding the jurisdictional amount. Is there diversity jurisdiction?

Your answer _____.

Q–7. Part 1. P, a citizen of Germany, sues D, a citizen of Great Britain, for damages exceeding the jurisdictional amount. Is there diversity jurisdiction?

Your answer _____.

Part 2. Assume Congress amends 28 U.S.C. § 1332(a) to include a new provision granting the district courts jurisdiction over civil actions between aliens. Does this confer federal question jurisdiction in part 1?

Your answer _____.

Answer to Q–6. Yes. Diversity jurisdiction exists because the amount in controversy is sufficient and the suit is between a citizen of a state and a citizen or subject of a foreign state. 28 U.S.C. § 1332(a)(2). This is commonly called alienage jurisdiction.

Answer to Q–7. Part 1. No. There is no diversity jurisdiction because the suit is between citizens of two foreign states and hence does not fall within 28 U.S.C. § 1332(a)(2).

Part 2. No. Even though the suit between two aliens would, in this hypothetical, fall within 28 U.S.C. § 1332, the statute would be unconstitutional. Article III, § 2 of the United States Constitution (reproduced at pages 30–31 grants the federal courts authority over only specific classes of cases, and a suit between two aliens is not included.

Note that in Q–6 and Q–7, the interpretation of the statute is consistent with the goal of protecting out-of-state litigants from actual or perceived bias that they might encounter if forced to sue in state court. Were a citizen of California or of France forced to sue an Iowa citizen in Iowa state court, there might be a real or perceived danger of bias in favor of the Iowa citizen. On the other hand, the state court would presumably be neutral in a suit between two aliens. As is often the case, the somewhat ambiguous language of the statute (conferring jurisdiction upon suits "between . . . citizens of a State and citizens or subjects of a foreign state") can be illuminated by reference to its underlying purpose.

Admittedly, the hodge-podge of rules about diversity jurisdiction cannot always be explained in terms of the supposed goal of preventing local bias. For example, a citizen of Virginia may institute a diversity suit against a citizen of Georgia in federal court in Virginia, despite the fact that there is no *a priori* reason to believe that a citizen of Virginia would need to fear bias from a home state court.

Q–8. P, a citizen of Texas, sues D, a citizen of the United States who is domiciled in Arkansas, for an amount in excess of the jurisdictional amount. Is there diversity jurisdiction?

Your answer _____.

Q–9. P, a citizen of Illinois, sues D, a citizen of Mexico who has been admitted to the United States for permanent residence and is domiciled in Illinois, for an amount in excess of the jurisdictional amount. Is there diversity jurisdiction?

Your answer _____.

Q–10. Part 1. P, a citizen of Florida, sues D, an American citizen who moved to Florida from Michigan three months prior to the commencement of the action. D was born and reared in Michigan, and voted there in the last election, but now has an abode in Florida and intends to remain there permanently. The amount in controversy exceeds the jurisdictional amount. Is there diversity jurisdiction?

Your answer _____.

Part 2. Assume the same facts as Part 1, except D moves to Florida three months after commencement of the action. Is there diversity jurisdiction?

Your answer _____.

Part 3. P and D were both citizens of Michigan at the time the claim arose. P moved to Florida and became a citizen there for the avowed purpose of creating diversity jurisdiction, then commenced the action. Is there diversity jurisdiction?

Your answer _____.

Answer to Q–8. Yes. A natural person who is a citizen of the United States is also a citizen of the state in which that person is domiciled. See *Scoggins v. Pollock,* at p. 35. Therefore, diversity of citizenship jurisdiction exists under 28 U.S.C. § 1332(a)(1).

Answer to Q–9. No. Although 28 U.S.C. § 1332(a)(2) would appear to grant jurisdiction in this situation since the suit is between "citizens of a State and citizens or subjects of a foreign state," there is no diversity of citizenship because 28 U.S.C. § 1332(a) provides that "[A]n alien admitted to the United States for permanent residence shall be deemed a citizen of the State in which such alien is domiciled." The intent of this provision is to restrict diversity jurisdiction. Accordingly, D will be deemed a citizen of Illinois, and since P is a citizen of Illinois, there is no diversity.

Answer to Q–10. Part 1. No. Since D has physically moved to Florida and intends to remain there permanently, D has become domiciled in Florida under the test set forth in *Scoggins v. Pollock,* at p. 35. D is consequently a citizen of Florida.

Part 2. Yes. Citizenship is determined as of the day of the commencement of the action. Diversity is not destroyed by later actions of the parties.

Part 3. Yes. Diversity is determined by the citizenship of the parties as of the day of commencement. P's motive in becoming a Florida citizen is not relevant. *See* CHARLES A. WRIGHT & MARY KAY KANE, THE LAW OF FEDERAL COURTS § 28 (6th ed. 2002). D might challenge P's intent to remain in the new state indefinitely, as was done in *Baker v. Keck,* but this question states P became a citizen of Florida.

Q–11. P, a citizen of Ohio, sues D, an American citizen who was born and reared in Ohio, but who left two months ago to work for the Peace Corps in Costa Rica. D does not know where she will live after she finishes her two-year stint in the Peace Corps, but she has a definite intention not to live in either Ohio or Costa Rica. The amount in controversy exceeds the jurisdictional amount. Is there diversity jurisdiction?

Your answer _____.

Q–12. P, a citizen of Oregon, sues D Corporation, which is incorporated in Delaware and has its principal place of business in Oregon, for an amount exceeding the jurisdictional amount. Is there diversity jurisdiction?

Your answer _____.

Q–13. P, a citizen of North Carolina, sues D, a citizen of New York, for $200,000 for personal injuries arising out of an automobile accident in Pennsylvania. Suit is brought in federal district court in North Carolina. D has never been to North Carolina and has no connection with it except for this suit. Is there diversity jurisdiction?

Your answer _____.

Answer to Q–11. No. Since D has not acquired a new domicile, she is deemed to have retained her old domicile in Ohio despite her intention not to return there. *See Scoggins v. Pollock,* at p. 35.

Answer to Q–12. No. The corporation has dual citizenship: Delaware and Oregon. 28 U.S.C. § 1332(c)(1) provides "[A] corporation shall be deemed to be a citizen of any State by which it has been incorporated and of the State where it has its principal place of business." Therefore, the plaintiff and defendant are citizens of the same state–Oregon–and there is no diversity jurisdiction.

Prior to the enactment of 28 U.S.C. § 1332(c) in 1958, a corporation was a citizen only of the state in which it was incorporated. Therefore, a corporation owned and operated in Oregon by Oregonians could litigate its local disputes in federal court if it were formally incorporated in another state, even though it would have no legitimate reason to fear prejudice at the hands of Oregon state courts. Section 1332(c) was amended to correct this anomaly.

Answer to Q–13. Yes. Diversity jurisdiction is a form of *subject matter jurisdiction.* It is based on the theory that a federal court is particularly competent, because of its neutrality, to decide cases involving citizens of different states. *Personal jurisdiction* is a separate jurisdictional requirement based upon the connection of the defendant to the forum state. Requirements of personal jurisdiction are designed to ensure that the suit is brought in a state that has power over the defendant and is a geographic location that is reasonably fair and convenient. *Venue* is also a separate requirement, dealing with convenience of the location of the action. Diversity jurisdiction exists here. The question does not ask about personal jurisdiction or venue; objection to either would likely result in dismissal.

Q–14. A, a citizen of Nebraska, sues D1, a citizen of Washington, and D2, a citizen of Tennessee, for a claim that arose at a luau while all three parties were vacationing in Hawaii. The claim exceeds the jurisdictional amount. P files the action in the District of Hawaii. Is there diversity jurisdiction?

Your answer _____.

Answer to Q–14. Yes. Diversity of citizenship exists between the parties. The fact that the suit was brought in Hawaii does not deprive the court of diversity jurisdiction. [Personal jurisdiction and venue are also likely proper here.]

This rule has been criticized on the ground a local state court would not likely be biased in a suit between two noncitizens. For example, there is no reason to believe the state court of Hawaii would favor one party or the other in a suit between a plaintiff from Nebraska and defendants from Washington and Tennessee. Hence, no reason exists to confer federal diversity jurisdiction upon that case. The purpose of diversity jurisdiction would seem to be served adequately by a rule that provided a federal forum for suits brought in a state in which one of the parties was domiciled; however, 28 U.S.C. § 1332 confers diversity jurisdiction upon all federal courts, regardless of whether any of the parties is a citizen of the state in which the suit has been brought. When one federal court has diversity jurisdiction, then all federal courts have diversity jurisdiction.

Q–15. P, a citizen of Delaware, sues D1, a citizen of New Jersey, and D Corporation, which is incorporated in Delaware and has its principal place of business in New Jersey, in the District of New Jersey. The amount in controversy exceeds the jurisdictional amount. Is there diversity jurisdiction?

Your answer _____.

Answer to Q–15. No. "Complete diversity" does not exist. There is no diversity of citizenship between P and D Corporation, since both are citizens of Delaware. There is diversity between P and D1. The issue, then, is whether minimal diversity, *i.e.,* between one plaintiff and one defendant, is sufficient to establish jurisdiction under § 1332. In *Strawbridge v. Curtiss,* 7 U.S. (3 Cranch) 267, 2 L.Ed. 435 (1806), Chief Justice John Marshall interpreted the language of a predecessor statute to § 1332(a)(1) to mean diversity of citizenship must exist between each plaintiff and each defendant. When one plaintiff and one defendant are citizens of the same state, the federal court has no jurisdiction, even if there is diversity among all other parties.

This rule of complete diversity has been criticized because it excludes federal jurisdiction in circumstances in which there may be a genuine danger of local prejudice. For example, P might have a genuine reason to fear prejudice in state court in New Jersey. Chief Justice Marshall himself is said to have expressed doubts about the wisdom of *Strawbridge,* but the rule of complete diversity remains good law. We do know today that complete diversity is required only by the statute, and not by Article III, § 2 of the Constitution. *See State Farm Fire & Cas. Co. v. Tashire,* 386 U.S. 523, 87 S.Ct. 1199, 18 L.Ed.2d 270 (1967).

2. Removal Jurisdiction

Q–16. P1, a citizen of New Mexico, and P2, a citizen of Colorado, sue D1, a citizen of Utah, and D2, a citizen of California, in Arizona state court. The claim arises under Arizona state law. The amount in controversy exceeds $75,000. May the defendants remove the action to federal court?

Your answer _____.

Q–17. Part 1. P, a citizen of Kentucky, sues D, a citizen of Indiana, in state court in the state of Kentucky. The claim arises under state law and the amount in controversy is $50,000. May D remove the case to federal court?

Your answer _____.

Part 2. Assume instead that the amount in controversy is $75,000. May D remove the case to federal court?

Your answer _____.

Q–18. Part 1. P sues D in state court in Connecticut. The claim arises under state law and the amount in controversy is $200,000. P was born and raised in Vermont, but moved to Connecticut shortly before the commencement of the action and intends to remain there permanently. D is domiciled in Connecticut. May D remove the action to federal court?

Your answer _____.

Part 2. P remains domiciled in Vermont until after she commences the action in Connecticut state court. D is domiciled in Connecticut. May D remove the action to federal court?

Your answer _____.

Q–19. P Corporation, which is incorporated and has its principal place of business in Massachusetts, sues X Corporation, which is incorporated and has its principal place of business in California, and Y Corporation, which is incorporated in Delaware and has its principal place of business in New York. The action is commenced in state court in New York. The claim is breach of a contract in which X Corporation promised to deliver widgets to P Corporation and Y Corporation issued a surety bond for performance. The amount in controversy is one million dollars and the claim arises under state law. May the defendants remove the case to federal court?

Your answer _____.

Answer to Q–16. Yes. The parties are of diverse citizenship and the requirements of 28 U.S.C. § 1441(a) have been met. The fact that the Arizona court has concurrent jurisdiction does not prevent removal of the case to federal court.

Answer to Q–17. Part 1. No. An action is removable only if the federal district court has original jurisdiction. *See* 28 U.S.C. § 1441(a). This action could not have been brought in federal court because the amount in controversy does not satisfy the jurisdictional amount.

Part 2. No, for the same reason. The jurisdictional amount is satisfied only when "the matter in controversy *exceeds* the sum or value of $75,000* * *." 28 U.S.C. § 1332(a).

Answer to Q–18. Part 1. No. The district court does not have original jurisdiction because both parties are citizens of Connecticut. P has acquired a domicile in Connecticut because the two elements of physical presence and intent to remain indefinitely are satisfied. *See Scoggins v. Pollock,* at p. 35.

Note that the technically correct answer to the question posed is yes, D may remove the case to federal court because a notice of removal operates automatically to remove the case from state to federal court. 28 U.S.C. § 1446(d). Since the case would not have properly been removed, however, plaintiff will succeed in a motion to remand the case to state court. 28 U.S.C. § 1447(c).

Part 2. No. Although the district court would have original jurisdiction over the action since the parties are of diverse citizenship, and plaintiff could have sued originally in federal court, the removal statute does not allow a defendant who is a citizen of the state in which the action was brought to remove. 28 U.S.C. § 1441(b). The rationale is that a defendant who is a citizen of the state need not fear local prejudice.

Answer to Q–19. No. Although the parties are of diverse citizenship and the district court would have original jurisdiction, Y Corporation is a citizen of New York because it has its principal place of business there [28 U.S.C. § 1332(c)(1)], so as in Q–18, part 2, the action is not removable because one of the defendants is a citizen of the state in which the action was brought.

The claim against the California corporation does not fit within 28 U.S.C. § 1441(c) for two reasons: no federal question is involved, and there is no "separate and independent claim or cause of action." *See* CHARLES A. WRIGHT & MARY KAY KANE, THE LAW OF FEDERAL COURTS § 39 (6th ed. 2002).

Q–20. P, a citizen of Alabama, sues D, a citizen of Louisiana, in state court of Louisiana. The action arises under a federal statute that confers concurrent jurisdiction upon state and federal courts. The amount in controversy exceeds the jurisdictional amount. May D remove the action to federal court?

Your answer ————————————.

B. Personal Jurisdiction

Q–21. Part 1. Defendant of Nebraska went to Colorado for a picnic. She stayed only a few hours. While in Colorado, she was served with process from a Colorado state court. The action arose from an automobile accident that occurred in Wyoming. Does Colorado have personal jurisdiction in the action?

Your answer ————————————.

Part 2. Same facts as Part 1, except that the defendant is a corporation. Its President goes to Colorado for a short personal errand and is served with process. Does Colorado have jurisdiction over the action?

Your answer ————————————.

Q–22. D Corporation was incorporated in Nevada solely to obtain the benefits of a favorable corporation law. D Corporation's only place of business is in Texas. Other than incorporation, it has no contacts at all with Nevada: no property, no business activity, no shareholders. P, a Texas resident, sues D Corporation in Nevada state court on an automobile accident that occurred in Texas. May Nevada exercise personal jurisdiction over D Corporation?

Your answer ————————————.

Q–23. D Corporation is incorporated and has its principal place of business in state A. It ships 2000 cases of beer a year to X, a wholesaler in state B. It does no other business in state B. P, a management consultant in state B, sues D Corporation in state court of state B claiming failure to pay for services he performed for D Corporation in state A. May state B exercise personal jurisdiction in the case of P v. D Corporation?

Your answer ————————————.

Q–24. Under a long-arm statute, a state court in state X can exercise personal jurisdiction over defendant based on defendant's minimum contacts with state X. Does a federal court sitting in state X also have personal jurisdiction over defendant?

Your answer ————————————.

Answer to Q–20. Yes. The subject matter jurisdiction of the federal court is based upon the existence of a federal question and therefore the action is removable "without regard to the citizenship or residence of the parties." 28 U.S.C. § 1441(b). Federal question cases are treated differently from diversity cases because federal question jurisdiction is not based upon fear of prejudice in state courts against non-citizens, but upon the special competency of the federal courts to decide questions of federal law.

Answer to Q–21. Part 1. Yes. Defendant was served in the state. Assertion of "transient" or "territorial" jurisdiction is of long standing, and has been upheld against constitutional attack even where defendant had no connection with the forum other than service in the state. *Burnham v. Superior Court,* 495 U.S. 604, 110 S.Ct. 2105, 109 L.Ed.2d 631 (1990).

Part 2. No. Transient jurisdiction normally applies only when the defendant is a natural person present within the state. A corporation is an artificial person. No other basis for personal jurisdiction exists here.

Answer to Q–22. Yes. Incorporation in a state gives the state power to subject the corporation to its courts. This is akin to service on a natural person within a state.

Answer to Q–23. No. First, even though D Corporation is transacting business in state B, that business has no connection with the claim. The long-arm statutes of many states require that the claim arise out of the events that take place in the state. *See, e.g.,* Uniform Interstate and International Procedure Act § 1.03(b), at pp. 43–44.

Second, even in those states that have long-arm statutes that reach to the limits of due process—whether by specific provision or court interpretation—D Corporation would not likely be found to have sufficient minimum contacts such as not to offend traditional notions of fair play and substantial justice in state B. This would be an attempted assertion of general jurisdiction by state B (the claim does not arise from the contacts), and courts require a high level of continuous and systematic business to establish minimum contacts with the state in such a case.

Answer to Q–24. Yes. Because Fed.R.Civ.P. 4(k)(1)(A) incorporates state long-arm statutes, a federal court may exercise personal jurisdiction whenever the state in which it is located would have personal jurisdiction. [A federal court may also exercise personal jurisdiction under Fed.R.Civ.P. 4(k) in a few situations when the state court could not, but these are not relevant here.]

Q–25. Part 1. D Corporation is incorporated and has its only place of business in state A. It contracts with P, a resident of state B, to ship 100 cases of whiskey from state A to state B. D Corporation fails to ship the whiskey, and consequently, P sues D Corporation in state court in B. May state B exercise personal jurisdiction over D Corporation?

Your answer _____.

Part 2. Same facts as Part 1, with the additional facts that D Corporation has shipped whiskey to P in state B for several years, P has always paid for those shipments with checks drawn on a bank in state B, and P has negotiated prices and other contract terms with D Corporation over the telephone and by mail from P's office in state B. May state B exercise personal jurisdiction over D Corporation?

Your answer _____.

Q–26. D Corporation, located solely in Michigan, has supplied component parts to Acme Manufacturing Co., located in North Carolina, for several years. Acme is D Corporation's primary customer. Acme uses the parts and ships the final product nation-wide. One of the parts fails and P is injured in New York. Does New York have personal jurisdiction over D Corporation?

Your answer _____.

C. Notice and Opportunity to Be Heard

Q–27. P landlord commenced an action to evict D tenant pursuant to state unlawful detainer law for failure to pay rent. Service was made on D by tacking the summons and complaint to D's apartment door, even though such notices had sometimes in the past disappeared from other tenants' doors. Is this constitution-ally sufficient notice to D?

Your answer _____.

Answer to Q–25. Part 1. No. The long-arm statute is likely to be satisfied. For example, Uniform Interstate and International Procedure Act § 1.03(a)(2), at p. 43, provides jurisdiction when the claim arises from defendant's "contracting to supply services or things in this state." Second, however, the defendant must have minimum contacts with the state so that exercise of jurisdiction over it would not offend traditional notions of fair play and substantial justice. On the facts here, D Corporation has no contact with state B other than a single, unperformed contract. A court will conclude the exercise of jurisdiction would violate due process.

Part 2. Yes. As in Part 1, the long-arm statute is satisfied. The additional facts clearly supply sufficient minimum contacts of D Corporation with state B for the court to exercise jurisdiction.

Answer to Q–26. Maybe. The first question is whether the long-arm statute reaches defendant's actions, so we would look at the New York statute. If we assume the New York statute is similar to Uniform Interstate and International Procedure Act § 1.03(a)(4), found at pp. 43–44, D Corporation did cause "tortious injury in this state by an act or omission outside this state;" the additional requirement is that D Corporation "derives substantial revenue from goods or services used or consumed in this state." This element will be more difficult to satisfy and will likely require production of a record to show the revenues.

The due process step may or may not be satisfied. D Corporation has placed its product into the stream of commerce, perhaps knowing that some portion will flow into New York. There are no other known contacts. The plurality opinion in *Asahi Metal Industry Co. v. Superior Court,* 480 U.S. 102, 107 S.Ct. 1026, 94 L.Ed.2d 92 (1987), disapproves the stream of commerce theory as a basis for personal jurisdiction. Two concurring opinions, commanding five votes, appear to approve the stream of commerce theory, but agree on dismissal for other reasons. Accordingly, the constitutional acceptability of the stream of commerce theory is in doubt. See n. 25, *supra.*

Answer to Q–27. No. Due process requires that P choose a method of notice that is reasonably calculated to give actual notice, "reasonably certain to inform those affected." *Mullane v. Central Hanover Bank & Trust Co.,* 339 U.S. 306, 315, 70 S.Ct. 652, 657, 94 L.Ed. 865, 874 (1950). Here P was aware of D's location and chose to notify by posting on a door to a common area, even though other such notices had disappeared. Such notice is constitutionally inadequate. *Greene v. Lindsey,* 456 U.S. 444, 102 S.Ct. 1874, 72 L.Ed.2d 249 (1982).

Q–28. State X's garnishment statute allows seizure when plaintiff alleges defendant is about to waste property in which plaintiff has an ownership interest. Plaintiff must file a detailed affidavit of the facts and post a bond. The garnishment order must be signed by a judge. Plaintiff is allowed a hearing on the seizure "no later than two weeks after the sheriff takes possession of the property." Does this procedure provide a constitutional opportunity to be heard?

Your answer _____.

Answer to Q–28. Maybe. The Supreme Court's earlier pre-judgment seizure cases seem to require four criteria be met for a constitutional seizure: 1) plaintiff must file a particularized affidavit, 2) plaintiff must post a bond, 3) a judge must approve the seizure, and 4) defendant must receive a right to an early hearing. The first three appear to be met. The question is whether a hearing "no later than two weeks" after the seizure is a "prompt post deprivation hearing." The Court has not specified a time limit. The Court's latest decision, *Connecticut v. Doehr,* 501 U.S. 1, 111 S.Ct. 2105, 115 L.Ed.2d 1 (1991), appears to turn more toward a balancing test to evaluate a pre-judgment seizure. The court is to balance the interest of the party from whom the property is seized, the interest of the party seizing the property, and the risk of erroneous deprivation. To apply such a balancing test in this question, we would need additional facts.

D. Venue

Q–29. P, a resident of South Dakota, sues D, a resident of Kansas, in federal district court in Nebraska on a claim based upon an automobile accident in Nebraska. Jurisdiction is based solely on diversity of citizenship. Is venue properly laid in Nebraska?

Your answer ————————————.

Q–30. Part 1. P, a resident of Illinois, sues D, a resident of Ohio, and D Corporation, which is incorporated and has its principal place of business in Indiana. D Corporation regularly does business and so is subject to personal jurisdiction in Illinois, Ohio, Indiana, and Kentucky. The sole basis for jurisdiction is diversity of citizenship. The claim arises from an automobile accident in California. Is venue properly laid in federal district court in Ohio?

Your answer ————————————.

Part 2. Could venue properly be laid in federal district court in Illinois?

Your answer ————————————.

Part 3. Could venue properly be laid in federal district court in Indiana?

Your answer ————————————.

Part 4. Would your answer to any of the above parts of this question be different if federal subject matter jurisdiction were based on a federal question instead of diversity of citizenship?

Your answer ————————————.

Answer to Q–29. Yes. A substantial part of the events or omissions giving rise to the claim–indeed the whole claim–arose in Nebraska, which is a permissible venue. 28 U.S.C. § 1391(a)(2). Another permissible venue would have been Kansas, where defendant lives. 28 U.S.C. § 1391(a)(1).

Answer to Q–30, Part 1. Yes. Both defendants reside in Ohio, so venue is proper under 28 U.S.C. § 1391(a)(1). D Corporation is deemed a resident of Ohio under § 1391(c) because it is subject to personal jurisdiction there when the action is commenced.

Part 2. No. The residence of the plaintiff is not a permissible venue under § 1391(a). Both defendants do not reside in Illinois, so § 1391(a)(1) does not apply, and no part of the claim arose there, so § 1391(a)(2) does not apply.

An argument that § 1391(a)(3) applies, allowing venue in a district "in which any defendant is subject to personal jurisdiction," would fail. As a fallback provision, § 1391(a)(3) applies only when "there is no other district in which the action may otherwise be brought." As can be seen in part 1, the action may be brought in Ohio under § 1391(a)(1). Also, the action may be brought in California under § 1391(a)(2).

Part 3. No. Venue may be laid, pursuant to § 1391(a)(1), in a district where "any defendant resides, if all defendants reside in the same State." Defendant D Corporation resides in Indiana, but defendant D does not. No part of the claim arose in Indiana. Since venue could be laid in either Ohio or California, the fallback provision cannot be used.

Part 4. No. The two venue statutes differ only in their third subsections. The "catch-all" federal question venue subsection, § 1391(b)(3), is worded differently from the "catch-all" diversity venue subsection, § 1391(a)(3), but both are similar in that they apply only when venue cannot properly be laid in another district. From parts 1 and 2, both Ohio and California would be proper venues.

III. COMPUTER EXERCISES

A. CALI CIV 03: Jurisdiction and Venue

1. Facts

You are a lawyer working for a firm in the state of Fraser. One of the firm's partners asks you to do some research on a personal injury action. Pam Pedestrian is a local resident who was involved in an accident in the state of Elliott while on summer vacation there. A truck driven by a servant of D Corporation collided with a car driven by David Driver, causing Driver's car to swerve onto the sidewalk and strike Pedestrian. The partner wants to sue both D Corporation and David Driver, and asks you to identify states where the action can be brought without being dismissed for lack of jurisdiction or improper venue. Pedestrian's claim will be based on negligence, and therefore arises under state law.

The partner hands you the file in Pedestrian's case. It yields the following information.

Pedestrian is a doctor who practices in Fraser. She owns a home in Fraser, where she was born and reared and plans to live out her days. She was injured in the accident, and if liability can be established, Pedestrian could realistically hope to recover about $250,000.

David Driver is a law student who lived at his parent's home in Fraser through high school. He next lived on campus while attending college at Fraser State University, and then moved to a small apartment in the state of Coffman when he became a student at Coffman Law School. Driver's parents support him while he attends law school, and he has frequently returned to his parent's home in Fraser during vacation periods. Driver is a third-year law student. Between his second and third years of law school, Driver was a summer associate for a law firm in Coffman. During the summer, he moved from the apartment he had rented for two years into the much larger apartment he now occupies.

Two months ago, Driver accepted a full-time job with a law firm in the state of Northrop. He obtained the job through interviews at Coffman Law School, and has not visited Northrop since accepting the job. He says he plans to remain in Coffman only until his graduation five months hence. Just recently, Driver inherited a $120,000 house in Northrop from a cousin. He has never occupied or even seen the house, and it is being rented to tenants on a lease that expires in six months. Driver told the law firm in Northrop that if he got an offer he would move to Northrop and live there permanently.

D Corporation is a shoe manufacturer incorporated in the state of Coffman. Its home office and manufacturing plant are located in the state of Northrop. Consequently, its corporate officers and all of its employees are located in Northrop, although a few of its sales representatives occasionally travel in neighboring states to take orders for shoes. D Corporation sells most of its shoes in Northrop, but it sells a substantial number of shoes on a regular basis to wholesalers in both Coffman and Fraser. D Corporation has not sold any shoes or conducted any other business activities, directly or indirectly, in Elliott. The truck involved in the accident was passing through Elliott while transporting a shoe display to an industrial fair in another state. With the exception of property specifically described above, neither defendant owns any attachable property in any states.

Your initial research shows that all states involved in this case have adopted the general American rules of personal jurisdiction described above at pages ___.

2. *Fact Summary*

   Fraser is

— Pedestrian's home state

— the home state of Driver's parents

— one of the states in which D Corporation sells shoes

   Coffman is

— the state where Driver is now attending law school

— one of the states in which D Corporation sells shoes

— the state in which D Corporation is incorporated

   Elliott is

— the site of the accident

   Northrop is

— the state of D Corporation's plant and home office

— the state of Driver's future law firm employer

— the state where the house inherited by Driver is located

— one of the states in which D Corporation sells shoes

3. *Questions for Computer Exercise*

   Please answer "yes," "no," or "maybe" to each of the following questions. Assume that the defendants will raise every objection to jurisdiction and venue available to them, and that none of the courts will dismiss on *forum non conveniens*.

The "maybe" answer should be used when you believe a categorical "yes" or "no" is inappropriate. When more facts are needed before a decision can be made, or if sufficient facts are known but both sides have substantial legal arguments, then answer "maybe." You should not base a "maybe" answer on conceivable but frivolous legal arguments or on factual possibilities that are unusual and improbable.

Q–1. COFFMAN–FEDERAL COURT

Can Pedestrian bring suit against both defendants in federal court in Coffman?

[Note: Your answer to this question should take into account all aspects of jurisdiction. The following questions will probe each of these aspects.]

Answer: _____

1a. Would the court have subject matter jurisdiction?

Answer: _____

Briefly state reasons for your answer: _____

_____

_____

_____

_____

_____

1b. Would the court have personal (including quasi in rem) jurisdiction?

Answer: _____

Reasons: _____

_____

_____

_____

_____

1c. Would venue be proper?

Answer: _____

Reasons: _____

_____

_____
_____
_____
_____

Q–2. COFFMAN–STATE COURT

Can Pedestrian bring suit against both defendants in state court in Coffman?

[Note: Since at least one court in the state system will be a court of general subject matter jurisdiction, and venue will always be proper in at least one state court, you need consider only whether the state has personal (including quasi in rem) jurisdiction to answer the state court questions.]

Answer: _____

Reasons: _____

_____
_____
_____
_____
_____

Q–3. ELLIOTT–FEDERAL COURT

Can Pedestrian bring suit against both defendants in federal court in Elliott?

Answer: _____

3a. Would the court have subject matter jurisdiction?

Answer: _____

Reasons: _____

_____
_____
_____
_____
_____

3b. Would the court have personal (including quasi in rem) jurisdiction?

Answer: _____

Reasons: _____

_____

_____

_____

_____

3c. Would venue be proper?

Answer: _____

Reasons: _____

_____

_____

_____

_____

Q–4. ELLIOTT–STATE COURT

Can Pedestrian bring suit against both defendants in state court in Elliott?

Answer: _____

Reasons: _____

_____

_____

_____

_____

Q–5. NORTHROP–FEDERAL COURT

Can Pedestrian bring suit against both defendants in federal court in Northrop?

Answer: _____

5a. Would the court have subject matter jurisdiction?

Answer: _____

Reasons: _____

_____

_____

_____

_____

5b. Would the court have personal (including quasi in rem) jurisdiction?

Answer: _____

Reasons: _____

_____

_____

_____

_____

5c. Would venue be proper?

Answer: _____

Reasons: _____

_____

_____

_____

_____

Q–6. NORTHROP–STATE COURT

Can Pedestrian bring suit against both defendants in state court in Northrop?

Answer: _____

Reasons: _____

_____

_____

_____

_____

Q–7. FRASER–FEDERAL COURT

Can Pedestrian bring suit against both defendants in federal court in Fraser?

Answer: _____

7a. Would the court have subject matter jurisdiction?

Answer: _____

Reasons: _____

_____

_____

_____

_____

_____

7b. Would the court have personal (including quasi in rem) jurisdiction?

Answer: _____

Reasons: _____

_____

_____

_____

_____

_____

7c. Would venue be proper?

Answer: _____

Reasons: _____

_____

_____

_____

_____

_____

Q–8. FRASER–STATE COURT

Can Pedestrian bring suit against both defendants in state court in Fraser?

Answer: _____

Reasons: _____

_____

_____

_____

_____

_____

_____

This concludes the questions. You are now ready to go to the computer to work through CALI CIV 03: Jurisdiction and Venue.

B. CALI CIV 19: Jurisdiction Over the Person

In addition to the computer exercise you have prepared above, you may wish to gain additional understanding of jurisdiction by doing the CALI computer exercise "Jurisdiction over the Person" by James M. Klebba.[35] A description of the exercise is reproduced below.

This exercise is designed for a student who has already read most of the material on personal jurisdiction in a typical first year civil procedure course. The topics covered include: the "minimum contacts" test as a measure of the due process clause of the 14th Amendment, the interpretation and application of typical longarm statutes, the interplay of statutory interpretation with the constitutional requirements, the difference between "specific" and "general" jurisdiction, the extent to which a defendant may contractually waive jurisdiction protections, an exploration of the different ways in which the jurisdictional rules apply depending on whether the defendant is an individual or a corporation, and the continued viability of the concept of "transient" jurisdiction. The above topics are explored through a series of hypotheticals, beginning with an extended variation on the facts of International Shoe. The two predominant jurisdictional statutes used in the exercise are the Uniform Interstate and International Procedure Act and the Rhode Island (California) statute which extends jurisdiction to the limits of the Due Process Clause. At appropriate points in the exercise students are able to refer back to the introductory fact situations, the Uniform Act, a list of important citations and previous related questions. The exercise is divided into three parts, so that one part can be conveniently done at a sitting.

35. Victor H. Schiro Professor of Law, Loyola University School of Law, New Orleans. The exercise is used with permission of CALI.

*

EXERCISE THREE

Pleading a Complaint

This exercise is about pleading, but more specifically, it is about pleading a complaint. Following discussion of the history of pleading under the common law and the codes, the exercise explores the requirements of pleading a complaint under the Federal Rules of Civil Procedure. It does not expand into the general topic of pleading, so subjects such as responses to a complaint, additional pleadings, and amendments to pleadings are not included. The exercise culminates in the pleading of a complaint for defamation, and to that end includes the facts of a hypothetical case plus discussion of the substantive law of defamation.

I. HISTORY OF PLEADING

A. Pleading under the Common Law

1. The Systems of Law and Equity

The judicial system in England developed two separate and distinct types of courts. These two systems of courts—law and equity—were independent of each other: they developed and expanded their jurisdictions separately and not as a complementary system. Even though these courts offered a litigant different types of relief, the litigant was forced to choose the correct court at his peril. A case commenced in one court could not be transferred to another court.

On one side of the divide were the three common law courts. King's Bench originally heard criminal cases and pleas of the crown. Common Pleas originally heard cases between subject and subject; it was held at a fixed place, which came to be Westminster. Exchequer originally heard revenue matters, then expanded its civil jurisdiction with the fiction that a person wronged by another person is less able to pay taxes, so such a case was in reality a revenue matter. The three common law courts contested with each other to expand their civil jurisdiction and eventually came to have essentially concurrent civil jurisdiction.

In these courts, a plaintiff pursued an "action at law" by filing a "claim" or "complaint" before a judge (or in the case of Exchequer, before a baron). The common law courts employed juries to decide questions of fact. The relief that these courts could grant was legal, which meant almost exclusively money damages. The common law courts developed a rigid system of writs that limited the types of actions that could be brought, as discussed in the next section. These courts also became somewhat hidebound by the accumulation of their precedents.

On the other side of the divide was the court of equity. The court of Chancery became available to prevent individual injustices that could occur through the rigid operation of the common law. This court developed parallel to, and independent of, the common law courts.

In Chancery, a plaintiff pursued a "suit in equity" by filing a "bill" before a chancellor. The court decided cases by the conscience of the chancellor, who would attempt to do justice in the individual case. To that end, Chancery originally refused to create precedents, but as the years passed, an oral tradition arose, and then written precedents developed. The chancellor decided all aspects of the case, including questions of fact. Chancery used no juries. The relief that this court could grant was equitable, which meant forms of relief—such as injunctions, specific performance, and rescission—that were designed to make the plaintiff whole when legal relief was not adequate.

This divided, independent system of law and equity flourished in England in the seventeenth and eighteenth centuries, so the system was imported into the American colonies. It became the legal system of the American states, and endured until the adoption of code practice in the mid-to-late nineteenth century (and in many states that refused the codes for long afterward). The English system itself was transformed in 1873 when Parliament combined all the courts into the Supreme Court of Judicature with both common law and equity jurisdiction.

2. The Writ System in the Common Law Courts

The part of the English common law system of most interest for study of the historical roots of pleading a complaint is the writ system.[1] Originally, a common law court secured jurisdiction over a civil case when the King, or later the Chancellor, issued a writ to the sheriff to arrest the defendant and bring him before the court. As the years passed, these writs took on differing forms that hardened into separate categories that became summaries of the type of case.

The primary contract (*ex contractu*) writs in the common law courts were debt (for a fixed sum of money or specific chattel owed), covenant (for breach of an obligation under seal), assumpsit (for breach of an obligation not under seal), and account (for receipts and disbursements in a continuing relationship). The primary tort (*ex delicto*) writs were trespass (for a direct and immediate injury to person or property),[2] case (for an indirect injury to person or property),[3] detinue (to recover a specific chattel), replevin (also to recover specific chattels), and trover (for money damages against a person who converted a chattel).

3. Problems with Common Law Pleading

The primary problem with the common law pleading system was it became more of a game of skill for lawyers than a method of resolving disputes on the merits. First, plaintiff's attorney was required to choose the correct writ to plead the case, for if the wrong writ were chosen, plaintiff would be out of court. In most cases, the choice would be easy, but in too many cases the facts lay between writs or in no writ at all. Second, pleadings did all the

---

1. *See generally* FREDERIC W. MAITLAND, THE FORMS OF ACTION AT COMMON LAW (1948); George B. Adams, *The Origin of English Equity*, 16 COLUM. L. REV. 87 (1916).

2. The writ of trespass was originally criminal, which developed to prevent breaches of the King's peace. The writ later further divided into trespass quare clausum fregit (q.c.t.) for injury to land, trespass de bonis asportatis (d.b.a.) for injury to chattels, and trespass vi et armis for injury to person.

3. The distinction between the writ of trespass and the writ of (trespass on the) case was the direct or indirect nature of the injury to plaintiff. It had nothing to do with intent of the defendant. For example, "[i]f a man throws a log into the highway, and in that act hits me, I may maintain trespass because it is an immediate wrong; but if as it lies there I tumble over it, and receive an injury, I must bring an action upon the case; because it is only prejudicial in consequence." Reynolds v. Clarke, 93 Eng. Rep. 747, 748 (K.B. 1726). Similarly, trespass lies against a defendant who feeds a dog poison; case lies against a defendant who leaves poison for a dog to find.

heavy lifting in cases, at least until the time of trial. Pleadings had the functions of 1) giving the opponent and the judge notice of the nature of the claim (or defense), 2) weeding out groundless claims (or defenses), 3) revealing the facts of the case, and 4) narrowing the issues. Third, because the pleading system had the goal of narrowing the case to a single issue of law or fact, the case might require many pleadings back and forth. For example, a defendant who responded with a plea of confession and avoidance (today an affirmative defense) did not deny plaintiff's complaint, so no issue was joined; plaintiff was required to replead a replication. Should that replication also plead in confession and avoidance, defendant was required to plead a rejoinder. The string could continue. Also, because the goal was a single issue, the common law severely restricted joinder of claims and parties.

B. Pleading under the Codes

1. Development of Code Pleading

The first great reform of pleading was the code system. The state of New York in 1848 adopted a code of civil procedure based on the work of a committee chaired by David Dudley Field. This Field code was intended and designed to simplify pleading and remove many of the technicalities from civil procedure. To that end, the Field code abolished the common law writs in favor of one form of action to be known as a "civil action," merged the systems of law and equity, simplified pleading and procedure, and allowed broad joinder of claims and parties.[4] The primary method by which the Field code accomplished this feat was through its requirement that a party plead only "a plain and concise statement of the facts constituting each cause of action (defense or counter-claim) without unnecessary repetition."

The Field code became a popular model for procedural reform. States over the ensuing years adopted their own codes of civil procedure based on the New York model. By the time of the promulgation of the Federal Rules of Civil Procedure in 1938, a substantial majority of states were code states.[5]

2. Problems with Code Pleading

The codes accomplished the primary goals of simplifying pleading and removing technicalities and traps for the unwary.

4. *See generally* JACK H. FRIEDENTHAL, MARY KAY KANE & ARTHUR R. MILLER, CIVIL PROCEDURE § 5.1 (3d ed. 1999).

5. *See* CHARLES E. CLARK, CODE PLEADING § 8 (2d ed. 1947).

Problems remained. First, a code by definition is a statute; this makes revisions and adjustments difficult because the legislature must take action. Second, the codes still required the pleadings to do the heavy pre-trial lifting of giving notice, weeding out groundless claims, revealing the facts, and narrowing the issues. Third, the most difficult problems grew out of the greatest reform of the codes: the centerpiece of the codes was the seemingly-simple requirement that a plaintiff need plead only "the facts constituting each cause of action." Both "facts" and "cause of action" soon became litigation-generating centers of controversy.

a. Pleading ultimate facts

From the first Field code in New York through all of the code states, the codes required the plaintiff to plead ultimate facts—as contrasted with conclusions of law or evidentiary facts. On the one hand, pleading conclusions of law was deficient. A plaintiff who pleaded only that defendants "trespassed," "assaulted" her, and caused her "to be confined" gave notice to the opponent and the court of theories of trespass, assault, and false imprisonment, but the complaint did nothing to reveal the facts, narrow the issues, or weed out baseless claims.[6] On the other hand, pleading evidentiary facts was deficient. A plaintiff who merely recited the evidence of a real estate transaction failed to plead the ultimate fact of the right of possession.[7] This could result in prolixity, and ambiguity of inference; for example, if plaintiff pleaded a decedent delivered $5000 to defendant, the inference of whether it was to be a loan or a gift was not clear.

A complaint that pleaded conclusions of law could be challenged. A complaint that pleaded only evidentiary facts could be challenged. Since they could be challenged, they often were challenged, especially because an "ultimate" fact was difficult to identi-

6. Gillispie v. Goodyear Serv. Stores, 258 N.C. 487, 128 S.E.2d 762 (1963), held the following complaint inadequate:

> On or about May 5, 1959 and May 6, 1959, the defendants, without cause or just excuse and maliciously came upon and trespassed upon the premises occupied by the plaintiff as a residence, and by the use of harsh and threatening language and physical force directed against the plaintiff assaulted the plaintiff and placed her in great fear, and humiliated and embarrassed her by subjecting her to public scorn and ridicule, and caused her to be seized and exhibited to the public as a prisoner, and to be confined in a public jail, all to her great humiliation, embarrassment and harm.

7. McCaughey v. Schuette, 117 Cal. 223, 48 P. 1088 (1897), held the following complaint inadequate: "Plaintiff contracted to buy real estate from defendant in exchange for cancellation of promissory notes. The notes were cancelled and the deed to the property delivered, but defendant refused to yield possession of the property."

fy. Consider this small hypothetical. Plaintiff wishes to sue for slander because at a student government meeting defendant announced that plaintiff stole books from his library carrel. How should the key allegation read? What is the ultimate fact? Here are three candidates:

—Defendant slandered plaintiff.

—Defendant said plaintiff stole books from him.

—Defendant imputed dishonesty to plaintiff.

The first allegation is insufficient as it is a conclusion of law. The second allegation is insufficient as it is an evidentiary fact. The third allegation is sufficient as it is an ultimate fact.

b. Pleading a cause of action

The codes required plaintiff to plead the facts constituting a "cause of action," but did not offer any definition of the term of art. Controversy quickly developed over what a cause of action required. Must the plaintiff state the legal theory of recovery? How many facts must the plaintiff plead? Perhaps even more important, how would a cause of action be defined and bounded for purposes of res judicata? Commentators disagreed vehemently. Courts at all levels, including the Supreme Court of the United States, labored to define a cause of action both in the individual case and in a comprehensive fashion.[8] Eventually, two major positions on "cause of action" emerged.

One position was the "primary right" theory, as advocated by Professors John Norton Pomeroy and O. W. McCaskill.[9] These advocates argued a cause of action was the intersection of a single legal right in plaintiff with a single legal duty in defendant. For example, when plaintiff and defendant had an auto accident, defendant rushed to plaintiff's car to punch him in the face, and seized plaintiff's wallet as preliminary compensation, plaintiff had three separate and distinct legal theories of recovery: negligence,

---

8. *Compare* Baltimore S.S. Co. v. Phillips, 274 U.S. 316, 321, 47 S.Ct. 600, 602, 71 L.Ed. 1069, 1072 (1927) ("A cause of action does not consist of facts, but of the unlawful violation of a right which the facts show.") *with* United States v. Memphis Cotton Oil Co., 288 U.S. 62, 67–68, 53 S.Ct. 278, 280, 77 L.Ed. 619, 623 (1933) ("[A cause of action is] something separate from writs and remedies, the group of operative facts out of which a grievance has developed.").

9. JOHN NORTON POMEROY, CODE REMEDIES § 347 (Thomas A. Boyle ed., 4th ed. 1904); O. W. McCaskill, *Actions and Cause of Action*, 34 YALE L.J. 614 (1925). McCaskill defined cause of action as "that group of operative facts which, standing alone, would show a single right in the plaintiff and a single delict to that right giving cause for the state, through its courts, to afford relief to the party or parties whose right is invaded." *Id.* at 638.

battery, and conversion. This meant plaintiff had three causes of action, Pomeroy and McCaskill asserted. Essentially, a cause of action was a single legal theory of recovery, and thus was closely akin to the common law "right of action." Plaintiff's inchoate three rights of action would become embodied in three causes of action when pleaded in the complaint.[10]

The other position was the "transactional" theory, as advocated by Professor Charles E. Clark.[11] Clark argued a cause of action was a single set of facts without regard to possible legal theories embedded within that set of facts: "The essential thing is that there be chosen a factual unit, whose limits are determined by the time and sequence and unity of the happenings, rather than by some vague guess or prophecy of potential judicial action."[12] Clark's cause of action was determined from a lay perspective on what facts would constitute a single transaction without regard to any legal theories a lawyer or judge might later apply to those facts. Accordingly, in the hypothetical in the paragraph above, Clark would answer plaintiff had one cause of action arising from a single set of facts, not three causes of action. As can be seen, Clark's cause of action was much broader than Pomeroy's and McCaskill's cause of action. This difference would be manifest in the facts necessary to plead a cause of action and also in unpleaded portions of a cause of action that might be barred by res judicata.

C. Pleading under the Federal Rules of Civil Procedure

1. Development of the Federal Rules

Because of these and other problems with the codes, an impetus developed in the early twentieth century for another round of sweeping reform in civil procedure. Congress passed the Rules Enabling Act in 1934 (28 U.S.C. § 2072), which allowed the Supreme Court to appoint an advisory committee to draft rules of civil procedure for the federal courts. The advisory committee, under the leadership of reporter Charles E. Clark, recommended a set of civil procedure rules to the Court, and the Court promulgated the Federal Rules of Civil Procedure in 1938.

10. *Id.* at 617.

11. Charles E. Clark, *The Code Cause of Action*, 33 YALE L.J. 817 (1924). Clark defined cause of action as "an aggregate of operative facts which give rise to one or more relations of right-duty between two or more persons. The size of such aggregate should be worked out in each case pragmatically with an idea of securing convenient and efficient dispatch of trial business." *Id.* at 837.

12. CHARLES E. CLARK, CODE PLEADING 143 (2d ed. 1947).

The Federal Rules have been successful. As amended, they govern procedure in the federal courts to this day. As were the codes, the federal rules in their turn have been popular in the states. A majority of American states today are rules states with rules patterned after the Federal Rules–yet because several states with large populations retained their codes, the majority of Americans today live in code states.

2. Pleading a Claim under the Federal Rules

The Federal Rules continue the great reforms of the codes: abolishing the common law writs in favor of a "civil action," merging law and equity, allowing broad joinder of claims and parties, and simplifying pleading and procedure. As to the latter, the rules simplify pleading by removing some of its duties. No longer is pleading required to reveal the facts, narrow the issues, or weed out groundless claims. Instead, the function of pleading under the rules is to give notice to the opposing party and the court of the nature of the claim (or defense). The Federal Rules are often called a notice pleading system.

The Federal Rules accomplish the feat of this simple, notice pleading system primarily by requiring plaintiff to plead only "a short and plain statement of the claim showing that the pleader is entitled to relief."[13] The intended simplicity of pleading a claim is reinforced by other parts of the rules.[14] The other functions of preparing a case for trial are delegated to other portions of the rules, primarily the discovery rules.

By requiring only a short and plain statement of a claim, the rules eliminate the two major sources of pleading litigation the codes generated. The codes required pleading of "facts." That requirement does not appear in Federal Rule 8. The codes required pleading of a "cause of action." That phrase does not appear in Federal Rule 8—or anywhere in the Federal Rules. It has been abolished in the federal courts and rules states. Use of the newly-coined term "claim for relief" in preference to "cause of

13. FED.R.CIV.P. 8(a)(2).

14. FED.R.CIV.P. 8(e)(1) instructs the pleader "[e]ach averment of a pleading shall be simple, concise, and direct. No technical forms of pleading or motions are required." FED.R.CIV.P. 8(f) instructs the court "[a]ll pleadings shall be so construed as to do substantial justice." FED.R.CIV.P. 84 instructs all that "[t]he forms contained in the Appendix of Forms are sufficient under the rules and are intended to indicate the simplicity and brevity of statement which the rules contemplate." For example, the allegation in form 9 for negligence that "defendant negligently drove a motor vehicle against plaintiff who was then crossing said highway" states a claim for relief, but would not have stated a cause of action under the codes.

action" was quite intentional on the part of reporter Clark and the committee—and therefore the Supreme Court–to eliminate these two pleading problems. Two corollaries follow from this choice by the Court: 1) the term cause of action is obsolete and should not be used in federal courts and rules states, and 2) the term claim embodies Clark's view that the proper litigation unit is an operative set of facts instead of a single legal theory.

The transition from cause of action to claim did not–and even today sometimes does not–come easily. Repeated attempts to reinstitute fact pleading and the cause of action have been made in the federal courts. These attempts have been beaten back. The most famous early case standing for the proposition that Federal Rule 8(a)(2) means what it says is *Dioguardi v. Durning*.[15] The district court dismissed plaintiff's hand-drawn, nearly unintelligible complaint for failure "to state facts sufficient to constitute a cause of action." The opinion reversing the dismissal was written by the same man who drafted the Federal Rules: now Judge Charles E. Clark of the Second Circuit. The court decided the complaint stated a claim because it gave basic notice to defendant of the nature of plaintiff's claim. Not long after *Dioguardi*, the Supreme Court stated "all the rules require is 'a short and plain statement of the claim' that will give the defendant fair notice of what the plaintiff's claim is and the grounds upon which it rests."[16] The Court even wrote "a complaint should not be dismissed for failure to state a claim unless it appears beyond doubt that the plaintiff can prove no set of facts in support of his claim which would entitle him to relief."[17] The most famous later case is *Leatherman v. Tarrant*

15. 139 F.2d 774 (2d Cir. 1944).

16. Conley v. Gibson, 355 U.S. 41, 47, 78 S.Ct. 99, 103, 2 L.Ed.2d 80, 85 (1957).

17. Perhaps the Supreme Court did not intend a literal reading of this language. One leading treatise says this:

> The rules require the pleader to disclose adequate information about the basis of the claim for relief as distinguished from a bare averment that the pleader wants relief and is entitled to it. It is true that in Conley v. Gibson the Supreme Court referred to "simplified 'notice pleading,' " but in context it is plain that the Court's statement was one of aim rather than definition. Only two sentences before the phrase in question the Court had emphasized that the rules require the complaint to give the defendant "fair notice of what the plaintiff's claim is and the grounds upon which it rests." Thus the Court recognized that the rule does contemplate the statement of circumstances, occurrences, and events in support of the claim presented, even though it permits these circumstances to be stated with great generality.

CHARLES A. WRIGHT & MARY KAY KANE, THE LAW OF FEDERAL COURTS § 68, at 475 (6th ed. 2002). The adjustment of courts to notice pleading and attempts to provide special rules for pleading certain types of cases are discussed in JACK H. FRIEDENTHAL, MARY KAY KANE & ARTHUR R. MILLER, CIVIL PROCEDURE §§ 5.8–5.9 (3d ed. 1999).

County Narcotics Intelligence & Coordination Unit.[18] The district court attempted to place heightened pleading requirements, *i.e.*, more factual detail, on complaints alleging certain civil rights violations. The Supreme Court rejected heightened pleading requirements as a violation of Federal Rule 8(a)(2).

In sum, the role of pleading under the Federal Rules is much less than it was under the common law or the codes. Pleading is no longer a fine art. A court construing a challenged complaint will not look to see if every jot and tittle is in place, but will ask whether the complaint gives fair notice of the claim.

II. DRAFTING A COMPLAINT UNDER THE FEDERAL RULES

A. Form of the Complaint

The complaint is composed of four major sections: the caption, the body, the demand for relief, and the signature.

The caption. Each complaint must have at the top of the first page an appropriate caption, which is a standardized heading including the name of the court, the names of the parties, the file number, and the designation of the pleading [here, the complaint].[19] A standard caption would be as follows:

UNITED STATES DISTRICT COURT
DISTRICT OF DAKOTA

PETER SCHULER,	)	
Plaintiff,	)	
v.	)	COMPLAINT
	)	
DAVID DOUR,	)	File Number _____
Defendant.	)	

The body. The body must first state "a short and plain statement of the grounds upon which the court's jurisdiction depends." Fed.R.Civ.P. 8(a)(1) (*see* II.B.1, *infra*). Second, the body must contain separate, numbered paragraphs,[20] which state "a

---

18. 507 U.S. 163, 113 S.Ct. 1160, 122 L.Ed.2d 517 (1993).

19. "Every pleading shall contain a caption setting forth the name of the court, the title of the action, the file number, and a designation as in Rule 7(a). * * * " FED.R.CIV.P. 10(a).

20. FED.R.CIV.P. 10(b).

short and plain statement of the claim showing that the pleader is entitled to relief." Fed.R.Civ.P. 8(a)(2) (*see* II.B.2, *infra*). The "complaints" at the end of this exercise are examples of the body section of the complaint. An introductory phrase to the body of the complaint, such as "For her complaint against defendant, plaintiff alleges as follows" is commonly used, but is not necessary.

Demand for relief. The complaint must include "a demand for judgment for the relief the pleader seeks." Fed.R.Civ.P. 8(a)(3). This demand is also called the ad damnum clause, or the wherefore clause. The following example is a common form:

WHEREFORE, Plaintiff demands judgment against Defendant in the amount of $100,000, plus interest and costs.

Many attorneys add a phrase such as "and for such other relief as the court may deem the plaintiff to be entitled," but Federal Rule 54(c), which provides a judgment "shall grant the relief to which the party in whose favor it is rendered is entitled, even if the party has not demanded such relief in the party's pleadings" renders such a phrase superfluous.

Signature. Fed.R.Civ.P. 11 requires a manual signature on the copy of the pleading filed with the court, plus information as to the address and telephone number of the attorney. A common form is as follows:

Lawyer, Argue & Case
by_____ /s/ C.C. Case
Attorneys for Plaintiff
111 Main Street
Capital City, Dakota 11111
(111)111–1111

B. Content of the Complaint

1. Jurisdictional allegations

The first requirement for a complaint in a federal court is that it include "a short and plain statement of the grounds upon which the court's jurisdiction depends." Fed.R.Civ.P. 8(a)(1). This statement is required because the federal courts are courts of limited subject matter jurisdiction [*see* Exercise Two, pp. 30–34]. Subject matter jurisdiction of the federal courts is never assumed, as it is in state courts of general subject matter jurisdiction (so a state rules system patterned on the federal rules will likely omit this requirement). An allegation of federal question jurisdiction will cite the federal law provision under which the claim is alleged to arise. An allegation of diversity jurisdiction will allege the citizenship of each of the parties and the amount in controversy. Examples of sufficient jurisdictional allegations are included in form 2 of the Federal Rules appendix of forms.

Later in this exercise, section III.D.1 contains several varying allegations of diversity jurisdiction. You will be asked to evaluate each for sufficiency.

2. The claim

The next requirement for a complaint in a federal court is that it include "a short and plain statement of the claim showing that the pleader is entitled to relief." Fed.R.Civ.P. 8(a)(2). While this sparse requirement, especially as reinforced by decisions of the Supreme Court, allows plaintiff to plead the facts of the case with generality (as discussed in section I.C.2, *supra*), it should not be taken as license to authorize sloppy pleading practices. An attorney who attempts to draft a complaint without having first thought through the elements of the claim and the facts necessary to establish those elements will draft a poor complaint. Even should the complaint survive a challenge to its sufficiency, damage will result in unnecessary time and effort defending that challenge, possible later complications in the litigation, and impairment of the attorney's reputation.

In order to draft a good complaint, plaintiff's attorney still must investigate the case, research the law, and then plead the facts necessary to place plaintiff's claim under that law. "The Rules didn't abolish the necessity for clear thinking."[21] In the absence of thinking through the legal nature of the claim to be pleaded, the plaintiff's attorney may well omit important facts, include irrelevant allegations, or even plead a defense to the claim. One treatise suggests pleaders under the Federal Rules should still continue to "make statements of claim that provide the opposing party and the court with a fairly definite picture of the transaction sued on and the legal theories implicitly used. This is the most that can be expected of pleadings."[22]

Pleading can be thought of as a syllogism. The form of a classic syllogism is this.

All men are mortal.	[major premise]
Socrates is a man.	[minor premise]
[Therefore] Socrates is mortal.	[conclusion]

---

21. Plastino v. Mills, 236 F.2d 32, 34 (9th Cir. 1956).

22. FLEMING JAMES, JR., GEOFFREY C. HAZARD, JR. & JOHN LEUBSDORF, CIVIL PROCEDURE § 3.6, at 191 (5th ed. 2001).

The applicable substantive law is the major premise. The facts of the case that fit the law are the minor premise. The conclusion follows that plaintiff wins. Traditionally, plaintiff need not plead the major premise since the court is presumed to know the law. Plaintiff need plead only the minor premise. Even so, a careful pleader will not leave the court to guesswork. For example, form 9 of the Federal Rules appendix of forms identifies the nature of plaintiff's claim as "defendant negligently drove." The allegations of the form do not recite the law of negligence, but they do notify the opposing party and the court that the claim is for negligence.

Later in this exercise, section III.D.2 contains several alternatives for allegations of the body of a complaint for defamation. You will be asked to evaluate each for sufficiency.

3. *Federal Rule 11 and ethical considerations in good faith pleading*

Prior to 1983, Fed.R.Civ.P. 11 required only a good faith certification that the attorney had "read the pleading," that it was on "good ground," and that it was "not interposed for delay." While this imposed an ethical requirement on the attorney filing a pleading, the rule provided no real means of enforcement. From the adoption of the Federal Rules in 1938 until 1983, few Rule 11 sanctions were sought, and fewer were granted.

This situation changed dramatically with amendment of Rule 11 in 1983. Responding to a burgeoning federal caseload and claims of abusive litigation practices, the Supreme Court rewrote Rule 11 in several ways. First, application of the rule was expanded beyond pleadings to include also motions and other papers. Second, any pleading, motion, or other paper not signed would be stricken. Third, the rule expanded improper purposes of pleading from delay alone to include harassment or needless expense. Fourth, violation of the rule would result in a mandatory sanction ("shall impose"). Finally, and most importantly, the rule required that the paper be signed only "after reasonable inquiry." That meant an attorney could no longer accept a client's story at face value, at least without some minimal level of additional investigation, as a basis for pleading. The Court summarized the obligations of Rule 11 in this fashion: "A signature certifies to the court that the signer has read the document, has conducted a reasonable inquiry into the facts and the law and is satisfied that the document is well-grounded in both, and is acting without any improper motive."[23]

23. Business Guides, Inc. v. Chromatic Comm'ns Enter., Inc., 498 U.S. 533, 542, 111 S.Ct. 922, 929, 112 L.Ed.2d 1140, 1153 (1991). The purpose of the rule

Some litigants and attorneys sought to avoid sanctions by claiming good faith, but the good faith defense was rejected. Rule 11 applied an objective, not a subjective, standard.[24] An attorney was required to meet the standard of a reasonable attorney. Failure to meet that standard resulted in a variety of sanctions, which commonly included reimbursement of attorney's fees to the opposing party who had been required to defend the objectively unreasonable pleading or other paper.

Ten years of controversy followed. Many thought Rule 11 had swung from the extreme of toothlessness to the extreme of excessively sharp fangs. This controversy induced the Supreme Court to revisit Rule 11 in 1993. The rule was both contracted and expanded.

On the contraction side, the new rule provides procedures for Rule 11 sanctions motions. First, a party seeking a Rule 11 sanction must make the request in a separate motion. Fed.R.Civ.P. 11(c)(1)A). Second, the party seeking a sanction must serve the motion on the offending party and then allow 21 days for withdrawal or correction of the offending material before filing the motion for sanctions with the court. Fed.R.Civ.P. 11(c)(1)(A). Third, the rule makes clear that the purpose of a sanction is deterrence, not compensation: "A sanction imposed for violation of this rule shall be limited to what is sufficient to deter repetition of such conduct or comparable conduct by others similarly situated." Fed.R.Civ.P. 11(c)(2). The sanction may be in the form of "directives of a nonmonetary nature," or if monetary, the sanction will ordinarily be paid into court, not to the moving party. Fed.R.Civ.P. 11(c)(2). This major change from the 1983 version of the rule certainly eliminates much of the incentive for seeking a sanction.

On the expansion side, the new rule places a continuing obligation on a pleader in later stages of the case: "[b]y presenting to the court (whether by signing, filing, submitting, *or later advocating*)." In other words, a Rule 11 violation occurs when an attorney advocates a position in violation of the rule even though the position had been justified by the law and facts at the time it was first asserted. For example, an allegation in a complaint might be proved untenable by later discovery, so it cannot be relied on in a motion for summary judgment. A second expansion is to fix liability on law firms for the violations of their attorneys. Finally, the

was to require reasonable investigation, not to interfere with argument or creativity: "The court is expected to avoid using the wisdom of hindsight and should test the signer's conduct by inquiring what was reasonable to believe at the time the pleading, motion or other paper was submitted." Advisory Committee Note to 1983 Amendments to Fed.R.Civ.P. 11, 97 F.R.D. 165, 199 (1983).

24. *Business Guides*, 498 U.S. at 542, 111 S.Ct. at 922, 112 L.Ed.2d at 1140.

representations made when a pleading, motion, or other paper is signed are expanded:

> **Representations to Court.** By presenting to the court (whether by signing, filing, submitting, or later advocating) a pleading, written motion, or other paper, an attorney or unrepresented party is certifying that to the best of the person's knowledge, information, and belief, formed after an inquiry reasonable under the circumstances,—
>
> (1) it is not being presented for any improper purpose, such as to harass or to cause unnecessary delay or needless increase in the cost of litigation;
>
> (2) the claims, defenses, and other legal contentions therein are warranted by existing law or by a nonfrivolous argument for the extension, modification, or reversal of existing law or the establishment of new law;
>
> (3) the allegations and other factual contentions have evidentiary support or, if specifically so identified, are likely to have evidentiary support after a reasonable opportunity for further investigation or discovery; and
>
> (4) the denials of factual contentions are warranted on the evidence or, if specifically so identified, are reasonably based on a lack of information or belief.[25]

The objective standard for evaluation remains.[26] An attorney's subjective good faith belief is not a defense against sanctions when an objective, reasonable attorney would not have held such a belief or would have undertaken a more thorough investigation.[27]

---

25. Fed.R.Civ.P. 11(b). *See generally* Charles A. Wright & Mary Kay Kane, The Law of Federal Courts § 69A (6th ed. 2002).

26. Perhaps the most difficult area to evaluate is Fed.R.Civ.P. 11(b)(2), which covers arguments for modification of existing law. One guide is the following:

> Argument for extensions, modifications, or reversals of existing law or for creation of new law do not violate subdivision (b)(2) provided they are "nonfrivolous." This establishes an objective standard, intended to eliminate any "empty-head pure-heart" justification for patently frivolous arguments. However, the extent to which a litigant has researched the issues and found some support for its theories even in minority opinions, in law review articles, or through consultation with other attorneys should certainly be taken into account in determining whether paragraph (2) has been violated.

Advisory Committee Note to 1993 Amendments to Fed.R.Civ.P. 11, 146 F.R.D. 586–87 (1993).

27. Many examples of reasonable, and unreasonable, investigations are collected in 5A Charles A. Wright & Arthur R. Miller, Federal Practice and Procedure: Civil 2d § 1335 (1990).

Similar concerns underlie Rule 3.1 of the Model Rules of Professional Conduct:

A lawyer shall not bring or defend a proceeding, or assert or controvert an issue therein, unless there is a reasonable basis for doing so, which includes a good faith argument for an extension, modification or reversal of existing law * * *.

The comment to the Model Rule states "the test in Rule 3.1 is an objective test." Consequently, a subjective, good faith belief in the truth of a pleading will not save the attorney who files an objectively false or frivolous pleading from professional discipline.

III. AN EXERCISE IN DRAFTING A COMPLAINT FOR DEFAMATION UNDER THE FEDERAL RULES: CALI CIV 01

This exercise includes the facts of a hypothetical case of defamation, discussion of the substantive law of the tort of defamation, and discussion of the procedural law of pleading a defamation complaint. Please read these materials and answer the preliminary questions asked in section III.D. You will then be ready to go to the computer terminal to work through CALI CIV 01: Drafting a Complaint. Take this exercise and a copy of the Federal Rules of Civil Procedure with you.

A. Facts of the Case

You are an attorney practicing with a law firm in Capital City, Dakota. One of the partners in your firm has just received a statement from a client, Peter Schuler. The partner hands you the statement, in which Schuler gives the following account:

"Until this past May, I was a student at Dakota College in College Town, Dakota. On April 30, one of the proctors caught me watching television in the dorm with my girlfriend. The college is strict and old-fashioned. Women aren't allowed in the mens' dorms after 8 p.m.

"The proctor turned me in. They scheduled a hearing before the Dakota College Disciplinary Board, which has the job of punishing student misbehavior. All of its members are faculty members. Dean William Roberts is always on the Board. The other professors take turns, two at a time. This time the other members were Professor Mary Trueblood and Professor David Dour.

"Professor Trueblood is a nice person. But having Professor Dour on the Board was a stroke of bad luck for me. He's always hated me.

"I went before the Board in Room 215 of Old Main on May 10 and apologized. They said that they would let me know what their decision was the next morning.

"The next morning Dean Roberts told me that the board had voted to suspend me from school for a year because I had violated the visiting hours rules. I have never heard of anyone else getting such heavy treatment. Even Dean Roberts admitted it was heavy.

"So I looked at the records that the student council keeps of all disciplinary hearings. Out of 50 cases in the last ten years, only three students have been suspended. The others have all received social probation or something less. The council records don't show the reasons for the suspensions, but I talked to five alumni who went to the hearings on those three suspensions when they were students. All three suspensions were given after the same hearing seven years ago. Four out of the five alumni told me definitely that the students were suspended for cheating on an exam.

"I couldn't figure out why I got that treatment. I went in to see Professor Trueblood. I knew her from field trips in geology and always thought she was O.K. She didn't want to talk to me at first, but after beating around the bush for a while she finally told me confidentially that the Dean had been very much influenced by what Professor Dour said after I left. According to Trueblood, Professor Dour said, 'Peter is a heavy user of crack cocaine.' Trueblood said that those were Dour's exact words. I don't know where Dour got the idea that I am a drug user. It's absolutely untrue and I can't think of anyone who would say that about me. Maybe he made it up. He must have known that Dean Roberts is paranoid about drugs. Anyway, Trueblood said that they suspended me because they thought I was a drug user.

"I had this great part-time job in a bank in College Town and I was planning on going into its management training program after I graduated. When I went in to work the week after the Disciplinary Board meeting, my boss, John Thompson, told me I was fired. At first he wouldn't say why, but eventually he admitted that he had heard I had a 'personal reputation incompatible with the banking industry.' I asked him if he was talking about gossip that I had been using drugs and he said 'All I can say to that is if such were the case, that would be incompatible with the best interests of banking.'

"I asked him if he knew Professor Dour and he said 'Yes, but he has nothing to do with this. He didn't tell me anything.' I think Thompson was lying and that either Dour told him the phony story about crack, or that somehow he heard about what was said at the disciplinary hearing.

"I don't want to go back to Dakota College—ever! I'm disgusted with the place. Anyway, everyone there thinks I'm weird. I'm now back home, where my dad is letting me work in his furniture store."

Your partner asks you to draft a complaint for Peter Schuler against David Dour. The case will be filed in federal district court in Dakota, since the backlog there is considerably shorter than in state court. One drawback to Dakota federal court is that the judge is quite punctilious about pleading, having been trained many years ago in a code pleading state. Accordingly, you should compose a complaint to survive close scrutiny, and it should be able to survive probable defense motions to require a more definite statement under Fed.R.Civ.P. 12(e), or to dismiss for failure to state a claim under Fed.R.Civ.P. 12(b)(6).

B. Substantive Law of Defamation

1. State Law

The *Erie* doctrine[28] requires the federal court in Dakota to follow state law concerning the elements of defamation, except where federal constitutional issues are involved.

Dakota law provides that a defendant who communicates a disparaging, damaging falsehood about plaintiff to a third person is liable in an action for defamation (slander).[29]

Under the decisional law of the state of Dakota, the elements of slander are as follows:

(1) **Publication.** The slanderous words must have been spoken by the defendant so that a third person could hear them. A purely private statement, heard only by the plaintiff, is not slander. (No court of record in Dakota has specifically ruled on the issue of whether publication to a third person is an element of the tort of

28. The *Erie* doctrine is based on Erie Railroad Co. v. Tompkins, 304 U.S. 64, 58 S.Ct. 817, 82 L.Ed. 1188 (1938). Under *Erie*, state law provides the rule of decision for certain issues that arise in cases tried in federal court. For purposes of this exercise, you need only remember that state law defines the substantive elements of defamation, while federal law determines which party must plead the elements of the claim and the degree of particularity with which they must be pleaded.

29. The term *defamation* encompasses both *libel* and *slander*. In a general sense, libel is defamation communicated in writing or other durable form, and slander is defamation communicated orally. Since the defendant made his communications orally, the action might be characterized as either for the tort of defamation or for the tort of slander. Both terms will be used in this exercise. On the tort of defamation, *see generally* DAN B. DOBBS, THE LAW OF TORTS §§ 400–23 (2000).

slander, but commentators have assumed that the Dakota courts would follow the law of other jurisdictions and require this element.)

(2) **Falsity.** The words must have been false.

(3) **Disparagement.** The words must have been disparaging, that is, they must have been words that would tend to cause a person to be disliked, shunned, ridiculed, or held in contempt by others. "Joan is a thief" would clearly be disparaging. On the other hand, "Joan is a taxpayer" is not disparaging, and there would be no recovery even though Joan might have been offended by the words.

(4) **Pecuniary Damage/Slander per se.** In many slander cases, the words must have caused some specific pecuniary damage, such as loss of business customers, loss of a contract, or discharge from employment. Recovery cannot be based on humiliation, damage to reputation, illness, or mental distress alone.

The requirement of pecuniary damage does not apply to words that are slanderous *per se*. Words are slanderous *per se* if they (1) charge the person with a serious crime involving moral turpitude, (2) indicate the person has a loathsome disease, or (3) derogate the person's ability or honesty in the person's trade, business, or profession.

Dakota courts have not to this date been called on to decide whether suspension from college causes "pecuniary damage." Similarly open questions are whether the use of crack is a "serious crime involving moral turpitude" or whether use of crack is sufficiently analogous to a "loathsome disease" to justify classifying a statement charging use of crack as slanderous *per se*.

Privilege. In some contexts the free exchange of information has been considered to be so important that the Dakota caselaw confers an absolute privilege upon false statements. The absolute privilege applies, for example, to statements made by legislators on the floor of the state legislature. As to such statements, an action for slander can be defeated by the defense of privilege even if the person making the statement knew it was false.

In other contexts, the free exchange of information has been considered sufficiently important to justify conferring a conditional privilege. For example, there is a conditional privilege in Dakota for statements made in giving a reference to a prospective employer of a person. Another conditional privilege exists for persons reporting crimes to the police. The existence of a conditional privilege will defeat a claim for slander unless the person making the statement acted in bad faith, with spite or ill will, toward the person defamed.

105

Whether a statement made by a college professor to another disciplinary board member about a student is covered by an absolute privilege, a conditional privilege, or no privilege at all is an open question of law in the state of Dakota.

2. Federal Constitutional Law

Although state law generally governs the elements of slander, federal constitutional doctrine must also be taken into account, and the law in this area is uncertain and changing. A dictum in *Gertz v. Robert Welch, Inc.*, 418 U.S. 323, 94 S.Ct. 2997, 41 L.Ed.2d 789 (1974), seems to indicate that the First Amendment prohibits states from imposing liability without fault in defamation cases, *i.e.*, the defendant must have been at least negligent in publication of a false statement. Arguably, the Supreme Court's decision means that a state cannot constitutionally impose liability for making a false statement when the defendant reasonably believed the statement to be true.

Such a conclusion was unsettled by the decision eleven years later in *Dun & Bradstreet, Inc. v. Greenmoss Builders, Inc.*, 472 U.S. 749, 105 S.Ct. 2939, 86 L.Ed.2d 593 (1985), which can be read to say that cases involving a plaintiff who is a private figure (not a public figure) concerning a matter of private concern do not require a showing of defendant's fault for liability. *Gertz* involved a private figure in a matter of public concern. No additional guidance has been provided by the Court.

C. Procedural Law: the Burden of Pleading

The court of appeals in your circuit has announced that under its interpretation of the *Erie* doctrine, Dakota law should be followed on substantive issues in a defamation case, but federal law should be followed on pleading issues, including the allocation of the burden of pleading. A party who has the burden of pleading an issue must raise that issue in the pleadings, or the issue will be resolved against that party.

One question to be answered is who has the burden of pleading privilege: is it an element of the claim that must be pleaded by plaintiff, or is it an affirmative defense that must be pleaded by defendant? While Fed.R.Civ.P. 8(c) does not include privilege in its list of 19 affirmative defenses, the rule provides "and any other matter constituting an avoidance or affirmative defense." Your research on federal caselaw on the pleading of slander has led you to conclude that privilege is an affirmative defense.

On the subject of pleading a defamation case in general, you have also found the following passage in a treatise on federal practice:

Although special pleading requirements have not been set out in the federal rules for libel and slander actions, the standard for successfully pleading defamation tends to be more stringent than ordinary civil suits because of the unfavored nature of this type of action and the desire to discourage what some believe to be basically vexatious litigation. Thus, many of the traditional attitudes toward pleading in this context have survived the adoption of the federal rules.

Of course, all plaintiff technically is required to do is state a claim for which relief may be granted. Contrary to the common law and the generally accepted code approach, some courts have held that it is not necessary to include in the complaint the exact statements upon which the action is based, although some courts have held to the contrary and others have indicated that the substance of the actionable words should be pleaded. It also has been held by at least one court that an allegation of falsity is required. A general allegation of publication and the place where the libel circulated will suffice in most instances. However, if defendant does seek by a motion under Rule 12(e) to have plaintiff fix the situs of the alleged tort, the motion may well be granted, although this seems to represent a technically improper use of the motion for a more definite statement.

If the defamatory character of the statement rests on extrinsic facts, those facts should be pleaded. And if the libelous character of the statement depends upon an interpretation of the words other than a meaning that usually is given to the statement, the special meaning should be specifically pleaded by way of innuendo, explanation, or colloquium. It also is necessary to show that the defamation pertained to plaintiff.

A complaint indicating that the uttered statements are not actionable per se has been held not sufficient to state a claim for relief in the absence of an allegation of special damages, as discussed under Rule 9(g); conversely, if a writing contains material that is libelous per se, allegations of special damages are not necessary.

Although some courts tend to be unwilling to construe the statement of the claim for relief liberally in a libel or slander action and require that all elements of the cause of action be specially pleaded, nothing in Rule 8 imposes a special burden on the pleader in these classes of cases. A number of federal courts have not insisted that each element of the underlying cause be specifically pleaded. In Garcia v. Hilton Hotels International, Inc. [97 F.Supp. 5 (D.P.R.1951)], plaintiff failed to allege in so many words that there had been a publication and defendant challenged the complaint under Rules 12(b)(6), 12(e), and 12(f). Although the court in Garcia inferred the existence of publication and denied the motion to dismiss, as is discussed in another section, it did grant defendant's motion for a more definite statement, inter alia, because of the vagueness resulting from plaintiff's failure to set out the substance of the utterance alleged to have been made slanderously or the facts relied upon to establish a publication. Thus, despite the fact that the Garcia case represents a liberal attitude toward the pleading requirements of the federal rules, it also indicates that traces of disfavor for defamation actions still exist. There is little doubt that because of the unfavored status of libel and slander actions, it is advisable for the pleader to set forth his claim for relief as clearly as possible, and that all the elements of his claim at least should be inferable from the allegations in the complaint.[30]

D. Preliminary Questions

Please answer the following questions before going to the computer to begin CALI CIV 01: Drafting a Complaint. [Note: if your professor has told you to omit the section on jurisdictional allegations, skip to section III.D.2, *infra,* and when you begin the computer exercise, tell the computer to start on Question 3.]

1. Jurisdictional allegations

Since every complaint filed in federal court must allege federal subject matter jurisdiction [Fed.R.Civ.P. 8(a)(1)], we review the diversity statute, 28 U.S.C. § 1332, and then examine nine possible jurisdictional allegations. The statute reads as follows:

(a) The district courts shall have original jurisdiction of all civil actions where the matter in controversy exceeds the sum or value of $75,000, exclusive of interest and costs, and is between—

(1) citizens of different States;

---

30. 5 Charles A. Wright & Arthur R. Miller, Federal Practice and Procedure: Civil 2d § 1245 (1990) (citations omitted).

(2) citizens of a State and citizens or subjects of a foreign state;

(3) citizens of different States and in which citizens or subjects of a foreign state are additional parties; and

(4) a foreign state, defined in section 1603(a) of this title, as plaintiff and citizens of a State or of different States.

For the purposes of this section, section 1335, and section 1441, an alien admitted to the United States for permanent residence shall be deemed a citizen of the State in which such alien is domiciled. * * *

———————

Which of the following jurisdictional allegations would be deemed completely satisfactory by the most punctilious judge? (The computer will ask you to list *all* of the completely satisfactory allegations.)

1. Plaintiff is a citizen of the state of Minnesota and defendant is a citizen of the state of Dakota. The amount in controversy exceeds, exclusive of interest and costs, the sum of seventy-five thousand dollars.

2. This action arises under the laws of the United States, as hereinafter more fully appears.

3. Plaintiff is a resident of the state of Minnesota and defendant is a resident of the state of Dakota. The amount in controversy exceeds, exclusive of interest and costs, the sum of seventy-five thousand dollars.

4. Plaintiff is a citizen of the state of Minnesota. Defendant's citizenship is unknown to plaintiff. The amount in controversy exceeds, exclusive of interest and costs, the sum of seventy-five thousand dollars.

5. Jurisdiction in this action is based on diversity of citizenship and jurisdictional amount, in accordance with the requirements of 28 U.S.C. § 1332(a).

6. Plaintiff is domiciled in the state of Minnesota and defendant is domiciled in the state of Dakota. The amount in controversy exceeds, exclusive of interest and costs, the sum of seventy-five thousand dollars.

7. Plaintiff is a citizen of Minneapolis, Minnesota and defendant is a citizen of College Town, Dakota. The amount in controversy exceeds, exclusive of interest and costs, the sum of seventy-five thousand dollars.

8. Plaintiff is a citizen of the state of Minnesota and defendant is not a citizen of the state of Minnesota. The amount in controversy exceeds, exclusive of interest and costs, the sum of seventy-five thousand dollars.

9. Plaintiff is a citizen of the state of Minnesota and defendant is a citizen of the state of Dakota.

2.   Substantive allegations

Before proceeding, you may wish to try your hand at drafting a complaint from scratch. You can then compare your draft to the model drafts that follow. [The computer will not ask for your complaint, so if you wish, you may skip to the next paragraph.] Your draft complaint should be in the proper form, including a caption, a body, a demand for relief, and a signature (*see* section II.A, *supra*). When drafting the body of the complaint, plead all of the necessary elements of defamation (*see* section III.B.1, *supra*). Keep in mind that defamation (slander) may require the pleading of special damages, and Fed.R.Civ.P. 9(g) requires "When items of special damage are claimed, they shall be specifically stated."

For the computer exercise, the caption, the demand for judgment, and the signature sections of the complaint will be omitted. You will be asked to frame the allegations only for the body of the complaint. Please frame the body of your complaint either by (a) choosing one of the six complaints set forth on the following pages or (b) composing a complaint by using paragraph two of one of the complaints and paragraph three of another.

In assessing complaints one through six, you should remember that you do not want a complaint only minimally acceptable under the Federal Rules. You want a complaint that is as nearly perfect as possible, so defendant's attorney will have no basis for attacking it on pleading grounds. Therefore, you want to compose a complaint that does not even arguably commit any of the following pleading errors:

Error 1: The complaint fails to allege an element of the claim. Example: Plaintiff sues defendant alleging that defendant negligently drove his automobile in such a fashion as to endanger plaintiff. She fails to allege any injuries. Plaintiff has omitted the fourth element of the tort of negligence (duty, breach, causation, damages), and since the burden of pleading on this issue is on plaintiff, this complaint would be subject to attack under Fed.R.Civ.P. 12(b)(6) for failure to state a claim.

You need plead only a "short and plain statement of the claim." Fed.R.Civ.P. 8(a)(2). At the same time, some federal courts continue to apply relatively strict pleading requirements in defamation cases (see pp. 104–06, supra), so you want to make sure that your complaint alleges facts establishing all of the elements of slander. Otherwise, a punctilious judge might dismiss under Fed. R.Civ.P. 12(b)(6).

Error 2: The complaint fails to give the defendant information necessary to frame an answer. Fed.R.Civ.P. 12(e) provides "If a pleading to which a responsive pleading is permitted is so vague or ambiguous that a party cannot reasonably be required to frame a responsive pleading, the party may move for a more definite statement before interposing a responsive pleading." You should avoid a complaint that—though it technically states a claim—omits facts the other party needs to know in order to determine what defenses to raise in the answer. While a motion for more definite statement is rarely granted,[31] you should not give the defendant's attorney cause, or even an opening, to make the motion.

Error 3: The complaint raises an affirmative defense and fails to avoid it. A plaintiff need not anticipate affirmative defenses in the complaint, but should the plaintiff allege facts establishing an affirmative defense, she must go further and allege other facts that avoid the defense. Example: Suppose that the statute of limitations for slander is three years, but the statute is tolled when the plaintiff is mentally incompetent. Under Fed.R.Civ.P. 8(c), the statute of limitations is an affirmative defense. Plaintiff alleges in the complaint a slander by defendant four years previously, but fails to allege she was mentally incompetent for two of the four intervening years. Plaintiff has raised an affirmative defense in the complaint without avoiding it, and her complaint is subject to dismissal under Fed.R.Civ.P. 12(b)(6).[32]

Normally, of course, a district judge will allow plaintiff to amend the complaint, but the 12(b)(6) motion might cause unwelcome delay. Filing and decision on the motion postpones the date upon which defendant must file the answer [see Fed.R.Civ.P. 12(a)(4)(A)].

31. The motion should be granted only when the defendant cannot reasonably respond and is never to be used to force additional particulars out of plaintiff. Charles A. Wright & Mary Kay Kane, The Law of Federal Courts § 66, at 464 (6th ed. 2002).

32. 5A Charles A. Wright & Arthur R. Miller, Federal Practice and Procedure: Civil 2d § 1357 n. 58 (1990).

Error 4: The complaint contains superfluous matter. A small amount of superfluity is usually nothing to worry about. Under Fed.R.Civ.P. 12(f), courts may order stricken from a pleading any "redundant, immaterial, impertinent, or scandalous matter," but a motion to strike is not favored and would certainly not be granted against a complaint as short as the ones set forth in this exercise. Even so, a careful pleader will not frame a complaint containing superfluous matter. The inclusion of unnecessary matter will seem amateurish, and may impair the pleader's effectiveness in persuading the court about other matters. Furthermore, the superfluous language may provide information to the opposing party that will help in preparation of the case.

Error 5: The complaint violates standards of professional responsibility. As discussed in section II.B, *supra*, Fed.R.Civ.P. 11 requires an attorney to sign the complaint and provides that the signature certifies several matters, including that the claim is warranted by both law and fact. Violation of the rule can subject both the lawyer and the client to sanctions.

Rule 3.1 of the Model Rules of Professional Responsibility [quoted on p. 102] imposes a similar requirement of objective good faith on the attorney signing a pleading. Violation of Model Rule 3.1 could subject the lawyer to professional discipline.

Each of the six "complaints" below contains three paragraphs for the body of the complaint. Assume that the date left blank is the most recent year. Before going to the computer terminal, please read the complaints and answer the questions that follow them.

COMPLAINT ONE

1. [Jurisdictional allegation]

2. On May 10, 20___, in Room 215 of Old Main on the campus of Dakota College, in College Town, Dakota, defendant slandered the plaintiff.

3. As a result, plaintiff has been injured in his reputation and career, and has suffered great pain and mental anguish, to his damage in the sum of $100,000.

COMPLAINT TWO

1. [Jurisdictional allegation]

2. On May 10, 20___, in Room 215 of Old Main on the campus of Dakota College in College Town, Dakota, defendant falsely stated ''Peter (referring to plaintiff) is a heavy user of crack cocaine.'' Defendant knew this statement to be false at the time that he made it, or acted in reckless disregard of the truth.

3. As a result, plaintiff has been injured in his reputation, suspended from college, has been unable to obtain any employment, and has suffered great mental anguish, all to his damage in the sum of $100,000.

COMPLAINT THREE

1. [Jurisdictional allegation]

2. On May 10, 20___, in Room 215 of Old Main on the campus of Dakota College, in College Town, Dakota, defendant slandered the plaintiff by falsely stating to William Roberts and Mary Trueblood, ''Peter (referring to plaintiff) is a heavy user of crack cocaine.'' These false and defamatory statements were reported to plaintiff by Mary Trueblood, who was present at the meeting.

3. As a result, plaintiff's reputation has been damaged, he has suffered great humiliation, he has been suspended from college for one year, and he has been discharged from employment by the First National Bank, all to his damage in the amount of $100,000.

COMPLAINT FOUR

1. [Jurisdictional allegation]

2. Defendant was a professor, and plaintiff a student, at Dakota College in College Town, Dakota, on May 10, 20___. On that date defendant stated falsely that ''Peter (referring to plaintiff) is a heavy user of crack cocaine.'' Said statement was made to William Roberts and Mary Trueblood. These persons were faculty members attending a Dakota College Disciplinary Committee meeting which had been called in Room 215 of Old Main for the purpose of disposing of a disciplinary action against the plaintiff. Defendant failed to exercise due care in ascertaining whether the statement was true before making it.

3. Plaintiff has been suspended from college; has suffered damage to his reputation, as well as great mental anguish; and was discharged from employment by the First National Bank; all to his damage in the amount of $100,000.

113

COMPLAINT FIVE

1. [Jurisdictional allegation]

2. Defendant slandered the plaintiff by falsely stating to third persons, including John Thompson of the First National Bank, that ''Peter (referring to plaintiff) is a heavy user of crack cocaine.'' Defendant knew this statement to be false when it was made, or he acted with reckless disregard for the truth, or he failed to exercise due care in determining whether it was true.

3. As a result of defendant's false statement, the plaintiff has suffered great mental anguish and has been injured in his reputation, and there is evidence that, as a result of defendant's false statement, plaintiff was suspended from college and discharged from employment by the First National Bank, all to his damage in the amount of $100,000.

COMPLAINT SIX

1. [Jurisdictional allegation]

2. On May 10, 20__, in Room 215 of Old Main on the campus of Dakota College, in College Town, Dakota, defendant falsely stated to William Roberts and Mary Trueblood, ''Peter (referring to plaintiff) is a heavy user of crack cocaine.'' Defendant knew these words to be false, or he spoke them in reckless disregard of the truth, or he failed to exercise due care in determining whether they were true.

3. Defendant's false statement was made by him to other members of the College Disciplinary Board while the Board was deliberating about whether to punish plaintiff for violating college visiting hours rules. The Board ultimately decided to suspend plaintiff from college. This penalty was ostensibly imposed because of a violation of visiting hours rules, but actually was the result of defendant's slanderous statement. The student council records indicate that only three of the fifty students disciplined in the past ten years have been punished by suspension, and those three students were all suspended in one hearing. Four out of the five witnesses to that hearing have stated definitely that the students involved were suspended for cheating. Another result of defendant's slanderous statement was that plaintiff was discharged from his employment at the First National Bank. The aforesaid suspension from school, discharge from employment, and attendant humiliation and mental

anguish, caused plaintiff to suffer damages in the amount
of $100,000.

—————

In preparing for the computer exercise, answer these questions:

(a) In composing a complaint, I would use the second paragraph of Complaint ___ and the third paragraph of Complaint ___.

(b) Is Complaint One fully satisfactory?

_____ (Yes or No)

(c) If you answered that Complaint One is not fully satisfactory, then identify the defect(s) in Complaint One by writing in a
number or numbers from the multiple-choice display below.

_____

(d) Is Complaint Two fully satisfactory?

_____ (Yes or No)

(e) If you answered that Complaint Two is not fully satisfactory, identify its defect(s) with a number or numbers from the display
below.

_____

(f) Is Complaint Three fully satisfactory?

_____ (Yes or No)

(g) If you answered that Complaint Three is not fully satisfactory, identify its defect(s) with a number or numbers from the
display below.

_____

(h) Is Complaint Four fully satisfactory?

_____(Yes or No)

(i) If you answered that Complaint Four is not fully satisfactory, identify its defect(s) with a number or numbers from the display
below.

_____

(j) Is Complaint Five fully satisfactory?

_____ (Yes or No)

(k) If you answered that Complaint Five is not fully satisfactory, identify its defect(s) with a number or numbers from the display
below.

_____

(*l*) Is Complaint Six fully satisfactory?

_____ (Yes or No)

(m) If you answered that Complaint Six is not fully satisfactory, identify its defect(s) with a number or numbers from the display below.

_____

PLEADING DEFECTS DISPLAY

(The computer will ask you to use this multiple-choice display to identify defects in the allegations of the complaints on the above pages.)

1. *Omission of an element.* The complaint arguably fails to allege an element of the claim.

2. *Rule 12(e) vulnerability.* The complaint is subject to a motion for a more definite statement because it arguably fails to give the defendant information necessary to frame an answer.

3. *Unavoided defense.* The complaint arguably raises an affirmative defense and fails to avoid it.

4. *Superfluity.* The complaint contains damaging superfluous matter that should be omitted for tactical or other reasons.

5. *Violation of rules of professional responsibility.* The complaint violates Fed.R.Civ.P. 11 and Model Rule of Professional Responsibility 3.1.

[This concludes the written materials. You are now ready to go to the computer to work through CALI CIV 01: Drafting a Complaint.]

EXERCISE FOUR

Demurrers and Judgments on the Pleadings

This computer-aided exercise presents a defamation action in the state of Dakota. The facts are the same as in Exercise Three, recounted on pp. 102–04, except that the action is filed in state court instead of federal court. Peter Schuler, a former student at Dakota College, claims that David Dour, a professor at the college, called him a user of crack cocaine. As the exercise progresses, the computer will describe the pleadings filed by the parties and ask you to identify the issues that would be raised on challenges to those pleadings.

Dakota is a code pleading state, so the first challenge to plaintiff's pleading will be a demurrer by defendant. Later you will be asked to consider a motion for judgment on the pleadings. Since this exercise explores code pleading, it will be of special interest to students planning to practice in a code pleading state. Relevance to students planning to practice in a rules state will be less direct. Indeed, in a rules state, "[d]emurrers, pleas, and exceptions for insufficiency of a pleading shall not be used." Fed.R.Civ.P. 7(c). Even so, this exercise has value for students focusing on rules procedures. The code procedure is historically enlightening and provides instructive contrast with rules procedure. This exercise considers both. Even if you have studied only federal pleading, you will be able to do this exercise. The preliminary text will tell you what you need to know about code pleading.

Please read the following description of Dakota's substantive and procedural law. Then answer the preliminary questions on pp. 121–24 before going to the computer to begin CALI CIV 02: Demurrers and Judgments on the Pleadings.

I. SUBSTANTIVE LAW

The substantive law of defamation in the state of Dakota is discussed in Exercise Three at pp. 104–06. Please reread those pages.

In reaction to the dictum in *Gertz v. Robert Welch, Inc.,* 418 U.S. 323, 94 S.Ct. 2997, 41 L.Ed.2d 789 (1974) [discussed at p. 106], the Supreme Court of Dakota recognized a defense of due care. This means that even should defendant Dour's statement be found false and not privileged, defendant still prevails if he exercised due care in attempting to ascertain that the statement was true.

II. PROCEDURAL LAW

A. Burden of Pleading

In Dakota, plaintiff has the burden of pleading the elements of slander (publication, falsity, disparagement, and pecuniary damage/slander *per se*). Defendant has the burden of pleading the affirmative defenses of truth,[1] privilege, and due care. When defendant raises the affirmative defense of qualified privilege, plaintiff has the burden of pleading malice to overcome the privilege.

To say that a party has the burden of pleading on a given issue means that the party must raise that issue in the pleadings, or the issue will be resolved against the party. Dakota follows the rule that ambiguities in the pleadings are to be resolved against the pleader.[2]

B. Sequence of Code Pleadings and Motions

1. Truth, on which the defendant has the burden of pleading, and falsity, on which the plaintiff has the burden of pleading, are of course only two sides of the same coin. One of the peculiarities of the law of defamation/slander is that some jurisdictions have held that both the plaintiff and the defendant have the burden of pleading on the issue of truth/falsity. See 5 CHARLES A. WRIGHT & ARTHUR R. MILLER, FEDERAL PRACTICE AND PROCEDURE: CIVIL 2D § 1245 (1990). If the plaintiff fails to plead that the statement was false, then the complaint is legally insufficient. If the plaintiff does plead falsity, then the defendant must raise truth as an affirmative defense; a denial of the allegation of falsity in the complaint is insufficient. Should defendant fail to raise truth as an affirmative defense, then the defense will be waived unless the court later permits defendant to amend the answer.

2. Note that the code rule of resolving ambiguities against the pleader contrasts with practice in federal courts and rules states, where pleading ambiguities and irregularities are normally resolved in favor of the pleader. "All pleadings shall be so construed as to do substantial justice." FED.R.CIV.P. 8(f).

Under Dakota law, plaintiff commences the action by filing a complaint. Defendant may respond with a special demurrer (raising issues that do not go to the merits, such as lack of jurisdiction or improper joinder), with a general demurrer (challenging the legal sufficiency of the complaint, as discussed below), or with an answer. In the answer, defendant must raise any affirmative defenses or they will be waived. When defendant does not raise any affirmative defenses, the pleadings close with the answer. When defendant raises affirmative defenses, plaintiff is required to file a reply, denying or avoiding[3] the averments of the affirmative defenses. This reply closes the pleadings.[4] Since the defendant is not permitted to respond to the reply, the allegations in the reply are taken as denied or avoided by the defendant.

After the pleadings have closed, either party may move for judgment on the pleadings.

C. The General Demurrer

Dakota's general demurrer is a procedural device used by the defendant to challenge the legal sufficiency of the plaintiff's complaint. Only issues of law may be decided; the demurrer is not a method of testing the facts. The usual maxim "law for the judge, facts for the jury" applies. The general demurrer is defendant's way of saying to plaintiff, "Admitting for the moment that all of the facts alleged in your complaint are true, you are still not entitled to relief as a matter of law." Put more colloquially, defendant is saying "Yeah, so what!"

The purpose of the general demurrer is to allow early dismissal of a complaint that is insufficient on its face. Suppose that the complaint alleges "The defendant stuck out his tongue. This offended me. Therefore, I am entitled to damages." Even if these facts were true, the plaintiff would not be entitled to relief. The sooner the case is dismissed, the better. The defendant should not

3. A party avoids the allegations of the opponent's pleading by introducing new matter that will entitle the party to judgment even if the allegations of the opponent's pleading are true. At common law, the plea was called confession and avoidance. For example, if a plaintiff pleaded that the defendant falsely called her a thief, and the defendant responded by admitting that the statement was made but alleging that it was made during a criminal trial, then the defendant would have confessed the allegations in the plaintiff's complaint but avoided liability by raising the affirmative defense of absolute privilege. The modern day affirmative defense is the descendant of the common law confession and avoidance.

4. Dakota's code pleading system extends the pleadings a step beyond the federal rules, which neither require nor permit a reply unless the court orders one or defendant interposes a counterclaim. FED.R.CIV.P. 7(a).

be required to file an answer, undergo discovery, and prepare for trial without being able to get a determination about whether the plaintiff's complaint is legally sufficient.

At common law, filing a general demurrer was a daring step, since defendant thereby made a binding concession that the facts alleged by the plaintiff were true. Should the court decide that the facts pleaded by plaintiff did support relief, defendant had lost. Under modern pleading systems, defendant no longer faces sudden death if the demurrer is not sustained. Defendant is still allowed to change strategy later by filing an answer denying that the facts alleged in the complaint are true.

When the demurrer is sustained, the court will usually grant the plaintiff leave to amend the complaint to cure the defect(s) in the pleading, so a demurrer is particularly useful when defendant believes plaintiff has pleaded all of the facts that she could conceivably prove. Should plaintiff's legal theory be tenuous, the demurrer allows both parties to obtain a ruling on the legal sufficiency of the cause of action[5] without incurring the expense of trial. The general demurrer is thus functionally equivalent to the Fed.R.Civ.P. 12(b)(6) motion to dismiss for failure to state a claim upon which relief can be granted.

Dakota follows the traditional rule that a demurrer cannot be a "speaking motion," that is, matters outside the challenged pleading can never be presented to the court for its consideration on a demurrer. A demurrer to a complaint examines only the face of the complaint. All of the facts asserted are taken to be true for purposes of deciding the legal sufficiency of the complaint.[6]

D. The Motion for Judgment on the Pleadings

5. The codes require plaintiff to plead a "cause of action." Because of procedural wrangling over the scope of a cause of action and the difficult niceties of pleading ultimate facts, the drafters of the federal rules discarded the concept of the cause of action in favor of the "claim." FED.R.CIV.P. 8(a)(2) requires "a short and plain statement of the claim showing that the pleader is entitled to relief." See the discussion of cause of action and claim in Exercise Three, pp. 92–96.

6. Practice under the rules is the same, yet the rules provides an escape valve that allows the court to consider matters outside the face of the complaint:

If, on a motion asserting the defense numbered (6) to dismiss for failure of the pleading to state a claim upon which relief can be granted, matters outside the pleading are presented to and not excluded by the court, the motion shall be treated as one for summary judgment and disposed of as provided in Rule 56, and all parties shall be given reasonable opportunity to present all material made pertinent to such a motion by rule 56.

FED.R.CIV.P. 12(b).

After the pleadings have closed, either party may make a motion for judgment on the pleadings. The motion may be used by the defendant as a sort of hang-fire demurrer, or by the plaintiff to challenge the legal sufficiency of the defendant's answer.

As with the demurrer, the motion for judgment on the pleadings cannot "speak."[7] The allegations of the party opposing the motion are taken as true; resolution of factual issues is reserved for trial. Nor can the movant rely upon an affirmative allegation in his pleading, unless it is admitted by the adversary. For example, suppose plaintiff sues defendant on a theory of invasion of privacy, alleging defendant used plaintiff's photograph for advertising purposes without permission. If defendant admits using the photograph but raises an affirmative defense, plaintiff would be entitled to judgment on the pleadings when his complaint is legally sufficient and defendant's affirmative defense is legally insufficient. If the defendant denied using the photograph, however, the plaintiff would be bound by that denial for purposes of the motion for judgment on the pleadings. Plaintiff could not introduce extrinsic evidence that the photograph had been used.

The motion for judgment on the pleadings "searches the pleadings." When plaintiff makes a motion for judgment on the pleadings, she exposes herself to the possibility that her complaint will be dismissed. Before examining the sufficiency of the defendant's answer, the court examines the sufficiency of the plaintiff's complaint, and if the plaintiff's complaint does not state a cause of action, it will be dismissed. A bad answer is good enough to withstand a bad complaint.

The general demurrer and the motion for judgment on the pleadings are not the only means for weeding out non-meritorious cases before trial. The motion for summary judgment is a more effective device. Summary judgment is the subject of Exercise Eight.

III. PRELIMINARY QUESTIONS

Study the following pleadings [assume the year is the most recent] and answer the following questions before going to the computer to work through CALI CIV 02: Demurrers and Judg-

---

7. In rules practice also, a motion for judgment on the pleadings looks only to the faces of the complaint and the answer. The rules have an escape valve here also. As with the Rule 12(b)(6) motion, *see* note 6, *supra*, a court ruling on a motion for judgment on the pleadings may consider "matters outside the pleadings," which automatically converts the motion into one for summary judgment. Fed.R.Civ.P. 12(c).

ments on the Pleadings. The computer will ask you the same questions, with the same numbers [note the numbers are nonconsecutive here]. The computer will also ask you some additional questions that are not posed here.

PART ONE—DEMURRER

Assume Peter Schuler commenced his suit against David Dour in Dakota state court by filing a complaint containing the following allegations as its body:

COMPLAINT ONE

1. On May 10, 20__, in Room 215 of Old Main at Dakota College, defendant falsely stated ''Peter (referring to plaintiff) is a heavy user of crack cocaine.''

2. As a result, plaintiff has been injured in his reputation and has suffered great pain and mental anguish, all to his damage in the sum of $100,000.

Defendant responded with a general demurrer.

Q–1. In this procedural posture, could the trial court properly decide whether plaintiff was a heavy user of crack?

Your answer _____

Q–3. In ruling on the demurrer, could the trial court properly decide whether the use of crack is a crime involving moral turpitude?

Your answer _____

Q–4. In ruling on the demurrer, could the trial court properly decide whether a disparaging statement has to be false to be actionable?

Your answer _____

Q–6. In ruling on the demurrer, can the trial court properly decide whether publication is an element of the tort of slander?

Your answer _____

Q–8. In ruling on the demurrer, could the trial court properly decide whether a conditional privilege applies to statements made by a college professor in a disciplinary hearing?

Your answer _____

Q–9. The trial court scheduled a hearing on the demurrer and requested briefs from the parties. Plaintiff's brief argued that using crack is a serious crime involving moral turpitude, and therefore he did not need to plead pecuniary damage. Must the trial court decide that plaintiff's position on this issue is wrong in order to sustain the demurrer?

Your answer _____

Please consider the issues that could be decided on demurrer had plaintiff instead filed the following complaint. The computer will ask you questions about it.

COMPLAINT TWO

1. On May 10, 20__, in Room 215 of Old Main at Dakota College, defendant falsely stated to Mary Trueblood and William Roberts: ''Peter (referring to plaintiff) is a heavy user of crack cocaine.''

2. As a result of defendant's false statement, plaintiff has suffered damage to his reputation and great pain and mental anguish, all to his damage in the sum of $100,000.

PART TWO—JUDGMENTS ON THE PLEADINGS

Assume plaintiff filed Complaint Two, reprinted immediately above.

Defendant responded with the following answer:

ANSWER

1. Now comes the defendant and denies each and every material allegation in plaintiff's complaint except the allegations in paragraph 1 of plaintiff's complaint.

2. Now comes the defendant and for a further defense avers that the statement made by the defendant was made in a hearing before the Disciplinary Board of Dakota College, when defendant, a Professor at Dakota College, was discussing the issue of whether plaintiff, a student, should be suspended from said college.

In response to defendant's answer, plaintiff filed the following reply:

REPLY

1. Plaintiff admits the allegations in paragraph 2 of defendant's answer.

2. Plaintiff further avers that defendant knew the statement ''Peter is a heavy user of crack cocaine'' was false at the time that he made it.

After the reply was filed, defendant moved for judgment on the pleadings.

Q–16. In ruling on defendant's motion, may the trial court properly decide whether plaintiff is a user of crack?

Your answer _____

Q–17. In ruling on defendant's motion, may the trial court properly decide whether using crack is a serious crime involving moral turpitude?

Your answer _____

Q–18. In ruling on defendant's motion, may the trial court properly decide whether a statement by a college professor before a disciplinary board is absolutely privileged?

Your answer _____

Q–19. If the trial court determined that a statement of a professor before a disciplinary board was absolutely privileged, would defendant be entitled to judgment on the pleadings?

Your answer _____

Q–20. If the plaintiff had denied that the statement was made before the disciplinary board, would the defendant be entitled to judgment on the pleadings if such statements were absolutely privileged?

Your answer _____

Q–21. On the motion for judgment on the pleadings, may the trial court properly decide whether publication is an element of the tort of slander?

Your answer _____

Q–22. Suppose that the plaintiff alleged publication and the defendant admitted making the statement to plaintiff, denied publication, and raised the affirmative defense of due care. In a motion for judgment on the pleadings, could the trial court properly decide whether publication is an element of the tort of slander?

Your answer _____

You are now ready to go to the computer to do CALI CIV 02: Demurrers and Judgments on the Pleadings.

EXERCISE FIVE

Motions to Dismiss and Waiver Under Federal Rule 12

I. RAISING, AND WAIVING, RULE 12 DEFENSES

Exercise Three explored pleading a complaint. This exercise explores one type of response to a complaint: a preliminary motion to dismiss under Federal Rule of Civil Procedure 12. Consequently, this exercise is narrower than Exercise Three. We do not explore the requirements of, or drafting, an answer, which is the responsive pleading to the complaint. We do not discuss other possible preliminary motions, such as a motion for more definite statement or a motion to strike. We discuss the assertion–and possible waiver–of the seven grounds found in Federal Rule 12(b) for dismissal of a complaint.

A. The Federal Rule 12(b) Defenses

1. Abandonment of the Special Appearance

The common law provided a plea in abatement to attack jurisdiction and a demurrer to attack the legal sufficiency of a complaint. The codes provided a demurrer to handle both tasks. In both systems, the defendant could make a *special appearance* to challenge jurisdiction. This can be seen in some of the older decisions that refer to the defendant having "appeared specially."

Special appearance was a term of art. Defendant would appear in the court for the sole purpose of challenging personal jurisdiction, and no other purpose. That was why the appearance was special. A defendant who attempted to present other defenses or motions before the court made a general appearance, and a general appearance amounted to a consent to personal jurisdiction. A defendant who challenged jurisdiction and at the same time pleaded to the merits of the complaint obviously called on the power of the court; this was a general appearance. A defendant could also consent, or waive objection, to personal jurisdiction more subtly. For example, a defendant made a general appearance by such actions as opposing plaintiff's motion to amend the complaint, engaging in discovery, challenging the legal sufficiency of the complaint, or possibly even informing the court that it chose not to appear. Consequently, a defendant wishing to challenge personal jurisdiction had to be careful; the challenge must have been to personal jurisdiction and nothing else.

When the special appearance was successful, the case was dismissed and defendant went home happy. When the special appearance was unsuccessful, the case proceeded. At that point, defendant might have a choice to make. Some states allowed defendant to proceed to defend on the merits while preserving the jurisdictional objection. Other states provided that a defendant who proceeded to defend on the merits waived the jurisdictional objection.

All of this has been swept aside in practice in federal courts and in state court systems patterned after the Federal Rules. Federal Rule 12(b) has abolished the special appearance: "No defense or objection is waived by being joined with one or more other defenses or objections in a responsive pleading or motion."

2. Assertion of Rule 12(b) Defenses

A defendant is required to serve an answer on plaintiff within "20 days after being served with the summons and complaint." Fed.R.Civ.P. 12(a)(1)(A). [A defendant waiving service is allowed a response time of 60 days (90 days if defendant was addressed outside any federal judicial district). Fed.R.Civ.P. 12(a)(1)(B)]. Instead of answering within that 20–day period, defendant may choose to make a preliminary Rule 12(b) motion to dismiss.[1] Should defendant choose that course of defense, and the motion prove unsuccessful, defendant is allowed 10 days after service of

---

1. Actually, defendant is not the only party who can raise these defenses. The plaintiff, for example, can raise the defenses in response to a counterclaim. The language of Fed.R.Civ.P. 12 is carefully drawn to cover any party responding to a claim, whether defendant, plaintiff, or third-party defendant. For convenience, this exercise will use the terms "plaintiff" and "defendant" in the usual context of a simple two-party action with no counterclaim.

the court's unfavorable decision on the motion to answer. Fed. R.Civ.P. 12(a)(4)(A).

The seven challenges that Federal Rule 12(b) specifically allows to be made by preliminary motion are the following:

—(1) lack of jurisdiction over the subject matter;

—(2) lack of jurisdiction over the person;

—(3) improper venue;

—(4) insufficiency of process;

—(5) insufficiency of service of process;

—(6) failure to state a claim upon which relief can be granted; and

—(7) failure to join a party under Rule 19.

A defendant wishing to raise any one of these seven challenges has two options. Option one is to raise any and all of the defenses in the answer. "Every defense, in law or fact, to a claim for relief in any pleading * * * shall be asserted in the responsive pleading thereto if one is required * * *. Fed.R.Civ.P. 12(b). The answer is the responsive pleading required to the complaint. Fed.R.Civ.P. 7(a). Option two is to raise any and all of these defenses in a preliminary motion, one made before the answer is pleaded. "[T]he following defenses may at the option of the pleader be made by motion: [listing the seven defenses]. A motion making any of these defenses shall be made before pleading if a further pleading is permitted." Fed.R.Civ.P. 12(b). Those are the only two options. A defendant who brings a preliminary motion to dismiss that asserts fewer than all of the defenses and later attempts to assert an additional Rule 12(b) defense for the first time in the answer will in most instances waive it, as discussed in the next section. Similarly, a defendant cannot make successive preliminary motions to dismiss; one is the quota allowed.[2]

The reason the rules limit defendant to one preliminary motion is rather obvious. That is the efficient method to dispose of all the threshold jurisdictional motions. Without that limitation, defendant could delay the proceeding for a long time by doling out the motions. For example, defendant could move to dismiss for im-

2. A party who makes a motion under this rule may join with it any other motions herein provided for and then available to the party. If a party makes a motion under this rule but omits therefrom any defense or objection then available to the party which this rule permits to be raised by motion, the party shall not thereafter make a motion based on the defense or objection so omitted, except a motion as provided in subdivision (h)(2) hereof on any of the grounds there stated. Fed.R.Civ.P. 12(g).

proper service of process; following denial of that motion, defendant could move to dismiss for improper venue. The string could continue through multiple preliminary motions.

All of the seven grounds for dismissal found in Federal Rule 12(b) are threshold issues that can and should be disposed of before the parties and the court proceed to the work of deciding the merits of the case.[3] With the exception of dismissal for failure to state a claim upon which relief can be granted, all of the grounds for dismissal are separable from the merits. With the exceptions of dismissal for failure to join a Rule 19 party and failure to state a claim, all of the grounds for dismissal render the court powerless to act in the case because of a defect in jurisdiction, venue, or service of process. By requiring defendant to assert these defenses early— either in preliminary motion or no later than the answer—the rules prevent defendant from laying in the weeds and springing such a ground for dismissal on plaintiff later should progress in the litigation not be favorable to defendant.

3. Waiving Rule 12(b) Defenses

While Fed.R.Civ.P. 12(g) requires a defendant who makes a preliminary motion under Rule 12 to consolidate all of its Rule 12(b) defenses into that motion, the enforcement provision is found in Fed.R.Civ.P. 12(h):

(1) A defense of lack of jurisdiction over the person, improper venue, insufficiency of process, or insufficiency of service of process is waived (A) if omitted from a motion in the circumstances described in subdivision (g), or (B) if it is neither made by motion under this rule nor included in a responsive pleading or an amendment thereof permitted by Rule 15(a) to be made as a matter of course.

(2) A defense of failure to state a claim upon which relief can be granted, a defense of failure to join a party indispensable under Rule 19, and an objection of failure to state a legal defense to a claim may be made in any pleading permitted or ordered under Rule 7(a), or by motion for judgment on the pleadings, or at the trial on the merits.

(3) Whenever it appears by suggestion of the parties or otherwise that the court lacks jurisdiction of the subject matter, the court shall dismiss the action.

---

3. "The defenses specifically enumerated (1)-(7) in subdivision (b) of this rule, whether made in a pleading or by motion, * * * shall be heard and determined before trial on application of any party, unless the court orders that the hearing and determination thereof be deferred until the trial." Fed.R.Civ.P. 12(d).

Since this exercise concerns waiver of defenses, we will work from back to front in this rule. First, Fed.R.Civ.P. 12(h)(3) provides that the defense of lack of subject matter jurisdiction [Fed.R.Civ.P. 12(b)(1)] cannot be waived. This of course follows from the fact that jurisdiction over the subject matter is granted by constitution and statutes, not by action of the parties. *See* Exercise Two, part I.A. Second, Fed.R.Civ.P. 12(h)(2) provides that the defenses of failure to state a claim [Fed.R.Civ.P. 12(b)(6)] and failure to join a Rule 19 party [Fed.R.Civ.P. 12(b)(7)] may be made as late as trial on the merits. In other words, these two rule 12 defenses are not waived by failure to consolidate them into a preliminary motion.

That leaves four rule 12 defenses that by the express provision of Fed.R.Civ.P. 12(h)(1) are waived if omitted from a preliminary motion to dismiss made "under this rule." These four waivable defenses are lack of jurisdiction over the person [Fed.R.Civ.P. 12(b)(2)],[4] improper venue [Fed.R.Civ.P. 12(b)(3)], insufficiency of process [Fed.R.Civ.P. 12(b)(4)], and insufficiency of service of process [Fed.R.Civ.P. 12(b)(5)].[5] These defenses must be consolidated into any preliminary motion brought under rule 12 [Fed. R.Civ.P. 12(g)]. Or in the absence of a preliminary motion to dismiss, these defenses must be consolidated into the answer. Or these defenses must be consolidated into an amendment to the answer that is allowed to be made as a matter of course.[6] Failure of defendant to assert one or more of these defenses in one of the preceding manners results in waiver of the defense(s).

II. WRITTEN EXERCISE

The following pages–and the accompanying computer-aided exercise–contain several questions to probe your understanding of

4. While the rule refers to lack of jurisdiction over the person, this is understood to include all bases of personal jurisdiction, including *in personam, in rem,* and *quasi in rem* jurisdiction. *See* Exercise Two, part I.A.

5. A motion to dismiss for insufficiency of process is properly brought only when the form of the process is defective. A motion to dismiss for insufficiency of service of process is properly brought to challenge the method of serving the process. *See* CHARLES A. WRIGHT & ARTHUR R. MILLER, FEDERAL PRACTICE AND PROCEDURE: CIVIL 2D § 1353 (1990).

6. FED.R.CIV.P. 12(h)(1) allows a defense omitted from the answer to be saved by amendment of the pleading made as a matter of course. FED.R.CIV.P. 15(a) allows the complaint to be amended as a matter of course "at any time before a responsive pleading [the answer] is served." Since no responsive pleading to the answer is usually permitted [unless the court orders a reply pursuant to FED.R.CIV.P. 7(a)], FED.R.CIV.P. 15(a) gives defendant 20 days after service of the answer on the plaintiff to amend the answer as a matter of course. Later amendment of the answer, as by consent or by leave of court, does not save the omitted defense.

the interrelationships of the federal rules and federal statutes involved in questions of waiver of defenses under Federal Rule 12. You will be required to exercise close scrutiny and interpretation of a complex set of interrelated provisions. The rules are Fed.R.Civ.P. 6(b), 7, 11, 12, and 15(a). The statutes are 28 U.S.C. §§ 1391(a) [venue] and 1404(a) [transfer of venue].[7] This exercise deals with the reasons for special treatment of Rule 12 defenses and analysis of the waiver provisions of the rule.

Instructions. The questions in this book are on the left-hand page, and the answers are on the right-hand page. Cover the right-hand page, write your answers to the questions in the spaces provided, and compare your answers to the suggested answers on the facing page.

7. 28 U.S.C. § 1391(a) is reproduced at p. 51, *supra.* 28 U.S.C. § 1404(a) is reproduced at p. 54, *supra.*

*

Q–1. Federal Rule of Civil Procedure 12(b) lists seven defenses that may be raised by the defendant prior to answering the complaint. A preliminary motion raising one of the Rule 12(b) defenses postpones the time for filing the answer until after the court has ruled on the motion. Fed.R.Civ.P. 12(a)(4)(A). The following questions are designed to probe why these defenses receive special treatment.

Q–1(a). Do the seven defenses in Rule 12(b) all involve matters that can be determined by the court on the face of the pleadings, without the necessity for testimony or findings of fact?

Your answer _____

Q–1(b). Is there a special need to decide the seven defenses before the rest of the lawsuit because they raise especially important issues?

Your answer _____

Q–1(c). Are the seven defenses suitable for early disposition because they involve trivial matters of form that should be corrected early in the lawsuit?

Your answer _____

Answer to Q–1(a). No. With the exception of the motion to dismiss for failure to state a claim (Rule 12(b)(6)), all of the listed defenses require findings of fact if the factual basis for them is contested. For example, the motion to dismiss for improper service of process, if contested, would require the trial court to make a finding about whether process was served upon an appropriate person. In a diversity case, the motion to dismiss for lack of subject matter jurisdiction can turn on whether a party acquired citizenship by moving to a new state, a matter that requires a finding of fact about the party's actions and intent. (Under Rule 43(e), the trial court could base factual findings on affidavits submitted by the parties, but would have the discretion to hear oral testimony or require depositions.)

Answer to Q–1(b). No. Not all of the issues are important. For example, the defense of insufficiency of process can involve the mere assertion that plaintiff omitted the summons or the complaint from otherwise proper process—a matter that cannot have much importance to a defendant who obviously knows of the lawsuit or she would not be making the motion. Similarly, the defense of improper service can be raised successfully if the plaintiff served an employee of a corporation who was not an officer, managing or general agent, or process agent within the meaning of Rule 4(h)(1). The sole purpose of allowing such motions seems to be to encourage parties to mind their formalities. The motions rarely terminate a lawsuit; instead, absent a statute of limitations problem, they merely result in a re-service of process.

Answer to Q–1(c). No. Some of the defenses are trivial, but others are important. The defense of lack of subject matter jurisdiction is considered near-sacred because it protects the division of powers between federal courts and state courts inherent in federalism. *See* CHARLES A. WRIGHT & MARY KAY KANE, THE LAW OF FEDERAL COURTS § 7 (6th ed. 2002).

Q–1(d). Do the seven defenses involve matters that can be severed for separate determination because they do not go to the merits of the lawsuit?

Your answer _____

Answer to Q–1(d). Yes, with minor qualifications. None of the defenses go to the merits, except the defense of failure to state a claim upon which relief can be granted. A Rule 12(b)(6) defense goes to the merits in the sense that it involves determination of whether the allegations, if true, present a meritorious claim. That defense, however, does not require or allow the court to look beyond the face of the complaint, and hence is a good defense to sever and consider early. Surely the lawsuit should not proceed further if the plaintiff's own statement of the claim, considered as true, provides no grounds for relief.

The other Rule 12(b) defenses have nothing to do with the merits of the case, so they are easy to separate and rule on prior to proceeding with the main lawsuit. Early disposition will promote judicial economy. When a defendant has a defense of improper venue or lack of jurisdiction, the court should rule on that defense before the parties develop the merits of the case, which may later be dismissed because it was brought in the wrong court. Finally, the trivial defenses concerning process might just as well be disposed of earlier as later; the possibility that separate treatment of these defenses will result in delay may not be too high a price to pay in order to encourage plaintiffs to adhere to the proper formalities, which after all have the significant purpose of making sure that defendants are given proper notice.

Q–2. Sally filed a complaint against George and process was served on Day 1. On Day 4, prior to his answer, George filed a motion raising the defenses of lack of subject matter jurisdiction, lack of personal jurisdiction, improper venue, insufficiency of service of process, and failure to state a claim upon which relief can be granted. Can George raise all of these defenses at the same time in the same motion?

Your answer _____

Q–3. Sally filed a complaint against George and process was served on Day 1. On Day 4, prior to his answer, George filed a motion under Rule 12(b)(1) to dismiss for lack of jurisdiction over the subject matter. The next day, George filed a motion under Rule 12(b)(3) to dismiss for improper venue. Has George waived his venue defense?

Your answer _____

Q–4. Sally filed a complaint against George and process was served on Day 1. On Day 4, prior to his answer, George filed a motion under Rule 12(b)(2) to dismiss for lack of jurisdiction over the person. The next day, George filed a motion under Rule 12(b)(1) to dismiss for lack of subject matter jurisdiction. Has George waived his subject matter jurisdiction defense?

Your answer _____

Q–5. Sally filed a complaint against George and process was served on Day 1. On Day 19, prior to his answer, George filed a motion under Rule 12(f) to strike impertinent matter from the complaint. The next day, George filed a motion under Rule 12(b)(2) to dismiss for lack of personal jurisdiction. Has George waived his personal jurisdiction defense?

Your answer _____

Q–6. Sally filed a complaint against George and process was served on Day 1. Without filing any preliminary motions, George filed an answer on Day 10 in which, in addition to responding to allegations in Sally's complaint, he raised the defenses of lack of jurisdiction over the person, lack of jurisdiction over the subject matter, failure to state a claim upon which relief could be granted, improper venue, and expiration of the statute of limitations. Does George have the right to raise all of these defenses in his answer without making any prior motions?

Your answer _____

Answer to Q–2. Yes. The defenses can be consolidated in the motion. Fed.R.Civ.P. 12(g). (Under some prior systems of pleading, the defendant was required to raise defenses in sequence, a time-consuming and inefficient procedure.)

Answer to Q–3. Yes. Rule 12(h)(1)(A) provides for waiver of the venue defense if it is omitted from a motion in the circumstances described in Rule 12(g). Rule 12(g) provides for consolidation of all Rule 12 motions that are "then available" to the movant. The purpose of these waiver provisions is to require that pre-answer motions be brought together, thereby preventing the delay that might arise from hearing the motions sequentially.

Answer to Q–4. No. Rule 12(h)(3) provides that the defense of subject matter jurisdiction may be raised at any time, or considered by the court on its own motion. Subject matter jurisdiction is granted by constitution and statutes, not by action of the parties. The federal subject matter jurisdiction defense is considered to be particularly consequential, since erroneous assertion of federal jurisdiction would be usurpation of state power. Hence, the defense is not waivable; the interests of speed and economy must yield to federalism.

Answer to Q–5. Yes. Rule 12(h)(1)(A) provides that a defense of lack of personal jurisdiction is waived "if omitted from a motion in the circumstances described in subdivision (g)." Rule 12(g) requires consolidation of any defenses "then available" in a "motion under this rule." Since a personal jurisdiction defense was "then available," and a Rule 12(f) motion is a "motion under this rule," the defense of personal jurisdiction was waived.

Answer to Q–6. Yes. Rule 12(b) provides that the designated defenses "may at the option of the pleader be made by motion." The defendant has two options: 1) raise the defenses in a preliminary motion, or 2) raise the defenses in the answer, provided that they have not been waived by omission from a preliminary motion. Since George made no preliminary motion, he did not waive any defenses by failing to join them with other defenses. They may all be consolidated in the answer, along with admissions, denials, and affirmative defenses.

Q–7. Sally filed a complaint against George and process was served on Day 1. On Day 10, George filed a Rule 12(b)(1) motion raising the defense of lack of subject matter jurisdiction. On Day 40, the trial court held a hearing on the Rule 12(b)(1) motion and ruled in favor of Sally. On Day 45, George filed his answer. (The answer was timely because the filing of the Rule 12(b)(1) motion extended the time for filing the answer until 10 days after notice of the court's action on the motion. Rule 12(a)(4)(A).) In his answer, George responded to the allegations in Sally's complaint and also raised the defenses of failure to state a claim upon which relief could be granted, lack of personal jurisdiction, expiration of the statute of limitations, res judicata, and improper venue.

Q–7(a). Has George waived the defense of failure to state a claim upon which relief could be granted?

Your answer _____

Q–7(b). Has George waived the defense of lack of personal jurisdiction?

Your answer _____

Q–7(c). Has George waived the defense of the statute of limitations?

Your answer _____

Q–7(d). Has George waived the venue defense?

Your answer _____

Answer to Q–7(a). No. The defense of failure to state a claim has not been waived. Rule 12(h)(2) preserves the defense and allows it to be asserted in a pleading, on a motion for judgment on the pleadings, or at the trial on the merits. The defense is considered too important to allow it to be waived by mistake.

Answer to Q–7(b). Yes. The defense of personal jurisdiction was waived by failure to join it in the Rule 12 motion. *See* Rule 12(h)(1)(A).

Answer to Q–7(c). No. The statute of limitations defense has not been waived because it is not a Rule 12 defense. This affirmative defense [*see* Rule 8(c)] could not have been raised in the Rule 12 motion, and therefore cannot be waived by omission from the motion.

Answer to Q–7(d). Yes. The defense of improper venue has been waived by the provisions of Rule 12(h)(1)(A).

Q–8. Sally filed and served a summons and complaint, and a set of interrogatories, on George on Day 1. On Day 10, George made a Rule 26(c) motion for a protective order, claiming that the interrogatories were burdensome and vexatious. On Day 15, George filed an answer responding to the allegations in Sally's complaint and raising the defense of improper venue. Has George waived the defense of improper venue?

Your answer _____

Q–9. Sally filed a complaint against George and process was served on Day 1. George did not file any preliminary motions. On Day 10, he served and filed an answer that denied all of the material allegations of Sally's complaint and raised the defenses of lack of subject matter jurisdiction and contributory negligence. Neither the parties nor the court took any further action until Day 25, when George attempted to amend his answer to include the defense of improper venue. Will this amendment save the venue defense?

Your answer _____

Q–10. Sally commenced an action alleging that George had defamed her by telling third persons that she is a drug addict. Process was served on Day 1. George did not make any preliminary motions. On Day 10, he filed an answer denying that he had ever said that Sally is a drug addict, and admitting all of the other allegations of Sally's complaint. On Day 35, George attempted to amend his answer to assert the defense of lack of personal jurisdiction. Will this amendment save the personal jurisdiction defense?

Your answer _____

Answer to Q–8. No. Rule 12(h)(1)(A) provides for waiver of a venue defense omitted from a Rule 12 motion in circumstances in which Rule 12 requires joinder. The operative language is in Rule 12(g), which requires consolidation when a motion has been made "under this rule," *i.e.*, under Rule 12. The Rule 26 motion for a protective order was not a Rule 12 motion, so omission of a venue defense did not trigger the waiver provisions of Rule 12(h)(1).

Answer to Q–9. Yes. George may amend the answer and save the venue defense. Rule 12(h)(1)(B) provides that the venue defense is waived if it is omitted from a Rule 12 motion, or no motion having been made, if it is omitted from a "responsive pleading or an amendment thereof permitted by Rule 15(a) to be made as a matter of course." Here the amendment is permitted "as a matter of course" because no responsive pleading is normally permitted to an answer [*see* Rule 7(a)], and 20 days have not passed since the answer was served [*see* Rule 15(a)].

Answer to Q–10. No. Here, the period during which the answer could be amended as a matter of course has elapsed, since no responsive pleading is normally permitted to an answer and more than 20 days have passed since service of the answer [*See* Rule 15(a)]. Therefore, under Rule 12(h)(1)(B), the defense of lack of personal jurisdiction has been waived.

III. COMPUTER EXERCISE: CALI CIV 09

You are now ready for further work in applying Rule 12 in CALI CIV 09: Waiver Under Rule 12. Be sure to take your Federal Rules of Civil Procedure with you to the computer.

*

EXERCISE SIX

Joinder and Supplemental Jurisdiction

I. INTRODUCTION

A. Joinder Devices Available under the Federal Rules

1. Common Law and Code Practice

Joinder was harshly restricted under the common law. Since a primary goal of common law pleading was reduction of the case to a single issue of law or fact [*see* Exercise Three I.A.3], the typical case was one plaintiff against one defendant on one theory of recovery. Joinder of claims or parties on the grounds of convenience or judicial economy was not considered desirable.

Joinder of differing theories of recovery was difficult and often impossible because of the common law writ system. Consider, for example, a plaintiff who wished to plead that defendant had both restrained him and announced to bystanders that he had caught a horse thief. Could plaintiff join these two theories in a single action? Since false imprisonment was properly brought under a writ of trespass, and slander was properly brought under a writ of case, the defendant could successfully demur for improper joinder. The same result followed should plaintiff wish to plead defendant had taken a horse (trespass) and refused to return it (case).

Similarly, joinder of parties was difficult because plaintiff was the master of his own case. While joinder of parties was possible, it depended on the substantive rights of the parties, which in turn depended on complicated rules that traced once again into the writ system.

Procedure in the court of equity was more flexible. Equity did not attempt to hold a case to a single issue. In fact, equity attempted to resolve an entire dispute in a single lawsuit; a popular equity maxim was "equity delights to do justice and not by halves." Accordingly, equity allowed plaintiffs to join various theories of recovery in a single suit, and equity allowed joinder of additional parties whose interests were implicated by the main controversy.

The middle 1800s brought on the wave of procedural reform of the codes. The codes borrowed from both common law and equity, and adopted several joinder concepts from the latter.[1] Joinder became easier. Problems remained. Joinder of theories of recovery was limited by narrow court interpretations of "transaction or transactions"[2] and also by the typical code provision that causes of action joined "must affect all the parties to the action." Joinder of parties was limited by narrow court interpretations of typical code provisions, such as that plaintiffs could join when they had "an interest in the subject of the action and in obtaining the relief demanded," or that defendants could be joined when they "claim an interest in the controversy adverse to the plaintiff."[3] A case, decided as late as 1925, illustrates these difficulties.[4] Plaintiff sued two defendants for wrongful death. The cause of action for negligence against the first defendant was for maintaining an attractive nuisance on which a boy hurt himself; the cause of action against the second defendant was for medical malpractice in treating the injuries. The decision was that parties and causes of action were misjoined since the causes of action did not arise out of the same transaction and they did not affect all the parties.

2. Federal Rules Joinder

The Federal Rules of Civil Procedure, promulgated in 1938, adopted the reforms of the codes and went further. Because the

---

1. CHARLES E. CLARK, CODE PLEADING chs. 6–7 (2d ed. 1947).

2. The typical pattern of a code was to list categories of causes of action that could be joined:

(1) contracts, express or implied; (2) injuries to the person; (3) injuries to the character; (4) injuries to the property; (5) actions to recover real property with or without damages; (6) actions to recover chattels with or without damages; (7) claims against a trustee by virtue of a contract or operation of law; (8) actions arising out of the same transaction or transactions connected with the same subject of action.

See CHARLES E. CLARK, CODE PLEADING 441 (2d ed. 1947).

3. See CHARLES E. CLARK, CODE PLEADING 365, 382 (2d ed. 1947).

4. Ader v. Blau, 241 N.Y. 7, 148 N.E. 771 (1925).

drafters were able to identify the problem areas that had developed in joinder under the codes, they were able to eliminate many of the problems. Joinder of both theories of recovery and of parties became easier. This increased ease of joinder was tongue-in-groove with the new role of pleading. Pleading under the Federal Rules was designed primarily to give the opponent notice and to leave the functions of revealing facts, narrowing issues, and weeding out meritless claims to discovery. Similarly, joinder was designed to promote broad convenience and judicial economy, and to leave problems of confusion that such joinder might create to devices such as separation and severance for trial [*see* Fed.R.Civ.P. 42].

A panoply of joinder devices is available under the Federal Rules. In fact, the number of devices and the similarity of some of the names of the devices can cause confusion. As a consequence, a person studying federal joinder must be sure to keep the various devices separate. The task may seem daunting at first, but understanding the purpose of each joinder device should greatly reduce the difficulty. This section provides the names and brief descriptions of all of the devices.[5] The next section of this exercise discusses each device in more detail. The Federal Rules joinder devices are the following:

—*joinder of claims* (party may join more than one claim against another party);

—*compulsory counterclaim* (claim against an opposing party that arises out of the same transaction or occurrence as the claim of the opposing party);

—*permissive counterclaim* (claim against an opposing party that does not arise out of the same transaction or occurrence);

—*cross-claim* (claim against a co-party);

5. This exercise does not consider certain topics related to joinder: real party in interest (action must be brought in the name of the person who will benefit from a recovery), and capacity to sue or be sued (ability of a person to represent his or her own interests in an action). *See* 6A CHARLES A. WRIGHT, ARTHUR R. MILLER & MARY KAY KANE, FEDERAL PRACTICE AND PROCEDURE: CIVIL 2D §§ 1542–73 (1990). This exercise does not consider standing to sue (ability of a person to challenge governmental action). *See* 13 CHARLES A. WRIGHT, ARTHUR R. MILLER, EDWARD H. COOPER & RICHARD D. FREER, FEDERAL PRACTICE AND PROCEDURE: JURISDICTION 2D §§ 3531 *et seq.* (1989 & Supp. 2004).

This exercise also does not consider class actions, a joinder device that allows a large number of persons to join as plaintiffs (or defendants) in a single litigation. The multiple nuances of that topic far exceed the scope of this brief treatment of joinder devices. *See generally* 7A–7B CHARLES A. WRIGHT, ARTHUR R. MILLER & MARY KAY KANE, FEDERAL PRACTICE AND PROCEDURE: CIVIL 2D §§ 1751–1820 (1986).

—*permissive joinder of parties* (allows joinder of multiple plaintiffs or multiple defendants);

—*compulsory joinder of parties* (requires joinder of multiple plaintiffs or multiple defendants);

—*third-party practice, or impleader* (party defending a claim may bring into the action a third person who may be derivatively liable for all or part of the claim);

—*intervention of right* (third person must be allowed to enter the action as a party);

—*permissive intervention* (third person may be allowed to enter the action as a party); and

—*interpleader* (person holding property potentially subject to multiple claimants may require claimants to assert their claims against the property in the same action—can be *statutory interpleader* or *interpleader under the rule*).

B. Supplemental Jurisdiction

1. The History of Pendent and Ancillary Jurisdiction.

As the preceding section discussed, the passage of years has brought more generous joinder. With this loosening of restrictions on the joinder devices themselves, attention in the field of joinder—at least in the federal courts—has shifted from the joinder devices to questions of federal subject matter jurisdiction.[6] For example, a plaintiff may be allowed as a matter of joinder of claims to attach a state law claim to a federal question claim, but why is a federal court allowed to adjudicate the state law claim? Or a defendant may be allowed as a matter of joinder to assert a state law cross-claim against a co-defendant, but why is a federal court allowed to adjudicate the state law claim?

The federal courts created two common law doctrines that expanded their jurisdictional reach over joined claims and parties: pendent jurisdiction and ancillary jurisdiction. Both of these common law doctrines have been subsumed into the statutory doctrine of supplemental jurisdiction.

Pendent jurisdiction allowed a plaintiff who asserted a federal question claim to add on, or append, additional state law theories of recovery arising out of the same facts as the federal claim.

6. The doctrine of supplemental jurisdiction applies only in federal courts, which are courts of limited subject matter jurisdiction. State courts of general jurisdiction do not have problems with limited subject matter jurisdictional reach, so joinder problems in state courts are limited to the joinder devices.

Assume, for example, plaintiff had been fired by her employer, and wished to assert three theories of recovery against defendant: a civil rights violation under Title VII, a breach of contract under state law, and the tort of intentional infliction of mental distress under state law. This three-count complaint could be filed in state court. Could all three counts be brought into federal court? Yes, said pendent jurisdiction. Since the two state-law theories arose out of a "common nucleus of operative facts," all formed part of the same "case" under Article III and the entire case could be heard in federal court.[7]

The pendent state law theories were limited to those factually intertwined with the federal law theory. In the example above, plaintiff could bring a three-count complaint for 1) Title VII violation, 2) breach of employment contract, and 3) intentional infliction of mental distress. Pendent jurisdiction would not allow 4) a factually-unrelated traffic accident between plaintiff and one of defendant's trucks. On the other hand, pendent jurisdiction would likely allow 4) defamation for a reference letter sent to one of plaintiff's prospective new employers.

Attempts were made to expand pendent jurisdiction to cover pendent parties as well as pendent "claims." These attempts to create pendent party jurisdiction achieved some success in lower federal courts, but were repeatedly rejected in the Supreme Court.[8]

While pendent jurisdiction assisted plaintiffs, ancillary jurisdiction assisted defendants. A defendant properly brought into federal court was allowed by the doctrine of ancillary jurisdiction to assert any claims it had that arose out of the same transaction or

---

7. United Mine Workers v. Gibbs, 383 U.S. 715, 725, 86 S.Ct. 1130, 1138, 16 L.Ed.2d 218, 227–28 (1966). The idea that federal courts have power to hear all aspects of a case traces back to Osborn v. Bank of the United States, 22 U.S. 738, 823 (1824):

> [W]hen a question to which the judicial power of the Union is extended by the constitution, forms an ingredient of the original cause, it is in the power of congress to give the circuit courts jurisdiction of that cause, although other questions of fact or of law be involved in it.

While the *Gibbs* opinion referred to the federal claim and the state law claim, the better terminology would be to refer to two theories of recovery within the same claim, since a claim is commonly recognized as all facts comprising a transaction or occurrence, which would be roughly synonymous with the "common nucleus of operative facts." Except for this looseness in language, *Gibbs* meshes nicely with the scope of the federal claim for relief. *See* Exercise Three I.C.2.

8. Finley v. United States, 490 U.S. 545, 109 S.Ct. 2003, 104 L.Ed.2d 593 (1989); Owen Equip. & Erection Co. v. Kroger, 437 U.S. 365, 98 S.Ct. 2396, 57 L.Ed.2d 274 (1978); Aldinger v. Howard, 427 U.S. 1, 96 S.Ct. 2413, 49 L.Ed.2d 276 (1976).

occurrence as the original, jurisdictionally-proper claim.[9] Thus, for example, a defendant was allowed to assert a compulsory counterclaim against the plaintiff because a compulsory counterclaim by definition arises out of the same transaction or occurrence as the claim.

Operation of ancillary jurisdiction in most cases became quite mechanical. The test for ancillary jurisdiction was whether the joined claim arose out of the same transaction or occurrence. The same test is found in many of the joinder devices. Therefore, when the joinder device was satisfied, ancillary jurisdiction was satisfied. Ancillary jurisdiction covered compulsory counterclaims, cross-claims, third-party claims, and intervention of right; it did not cover permissive counterclaims and permissive intervention.

The concept of the same transaction or occurrence in its essence means a single set of facts, so the kinship of ancillary jurisdiction to pendent jurisdiction's "common nucleus of operative facts" is readily apparent. Therefore, merger of the two doctrines became sensible.

2. Supplemental Jurisdiction

Congress decided in 1990 to merge the two jurisdictional doctrines by statute, and to call the result "supplemental jurisdiction":

(a) Except as provided in subsections (b) and (c) or as expressly provided otherwise by Federal statute, in any civil action of which the district courts have original jurisdiction, the district courts shall have supplemental jurisdiction over all other claims that are so related to claims in the action within such original jurisdiction that they form part of the same case or controversy under Article III of the United States Constitution. Such supplemental jurisdiction shall include claims that involve the joinder or intervention of additional parties.

(b) In any civil action of which the district courts have original jurisdiction founded solely on section 1332 of this title [diversity jurisdiction], the district courts shall not have supplemental jurisdiction under subsection (a) over claims by plaintiffs against persons made parties under Rule 14, 19, 20, or 24 of the Federal Rules of Civil Procedure, or over claims by persons proposed to be joined as plaintiffs under Rule 19 of such rules, or seeking to intervene as plaintiffs under rule 24 of

---

9. *See* 13 CHARLES A. WRIGHT, ARTHUR R. MILLER, EDWARD H. COOPER & RICHARD D. FREER, FEDERAL PRACTICE AND PROCEDURE: JURISDICTION 2D § 3523 (1984 & Supp. 2004).

such rules, when exercising supplemental jurisdiction over such claims would be inconsistent with the jurisdictional requirements of section 1332.[10]

In later sections of this exercise, we will explore this statute in depth and apply it in a wide variety of joinder situations. We will see that it is not a paragon of legislative drafting and has several unintended consequences. For now, we note that in many ways § 1367 does exactly what it was intended to do. It brings together pendent jurisdiction and ancillary jurisdiction into the new doctrine of supplemental jurisdiction. It establishes the test for supplemental jurisdiction as "the same case or controversy under Article III," which is largely synonymous with the common nucleus of operative facts and the transaction or occurrence. It creates pendent party jurisdiction in the last sentence of paragraph (a). It restricts the use of supplemental jurisdiction in diversity cases in paragraph (b) so as not to tread on the doctrine of complete diversity.

Consequently, any joinder question requires a series of analytical steps. The first step is to determine whether the joinder device permits the joinder. The second step is to determine whether the federal court has independent subject matter jurisdiction over the claim or party to be joined. When the federal court has independent jurisdiction, this second step is satisfied. When, however, the federal court does not have independent jurisdiction over the added claim or party, then the supplemental jurisdiction statute must be consulted. The third step is to determine that the claim or party to be added is part of the same case or controversy under Article III as required by § 1367(a). If so, and federal jurisdiction is not based solely on diversity, the analysis is at an end. If the federal jurisdictional basis is diversity, then a fourth step is required. The fourth step demands careful parsing of § 1367(b) to make sure that it does not take away the federal supplemental jurisdiction that § 1367(a) granted. As can be seen, only the first step involves operation of the actual joinder device.

II. THE JOINDER DEVICES

A. Claims

1. Joinder of Claims

As stated previously, the common law sharply restricted joinder of claims in its search for a single issue in an action. The codes

---

10. 28 U.S.C. § 1367(a)-(b). Paragraph (c) outlines situations in which the federal court may decline to exercise supplemental jurisdiction. Paragraph (d) is a saving statute for statute of limitations purposes should the court send a state claim back to state court. Paragraph (e) defines state for purposes of the statute.

broadened claim joinder by enumerating several possibilities for joinder, but the courts became caught up in technical and narrow definitions of the terms in those statutes.

The Federal Rules removed any possible questions about joinder of claims. Joinder of claims under Federal Rule 18 is unrestricted: "A party asserting a claim to relief * * * may join, either as independent or as alternate claims, as many claims, legal, equitable, or maritime, as the party has against an opposing party." The overriding policy is efficiency, allowing both the court and the parties to resolve all disputes in a single lawsuit. That means a plaintiff who has a conglomeration of totally unrelated claims against a defendant may join them all in one action–although Federal Rule 10 suggests strongly that unrelated claims be stated in separate counts. It means also that other parties who properly bring a transactionally-related claim, such as a counterclaim or a cross-claim, are able to add unrelated claims.

Should a confusing mess result, the solution of the rules is to allow the court to use its discretion under Federal Rule 42(b) to order separate trials. Joinder of claims is not a pleading problem; it is a trial problem.

Of course the rule makes clear that claims "may" be joined. A party may choose either to add another claim, or to save it for a later lawsuit. A party choosing the latter course must be wary of the preclusion doctrines. Should the unasserted matter actually be part of the same claim asserted in the first suit, it would be lost under the doctrine of claim preclusion (res judicata). Even should the unasserted matter truly be a separate claim, one or more common issues may be litigated and decided in the first lawsuit, raising the possibility of issue preclusion (collateral estoppel). *See* Exercise Eleven.

2. *Supplemental jurisdiction for Joinder of Claims*

Pendent jurisdiction allowed a claimant asserting a federal question to add a state law theory of recovery when both arose from a "common nucleus of operative facts." The same result is allowed under supplemental jurisdiction since the common nucleus of operative facts is equivalent to the "same case of controversy under Article III" as required by § 1367(a).

What about the situation when plaintiff has two factually unrelated claims against defendant? When federal jurisdiction is based on a federal question, the second, state law claim would not qualify for supplemental jurisdiction because—being factually unrelated—it would by definition not qualify as "part of the same case or controversy under Article III." When the federal basis is diversity, then supplemental jurisdiction is not necessary because diversity exists and plaintiff will likely be able to aggregate the amounts of all the claims.

B. Counterclaims

A counterclaim is asserted against an "opposing party." Fed. R.Civ.P. 13(a), (b). Essentially that means a counterclaim crosses the "v" of the lawsuit. A defendant may assert a counterclaim against plaintiff. A plaintiff may assert a counterclaim against a counterclaiming defendant. A third-party defendant may counterclaim against a third-party plaintiff. A claim that does not cross the "v," as for example a defendant against another defendant, is not a counterclaim.

The roots of counterclaim practice can be found in the common law. The practices of recoupment and setoff were available, but each had limitations. Recoupment by a defendant was limited to a claim arising from the same contract or transaction as the plaintiff's claim. As such, it could reduce or eliminate plaintiff's recovery, but could not provide a positive recovery for defendant. Setoff was created in equity to remedy these weaknesses of recoupment. Setoff allowed a positive recovery, and the defendant's claim did not have to arise from the same transaction as the plaintiff's claim. Yet setoff had its own weaknesses: the claim to be set off had to be liquidated or subject to ready computation. The right of setoff had to be mutual. Most importantly, since setoff was an equitable procedure, the circumstances had to call for the action of equity. For example, when A and B owed each other money, and A sued B for the debt, B could use setoff only when A was insolvent; otherwise B could bring a separate action.

The codes invented the counterclaim. Typically, they limited its use to situations where the counterclaim arose from the same transaction, or from the same contract, as the claim.

The Federal Rules create two types of counterclaims: compulsory counterclaims and permissive counterclaims.

1. Compulsory counterclaims

A compulsory counterclaim is a counterclaim that arises out of the same transaction or occurrence as the claim.[11] Other counter-

11. A pleading shall state as a counterclaim any claim which at the time of serving the pleading the pleader has against any opposing party, if it arises out of

claims are permissive counterclaims. Courts are therefore required to determine the scope of the "transaction or occurrence." While that phrase cannot be precisely defined, in its essence a transaction or occurrence is a single set of facts. It is not tied to legal theories or defenses. When cars driven by A and B collide, and then driver B gets out of his car and punches driver A presents one transaction or occurrence (only one event), not one for negligence and another for battery. Clearly, the transaction or occurrence is close kin to the claim for relief [*see* Exercise Three I.C.2], to the common nucleus of operative facts of pendent jurisdiction, to the Article III case or controversy of supplemental jurisdiction, and to the scope of a claim for purposes of res judicata [*see* Exercise Eleven II.A.3].

Unfortunately, many federal courts have felt a need to gloss the rule. One treatise summarizes the four popular glosses as follows:

> A number of courts have sought more concrete standards and four additional tests have emerged for deciding whether a counterclaim is compulsory. First, would res judicata bar a subsequent suit on defendant's claim absent the compulsory counterclaim rule? Second, are the issues of fact and law raised by the claim and counterclaim largely the same? Third, will substantially the same evidence support or refute plaintiff's claim as well as defendant's counterclaim? And fourth, is there any logical relationship between the claim and the counterclaim?[12]

Why "transaction or occurrence" requires gloss is puzzling. Courts that look to a single set of facts will be following the language of the rule, not an unnecessary addition. The logical relationship standard may make sense for the more difficult decision of when to tie transactions together into the same claim, as is sometimes necessary to decide for a question of joinder of parties [*see* II.E.1, *infra*] or in the field of res judicata.[13] It should be unnecessary here.

---

the transaction or occurrence that is the subject matter of the opposing party's claim and does not require for its adjudication the presence of third persons of whom the court cannot acquire jurisdiction.

Fed.R.Civ.P. 13(a). As can be seen, the pleader need not state a counterclaim it does not have at the time of serving the pleading. The rule also contains other escape valves, including that the potential counterclaim is already "the subject of another pending action." *See generally* Jack H. Friedenthal, Mary Kay Kane & Arthur R. Miller, Civil Procedure § 6.7, at 361 (3d ed. 1999).

12. Jack H. Friedenthal, Mary Kay Kane & Arthur R. Miller, Civil Procedure § 6.7, at 359 (3d ed. 1999).

13. Claim preclusion covers all parts of the plaintiff's claim that were or should have been adjudicated. Most courts today accept the transactional definition of claim found in Restatement (Second) of Judgments § 24 (1982): "the claim extin-

The party possessing a compulsory counterclaim "shall state" it. Even though a defending party is thus required to litigate its claim in a forum of the opposing party's choosing, the drafters decided that this inconvenience was justified by the efficiency of litigating all claims arising from the same transaction or occurrence in one proceeding. A compulsory counterclaim that is not stated is lost, although courts vary on the theory of loss, some using preclusion, others using an estoppel, and others using a sanction for violation of the rules.[14] Clearly, the safe course for an attorney in doubt as to whether her client's potential counterclaim is compulsory or permissive is to plead it.

2. Permissive counterclaims

The Federal Rules define a permissive counterclaim by exclusion. A permissive counterclaim is any counterclaim that is not compulsory. "A pleading may state as a counterclaim any claim against an opposing party not arising out of the transaction or occurrence that is the subject matter of the opposing party's claim." Fed.R.Civ.P. 13(b).

As the name suggests, a party may assert the permissive counterclaim in the action or may instead sue on it in a separate action–at a time and place of the party's choosing. Since by definition the permissive counterclaim does not involve the same subject matter as the claim, little efficiency is lost. A party choosing not to bring a permissive counterclaim must at the same time be careful that it is not lost through the operation of issue preclusion; to the extent that the counterclaim has an issue (or issues) in common with the claim, the decision on that issue in the litigation of the claim may well be preclusive in a later, separate action on the counterclaim. See the discussion of issue preclusion in Exercise Eleven.

3. Supplemental Jurisdiction for Counterclaims

Prior to the enactment of supplemental jurisdiction, the law in the area was clear. Compulsory counterclaims, arising out of the same transaction or occurrence, qualified for ancillary jurisdiction; permissive counterclaims, not arising out of the same transaction or occurrence, did not qualify for ancillary jurisdiction.

guished includes all rights of the plaintiff to remedies against the defendant with respect to all or any part of the transaction, or series of connected transactions, out of which the action arose."

14. *See* 6 CHARLES A. WRIGHT, ARTHUR R. MILLER & MARY KAY KANE, FEDERAL PRACTICE AND PROCEDURE: CIVIL 2D § 1417 (1990).

Enactment of § 1367 in 1990 was not intended to change, and did not change, these results. Compulsory counterclaims ride into federal court on supplemental jurisdiction. Permissive counterclaims do not.

Compulsory counterclaim. Looking first to § 1367(a), the court must decide whether the counterclaim is part of the same case or controversy under Article III. By definition, a compulsory counterclaim, because it must arise out of the same transaction or occurrence, is part of the same Article III case or controversy. Looking next to § 1367(b), the court will recognize that in diversity cases, "claims by plaintiffs against persons made parties under Rule 14, 19, 20, or 24" are not within supplemental jurisdiction. A counterclaim is asserted under Rule 13. Since that rule is not on the list, § 1367(b) does not apply, and the court is back to § 1367(a). A compulsory counterclaim is carried into federal court by supplemental jurisdiction.

Permissive counterclaim. Looking first to § 1367(a), the court must decide whether the counterclaim is part of the same case or controversy under Article III. By definition, a permissive counterclaim, because it does not arise out of the same transaction or occurrence, is not part of the same Article III case or controversy. The court need not even consider § 1367(b).

C. Cross-claims

1. Joinder of Cross-claims

The cross-claim traces back into the equity courts, which allowed a party to assert a cross-bill against another party. This procedure found its way into the federal equity rules of 1912. Many code states adopted the procedure, usually renaming the device a cross-complaint.[15]

The Federal Rules carried forward the possibility of asserting a claim against another party to the action, either as a counterclaim against an opposing party or as a cross-claim against a co-party. A co-party is a party on the same side of the "v." In other words, a cross-claim is by a defendant against another defendant. Or a cross-claim is by one plaintiff against another plaintiff. For example, assume plaintiff A and plaintiff B sue defendant C and defendant D. C could cross-claim against D since they are co-parties. [Note that should C assert such a cross-claim, C and D would then become opposing parties, and a claim by D back

---

15. JACK H. FRIEDENTHAL, MARY KAY KANE & ARTHUR R. MILLER, CIVIL PROCEDURE § 6.7 (3d ed. 1999).

against C would be a counterclaim.] Or C and D could assert a counterclaim against A and B. A might then plead a cross-claim against B (perhaps for indemnity).

Federal Rule 13(g) governs cross-claims in federal practice: "A pleading may state as a cross-claim any claim by one party against a co-party arising out of the transaction or occurrence that is the subject matter either of the original action or of a counterclaim * * *." The rule accordingly makes four things clear. First, a cross-claim is a claim against a co-party. Second, a cross-claim is always permissive. Third, the party must state a "claim;" an assertion that a co-party is entirely liable should be pleaded as a denial, not as a cross-claim. Fourth, the cross-claim must arise "out of the transaction or occurrence" of the original claim or counterclaim. The concept of transaction or occurrence means in its essence the same set of operative facts [see II.B.1, supra].

Allowing parties to add factually related claims to an existing action makes efficient sense for the court; allowing the addition of unrelated claims to an existing action would serve no efficiency purpose. That is why a cross-claim must be part of the same transaction or occurrence. This reasoning is undercut somewhat, however, by the fact that once a party is able to plead a cross-claim, the party is then able to add other, completely unrelated claims to the same action. This is so because of the broad federal joinder of claims rule, which allows the joinder of all claims against a party. See II.A.1, supra.

2. Supplemental Jurisdiction for Cross-claims

Prior to the enactment of supplemental jurisdiction, cross-claims qualified for ancillary jurisdiction because by rule they are required to arise from the same transaction or occurrence as the claim, and the same transaction or occurrence was also the test for ancillary jurisdiction. Enactment of § 1367 in 1990 was not intended to change, and did not change, this result.

As with any question of supplemental jurisdiction, we begin with § 1367(a). It provides supplemental jurisdiction extends to "all other claims that are so related to claims in the action within such original jurisdiction that they form part of the same case or controversy under Article III * * *." A cross-claim, because it must arise from the same transaction or occurrence, is part of the same case or controversy. Supplemental jurisdiction exists. We then consult § 1367(b). It provides supplemental jurisdiction does not exist in diversity cases when joinder is accomplished under certain enumerated rules. Rule 13(g) is not on the list. Consequently, cross-claims will always be covered by supplemental jurisdiction.

D. Third-party claims [also known as Impleader]

1. Joinder of Third-party Claims

Third-party practice is commonly called impleader, and the two terms are synonymous. The only difficulty with use of the term impleader is that it is another joinder device beginning with "i," and sometimes this causes confusion. A person must remember that *impleader* is used by a party to bring a person not a party (a third party) into the action, *intervention* is used by a person not a party to the action to force his way into the action, and *interpleader* is used by a person subject to multiple claims to the same property to force all claimants to assert those claims in a single action.

Third-party practice finds its origins in a common law procedure called "vouching in," or "vouching to warranty." This procedure allowed a defendant to vouch in another person who would be liable (originally because the third person had given a warranty on the property sought from defendant); this allowed the vouched in party to assume defense of the action. A judgment against the original defendant would then also be conclusive on the vouched in party. The weakness of this procedure was that the original defendant was still required to bring a second, separate action against the vouched in party to obtain a judgment. Third-party practice was adopted by several of the code states, and subsequently by the Federal Rules.

The advantage of third-party practice lies in this example. Plaintiff consumer sues defendant retailer for selling a defective product. The retailer can defend the action, and–should it lose–later sue the manufacturer of the product in a separate action. When the retailer wins that second action, the manufacturer ultimately pays the damages. The retailer is removed from the middle. Drawbacks exist with this plan, however. First, inconsistent results might occur: the jury in the first action may decide the product was defective, and the jury in the second action may decide the product was not defective. Second, delay results. The retailer might have to pay the first judgment years before the second case proceeds to judgment. Even worse, during the time lag the statute of limitations on the second action might expire. Third, the retailer will incur the expense of litigating two separate actions.

Impleader removes these problems. By impleading the manufacturer into the original action, the retailer removes the possibility of inconsistent results since the same jury will decide the entire action. Judgment will be entered on both the original claim and the third-party claim at the same time, so no delay results. Both claims will be determined in the same litigation, so little added expense will result.

Federal Rule 14(a), governing third-party practice, appears to be the longest and most complicated of all the joinder rules. Certainly it is long. When we parse out each sentence of the rule, however, it is not really complicated. Here is the relevant portion of Federal Rule 14(a), interspersed with our comments in italics.

> At any time after commencement of the action, a defending party, as a third-party plaintiff, may cause a summons and complaint to be served upon a person not a party to the action who is or may be liable to the third-party plaintiff for all or part of the plaintiff's claim against the third-party plaintiff.

Impleader may be used only against "a person not a party to the action." A claim against an opposing party is a counterclaim. A claim against a co-party is a cross-claim. When plaintiff sues defendant, and defendant brings in a third party, defendant then becomes known as "defendant and third-party plaintiff." The original plaintiff remains the plaintiff, and the third-person brought into the action is the third-party defendant.

This language also contains the most important thing to remember about the joinder device: impleader liability must be derivative. A third-party claim asserts the third-party defendant "is or may be liable" to the original defendant for the defendant's liability to the plaintiff. Impleader is not a device to offer up an alternative defendant to the plaintiff. For example, plaintiff homeowner sues defendant waterproofing company because the basement continues to leak. Defendant can implead the manufacturer of the waterproof paint it used. That is derivative liability. Defendant cannot implead the architect of the house on the theory that the fault lies in the house design instead of the waterproofing job. That is an alternate defendant, not derivative liability. Rule 14 cannot be used for that purpose. Defendant should plead a denial.

> The third-party plaintiff need not obtain leave to make the service if the third-party plaintiff files the third-party complaint not later than 10 days after serving the original answer. Otherwise the third-party plaintiff must obtain leave on motion upon notice to all parties to the action.

The original defendant may implead as a matter of right within 10 days of serving the original answer (although another party may

157

later move to strike the third-party complaint, so impleader in the end is always discretionary with the court); of course, the common practice is to serve the third-party complaint as part of the same document as the answer. After the 10–day period has expired, defendant must obtain leave of court to use third-party practice. The court will decide whether the increased efficiency of a single action will outweigh any prejudice to a party.[16]

The person served with the summons and third-party complaint, hereinafter called the third-party defendant, shall make any defenses to the third-party's claim as provided in Rule 12 and any counterclaims against the third-party plaintiff and cross-claims against other third party defendants as provided in Rule 13. The third-party defendant may assert against the plaintiff any defenses which the third-party defendant has against the plaintiff's claim.

The third-party defendant can defend the third-party claim, counterclaim against the third-party plaintiff (original defendant), cross-claim against other third-party defendants (if any—this is unlikely), and defend—assist in defense of—the original claim. After all, if the original claim fails, no liability will pass through.

The third-party defendant may also assert any claim against the plaintiff arising out of the transaction or occurrence that is the subject matter of the plaintiff's claim against the third-party plaintiff.

The third-party defendant may assert a claim directly against the original plaintiff, but that claim must be related to the action or efficiency would not result; accordingly, the claim must arise "out of the same transaction or occurrence as the plaintiff's claim." The proper title for such a claim is a Rule 14 claim; it is not a counterclaim since the third-party defendant and the plaintiff are not opposing parties until such a claim is asserted, and it is not a cross-claim since they are not co-parties.

The plaintiff may assert any claim against the third-party defendant arising out of the transaction or occurrence that is the subject matter of the plaintiff's claim against the third-party plaintiff, and the third-party defendant thereupon shall assert any defenses as provided in Rule 12 and any counterclaims and cross-claims as provided in Rule 13.

The original plaintiff is allowed to assert a claim directly against a third-party defendant who the original defendant has brought into the action, so long as the claim is transactionally

---

16. *See generally* JACK H. FRIEDENTHAL, MARY KAY KANE & ARTHUR R. MILLER, CIVIL PROCEDURE § 6.9 (3d ed. 1999).

related. The third-party defendant is then allowed to defend the claim as would an original defendant. Should a claim by the plaintiff against the third-party defendant be asserted first, it would be a Rule 14 claim; should it be asserted after the third-party defendant has asserted a claim directly against plaintiff, it would be a counterclaim since the two parties have become opposing parties.

Any party may move to strike the third-party claim, or for its severance or separate trial.

As mentioned above, the court will decide whether efficiency outweighs any possible prejudice to a party of trial in a single action.

A third-party defendant may proceed under this rule against any person not a party to the action who is or may be liable to the third-party defendant for all or part of the claim made in the action against the third-party defendant.

This would be properly termed a fourth-party action. The third-party defendant would become the "third-party defendant and fourth-party plaintiff." The above portions of Rule 14 apply, just as they do to a third-party action. And the chain of actions can, at least in theory, continue.

2. Supplemental Jurisdiction for Third-party Claims

Prior to the enactment of supplemental jurisdiction, third-party claims qualified for ancillary jurisdiction (a derivative claim must arise from the same transaction or occurrence). Enactment of § 1367 in 1990 was not intended to change, and did not change, this result.

In the standard third-party practice situation, defendant impleads the third-party defendant. The statute provides that supplemental jurisdiction extends to "all other claims that are so related to claims in the action within such original jurisdiction that they form part of the same case or controversy under Article III * * *." A third-party claim, because it must arise derivatively through the original claim, is part of the same case or controversy. Supplemental jurisdiction exists under § 1367(a). We then consult § 1367(b). It provides supplemental jurisdiction does not exist in diversity cases for joinder "over claims by plaintiffs against persons made parties under Rule 14 * * *." This sentence does not apply: even though joinder is accomplished under Rule 14, the third-party claim is not a claim by a plaintiff. It is a claim by a defendant. Consequently, supplemental jurisdiction exists over the third-party claim.

The same result was intended to apply, and does apply, in two other third-party practice situations. When the third-party defendant brings in a fourth-party defendant, that also is not a claim by a plaintiff, so supplemental jurisdiction attaches. Similarly, when the third-party defendant asserts a claim directly against the original plaintiff, that also is not a claim by a plaintiff, so supplemental jurisdiction applies.

The opposite result was intended to apply, and does apply, when the original plaintiff asserts a claim directly against the third-party defendant. Even though this claim must arise from the same transaction or occurrence, so § 1367(a) is satisfied, it is a claim by a plaintiff against a person made party under Rule 14, so § 1367(b) eliminates the supplemental jurisdiction.[17]

E. Joinder of Parties

1. Permissive Joinder of Parties

The common law, in its search for a single issue, made joinder of parties difficult. It tied joinder to the substantive rights of the parties and the forms of action. It distinguished between joint interests in which joinder was possible and several interests in which joinder was not possible. The codes allowed joinder more generously, although they added their own artificial categories for when joinder of parties would be permitted.[18]

While joinder of parties under Federal Rule 20 is not freely allowed as is joinder of claims under Federal Rule 18 [*see* II.A.1, *supra*], the two requirements of Federal Rule 20(a) for permissive joinder of parties are minimal:

—the relief sought arises from the same transaction or occurrence, or series of transactions or occurrences, and

—a common question of law or fact will arise.[19]

---

17. In Owen Equip. & Erection Co. v. Kroger, 437 U.S. 365, 98 S.Ct. 2396, 57 L.Ed.2d 274 (1978), the Supreme Court held that ancillary jurisdiction did not extend to such a claim. The Court expressed concern that ancillary jurisdiction was a doctrine extended to defendants brought involuntarily into court and that a collusive plaintiff and defendant could defeat the requirements of diversity by the technique of defendant bringing in a third-party defendant not diverse to plaintiff so that plaintiff could assert the real claim against that defendant. The drafters intended to, and did, carry this result forward in § 1367.

18. *See generally* JACK H. FRIEDENTHAL, MARY KAY KANE & ARTHUR R. MILLER, CIVIL PROCEDURE § 6.4 (3d ed. 1999).

19. FED.R.CIV.P. 20(a) reads in relevant part as follows:

The transaction or occurrence test arises throughout the federal joinder devices We have already discussed its meaning with regard to compulsory counterclaims, for example [*see* II.B.1, *supra*]. The essence of a transaction or occurrence is a single set of facts; it is not in any way tied to legal theories of recovery or defenses. Federal Rule 20 goes even further than a single transaction or occurrence: it allows permissive joinder when the relief arises from a series of transactions or occurrences. Perhaps, for example, plaintiff is injured in an auto accident, and several months later the physician treating her for the accident injuries commits malpractice. Plaintiff can join the driver and the physician permissively as defendants since this is a series of transactions or occurrences—even though separated in time by several months. Or perhaps a salesman of worthless securities sells them to plaintiff A over the telephone and some time later sells them to plaintiff B during an in-home presentation. The court would likely determine this to be a series of transactions or occurrences so that the two buyers could join permissively as plaintiffs in a single action. Here is where the logical relationship test, considering judicial economy and convenience, makes sense [*see* II.B.1, *supra*].

The common question requirement is even easier to satisfy. The question may be law or fact. In the first example above, the extent and valuation of plaintiff's combined injuries would provide a common question of fact. In the second example, the fraudulent nature of defendant's securities sales would provide a common question of law. The rule does not require a majority of common questions, or even a multitude of common questions. It requires only a common question. Once again, consideration of whether a common question is presented will prompt the court to consider economy and convenience of trying the case in a single proceeding.

Should the court determine that parties are misjoined, the remedy is to drop the misjoined party, not to dismiss the case. *See* Fed.R.Civ.P. 21.

2.   Compulsory Joinder of Parties

> All persons may join in one action as plaintiffs if they assert any right to relief jointly, severally, or in the alternative in respect of or arising out of the same transaction, occurrence, or series of transactions or occurrences and if any question of law or fact common to all these persons will arise in the action. All persons * * * may be joined in one action as defendants if there is asserted against them jointly, severally, or in the alternative, any right to relief in respect of or arising out of the same transaction, occurrence, or series of transactions or occurrences and if any question of law or fact common to all defendants will arise in the action. * * *

The common law required joinder of parties in certain limited situations, chiefly when a joint interest was involved. The codes generally carried this requirement forward. In interpreting this requirement in 1855,[20] the Supreme Court distinguished between merely necessary parties, without whom the action could proceed, and indispensable parties, without whom the action could not proceed. A party was deemed indispensable when the action would affect the absent party's interest or the action could not provide complete relief without the absent party. Over the following years, courts tended to sidestep the facts of the individual case in their haste to apply one of these two conclusory labels.

When Federal Rule 19 was originally promulgated in 1938, it adopted this system. The title of the rule was "Necessary Joinder of Parties," and it referred to "persons having a joint interest" who "shall be made parties." The same difficulties of the code systems accompanied the new rule. Courts had great difficulty distinguishing between "indispensable" and "necessary" parties, and tended to slap conclusory labels on them. This resulted in complete rewriting of Federal Rule 19 in 1966.

The title of Federal Rule 19 is now "Joinder of Persons Needed for Just Adjudication." It attempts to avoid the labels of necessary and indispensable parties and directs the court faced with a question of whether a third party must be joined in an action to make a pragmatic decision based on the individual case.

First, a court must consider Rule 19(a) to determine whether the person is "to be joined if feasible." The inquiry is designed to investigate how strong the third party's interest is in the case.[21] The rule provides guidelines to the court, primarily considering whether the absent person's interest will be affected or whether complete relief is possible without the absent person. Should the court decide the person is one who "shall be joined," the court "shall order that the person be made a party.

In the event joinder of the person is not feasible (joinder would destroy diversity or the person is not subject to personal jurisdiction), then the court must proceed to Rule 19(b). That rule leads the court through consideration of four practical factors determine whether the better course is to proceed without the absent person or to dismiss the action. The rule requires the court to place the conclusion where it belongs: at the end of the analysis. Only after considering all the factors and deciding that the fairer of

20. Shields v. Barrow, 58 U.S. (17 How.) 130, 15 L.Ed. 158 (1855).

21. 7 CHARLES A. WRIGHT, ARTHUR R. MILLER & MARY KAY KANE, FEDERAL PRACTICE AND PROCEDURE: CIVIL 2D §§ 1601–04 (2001).

the two options is to dismiss the action will the label of "indispensable" party be applied. The label is a conclusion, not a substitute for practical considerations and analysis.[22]

Even though the absent person is commonly called an indispensable party, the rules reinforce that until analysis is completed, this conclusory label should not be applied. The motion to dismiss is to be made for "failure to join a party under Rule 19." FED.R.CIV.P. 12(b)(7). Accordingly, the proper term for such a party is a "Rule 19 party."

3. Supplemental Jurisdiction for Joinder of Parties

As discussed above [see I.B.1, *supra*], pendent and ancillary jurisdiction were devices that supported joinder of additional claims in a federal lawsuit. Despite several attempts by lower federal courts to establish a doctrine of pendent party jurisdiction, these efforts were uniformly rejected by the Supreme Court [see n. 8, *supra*].

With the adoption of supplemental jurisdiction in 1990, the possibility of supplemental jurisdiction over additional parties to a lawsuit arose. First, § 1367(a) provides "[s]uch supplemental jurisdiction shall include claims that involve the joinder or intervention of additional parties." Second, § 1367(b) applies only to diversity cases.

Consequently, a case in federal court on any basis save diversity alone will allow the joinder of additional, nondiverse parties. Consider the facts of Finley v. United States, 490 U.S. 545, 109 S.Ct. 2003, 104 L.Ed.2d 593 (1989). Plaintiff, a citizen of California, sued the United States when her husband's airplane crashed at the San Diego airport; she sought to join another party, the city of San Diego, a California citizen, on a state law tort claim arising out of the same crash. The Supreme Court refused pendent party jurisdiction. Today, both of these claims could be brought into federal court. Plaintiff's suit against the United States comes in because the United States is a party. 28 U.S.C. § 1346. Plaintiff's claim against the city comes in by supplemental jurisdiction. This is so because § 1367(a) requires the two claims be part of the "same case or controversy under Article III." Only one airplane crashed; everything arose out of that single accident. Further, the statute specifically covers "claims that involve the joinder or intervention

---

22. This point was driven home forcefully by the Supreme Court in a major decision rendered only two years after the rewriting of FED.R.CIV.P. 19. Provident Tradesmens Bank & Trust Co. v. Patterson, 390 U.S. 102, 88 S.Ct. 733, 19 L.Ed.2d 936 (1968).

of additional parties." That is the end of the jurisdictional analysis since § 1367(b) applies only to a "civil action of which the district courts have original jurisdiction founded solely on section 1332."

And an unintended glitch in the statute may even allow permissive joinder of plaintiffs who fail to meet the diversity requirements. Consider, for example, two subcontractors, both citizens of state A, who wish to sue defendant contractor, a citizen of state B, for breach of their separate contracts in the same construction project. One plaintiff seeks $400,000, but the other plaintiff seeks only $27,000. Clearly, one plaintiff satisfies diversity requirements, but the other does not. Can the two plaintiffs join permissively to sue together in federal court?

The question of joinder is easily answered. Both parties sue on contracts arising from the same construction project, so the same transaction or occurrence is involved (one building project); at least one common question may arise on the events of the project or in interpretation of the standard-form contracts.

The more interesting question is whether diversity jurisdiction between plaintiff one and defendant allows supplemental jurisdiction over plaintiff two. We first look to § 1367(a) and determine that all parties were involved in one constitutional case or controversy (only one building project). Then we look at § 1367(b), which applies since the sole basis for federal jurisdiction is diversity. The statute reads "the district courts shall not have supplemental jurisdiction under subsection (a) over claims by plaintiffs against persons made parties under Rule * * * 20 * * *." This is a claim *by* a person made party under Rule 20, not a claim *against* a person made party under Rule 20, so § 1367(b) does not speak to this situation. How should a court respond to this apparent drafting error—a glitch in the statute? Some federal courts read the statute as it is written and allow supplemental jurisdiction.[23]

F. Intervention

A person who is not a party to a lawsuit can force his way in and become a party through the joinder device of intervention. The outsider can intervene into the lawsuit, either as a plaintiff or as a defendant. Should the intervention be successful, the intervenor becomes a full-fledged party to the suit.

Intervention originated in Roman law to give a nonparty a means to protect an interest when that interest might be affected by

23. *E.g.*, Stromberg Metal Works, Inc. v. Press Mechanical, Inc., 77 F.3d 928 (7th Cir. 1996).

a decision in a lawsuit that the losing party chose not to appeal; it developed in different forms in the common law and equity courts.[24] The device was taken into practice under the codes, and a typical code required the nonparty to show she had an interest in the subject matter of the lawsuit that was not represented by the current parties.

Federal Rule 24 provides two types of intervention: of right and permissive. When the nonparty satisfies the requirements of Rule 24(a), it has a right to intervene. When the nonparty is unable to satisfy that rule, it still may intervene permissively under Rule 24(b) in the discretion of the court. Of course, since the court must decide whether the requirements of Rule 24(a) are satisfied, in a large sense all intervention is permissive.

In a second sense, all intervention is permissive. A nonparty is never required to intervene. It can choose to remain outside a lawsuit and attempt to protect its interests in a separate suit. Due process prevents binding nonparties with the result of a lawsuit.

The joinder device of intervention balances a number of interests. It prevents persons from impairing the rights of nonparties through a lawsuit. It promotes efficiency by allowing entire controversies to be resolved in a single lawsuit. It balances the control of the litigation by the original parties with control shared with the new party; this seems to be part of the general trend toward dilution of party control toward court governance of a lawsuit.

1. Intervention of Right

Federal Rule 24(a) places three essential requirements on a party seeking to intervene of right. First, the application for intervention must be *timely*. The rule provides no guidelines of timeliness, so the court will consider the matter on an individual case basis. The court will consider such things as the stage of the litigation, the reasons for any delay in application, and any possible prejudice to the existing parties should the intervention be allowed. Certainly an application to intervene made during the pleading stage of the litigation will be timely; later applications raise possible delay for the original parties.

Second, the nonparty must show (a statute granting a right to intervene or) "*an interest* relating to the property or transaction which is the subject of the action and the applicant is so situated that the disposition of the *action may as a practical matter impair*

---

24. *See* Jack H. Friedenthal, Mary Kay Kane & Arthur R. Miller, Civil Procedure § 6.10 (3d ed. 1999).

or impede the applicant's ability to protect that interest." Fed. R.Civ.P. 24(a). A person who claims the proceeds of an insurance policy has an interest in that policy that would support intervention into a suit between another claimant for the proceeds and the insurance company. A lienholder of a property has an interest in a lawsuit involving that property. The interest need not always be economic. The federal courts have recognized a broad range of interests to support intervention, including economic, environmental, and educational.[25]

The rule also requires that the nonparty's interest may be impaired or impeded. Early cases held that the nonparty had to be bound by the potential adverse decision. This standard was almost impossible to satisfy since due process prevents binding a nonparty. Therefore, the rule was rewritten a number of times so that today it requires only that the nonparty's interest may be impaired or impeded as a practical matter. For example, in a challenge by environmentalists to pollution caused by an industrial plant, potential relief might include closing the plant. Employees, businesses in the locality, and even the county that might have its tax basis eroded would likely be held to have interests that as a practical matter might be impaired.

Third, the nonparty must show that its interest is *not adequately represented* by the existing parties. For example, when a nonparty also seeks the proceeds of an insurance policy, neither other claimants to the proceeds nor the insurance company represents the nonparty's interest in any way. On the other hand, assume a town zones land for open space. The landowner sues the town for a declaratory judgment that the ordinance is invalid. Will an environmental group that supports zoning the land for open space be entitled to intervene of right? The answer is no because the town is already defending the zoning. That interest is adequately represented.

This requirement that representation not be adequate can interplay with the timeliness requirement. For example, assume parents of schoolchildren sue the school board for racial discrimination. Other parents support the board policies, but they cannot intervene because the board is adequately representing their interests. The lengthy litigation results in a judgment by the trial court that the policies are discriminatory. The school board, for various reasons, decides not to appeal. Can the parents supporting the board's policies now intervene for purpose of prosecuting the appeal? Their interests for the first time are not represented, yet

---

25. *See* 7C Charles A. Wright, Arthur R. Miller & Mary Kay Kane, Federal Practice and Procedure: Civil 2d § 1908 (1986).

post judgment in the trial court is hardly timely. A well-known case allowed intervention,[26] but not all courts have agreed that such intervention is timely.

2. Permissive intervention

When the nonparty cannot qualify for intervention of right, it may still seek leave of court to intervene permissively. Federal Rule 24(b) requires only a timely application and a showing that (a federal statute confers a conditional right to intervene or) "applicant's claim or defense and the main action have a question of law or fact in common."

As with permissive joinder of parties [see II.E.1, supra], a common question is usually easy to find. Since the sole requirement of a common question is so minimal, much will depend on the discretion of the court.[27] The court will consider such things as the strength of the intervenor's interest, possible prejudice to existing parties, and possible dilution of the control of the lawsuit by the original parties.

3. Supplemental Jurisdiction over Intervenors

Prior to 1990, persons intervening of right generally qualified for ancillary jurisdiction while persons intervening only permissively had to establish their own independent basis for federal jurisdiction. The advent of supplemental jurisdiction in 1990 tilted the scale strongly toward the requirement of an independent basis of federal jurisdiction for all intervenors.

As with any question of supplemental jurisdiction, we first consider § 1367(a), which requires that the claim to be added "be so related to claims in the action within such original jurisdiction that they form part of the same case or controversy under Article III." The court will look closely at the intervenor's interest/claim to determine whether it is part of the same constitutional case. Since a constitutional case is essentially a common nucleus of operative facts, supplemental jurisdiction over an added claim by a nonparty is possible.

Next, we consider § 1367(b). When the basis for federal jurisdiction is diversity alone, this subsection applies, and it clearly

26. Smuck v. Hobson, 408 F.2d 175 (D.C.Cir. 1969).

27. See 7C Charles A. Wright, Arthur R. Miller & Mary Kay Kane, Federal Practice and Procedure: Civil 2d § 1913 (1986).

eliminates any possibility of supplemental jurisdiction over intervenors:

> the district courts shall not have supplemental jurisdiction under subsection (a) over claims by plaintiffs against persons made parties under Rule * * * 24 of the Federal Rules of Civil Procedure, or over claims by persons * * * seeking to intervene as plaintiffs under Rule 24 of such rules * * *.

Here the statute is clear. It specifically eliminates supplemental jurisdiction in diversity cases over both intervening defendants and intervening plaintiffs.

G. Interpleader

We reach the last of the joinder devices, and the last of the joinder "i"s. Interpleader is unique, and is structurally different from all of the other joinder devices. One of your authors likes to introduce interpleader by reading a newspaper story that appeared on the Associated Press wire several years ago:

> The scramble is on over who gets to keep $22,350 found in a room in the Excel Inn in Bloomington [Minnesota].

> The money was in $10, $20, $50 and $100 bills when [Mary Roe], a maid, found it in a brown leather briefcase while cleaning a room being rented by [John Doe] of St. Cloud [Minnesota], she said.

> Roe, following the 'finders keepers' theory of law, has filed a claim for the cash. Doe, who returned for the money the day after he discovered it was missing, says the money belongs to him. He told the Bloomington police that he found it five days earlier in a paper bag near a parked car in north Minneapolis [on the day after the Super Bowl].

> The situation became even more complicated when the police, who had some doubts about Doe's story, notified the Internal Revenue Service. The IRS now says Doe owes $33,963 in back taxes and therefore is also laying claim to the money.

> In addition, Excel Inns Limited Partnership, which owns the motel, and Excel Management Associates, which operates it, have filed a claim to the money on the theory that they may have more legal right to the cash than Roe.

> The city of Bloomington, which has custody of the money, [will sue] to have the ownership question decided in court.

What type of action will the city file? The stakeholder (the city) is willing to hand over the stake (the briefcase of cash) to one of the claimants, but does not want to hand it over to one claimant, be sued by another for it, and have to pay twice. The joinder device of interpleader was created for exactly this situation.

Originally, a true bill in interpleader required the stakeholder to deposit the stake into court and step back to allow the claimants to compete for it. More recently, (an action in the nature of) interpleader allows the stakeholder also to claim the property.

Although interpleader provides a joinder device to bring all potential claimants into a single action, it does not supply personal jurisdiction over all the claimants. Because of this weakness, the first federal interpleader act was passed in 1917. Today, it provides a method of nationwide service on claimants. This is known as statutory interpleader. A second type of federal interpleader is also available under Federal Rule 22. This is known as interpleader under the rule. Both types of federal interpleader have differing subject matter jurisdiction, personal jurisdiction, service, and other requirements, so the stakeholder may choose one or the other depending on how the situation fits each.

1. Statutory Interpleader

Statutory interpleader is spread through three sections of title 28: §§ 1335, 1397, and 2361. Taken together, these sections eliminate many of the jurisdictional problems that otherwise would exist in federal court. Only minimal diversity is required between two or more claimants to the property (§ 1335); the citizenship of a plaintiff bringing the interpleader is thus irrelevant unless the plaintiff is also a claimant (an "action in the nature of interpleader"). A minimum jurisdictional amount of $500 is required (§ 1335). The stakeholder must pay or place the stake into court (§ 1335). Venue may be laid in a district where any claimant resides (§ 1397). Process may be served nationwide (§ 2361). The district court may enjoin claimants from pursuing the property in any other state or federal court (§ 2361).

2. Interpleader under the Rule

Interpleader under Federal Rule 22 in many ways is less desirable than statutory interpleader, yet because of the differing jurisdictional requirements, it may be the only one of the two types of federal interpleader available to the stakeholder.

Interpleader under the rule has no special diversity jurisdiction provisions, which means that standard diversity requirements apply. The plaintiff stakeholder must be of citizenship diverse from all defendants/claimants (§ 1332). The stake must be of a value exceeding $75,000 (§ 1332). Venue must be laid under standard venue rules (§ 1391). A defendant may seek interpleader by way of a counterclaim (statutory interpleader is silent on this possibility). The rule is silent on whether the court may enjoin claimants from proceeding against the stake in other actions.

III. QUESTIONS ON JOINDER

Instructions. The questions are on the left-hand page, and the answers are on the right-hand page. Cover the right-hand page, write your answers to the questions in the spaces provided, and compare your answers to the suggested answers on the facing page. P represents plaintiff, and D represents defendant. For all questions, assume you are in federal court.

*

A. Counterclaims

Q–1. Part 1. P sues D for negligence in an auto accident. D wishes to counterclaim against P for negligence in the same auto accident. Is this a compulsory counterclaim?

Your answer _____

Part 2. Does this counterclaim qualify for supplemental jurisdiction?

Your answer _____

Q–2. Part 1. P sues D for negligence in an auto accident. D wishes to counterclaim against P for an antitrust violation arising out of a previous business relationship. Is this a compulsory counterclaim?

Your answer _____

Part 2. Does this counterclaim qualify for supplemental jurisdiction?

Your answer _____

Part 3. D asserts this antitrust counterclaim against P. P has a state tort law unfair competition claim against D arising from their previous business relationship. Is this a compulsory counterclaim?

Your answer _____

Part 4. Does this counterclaim qualify for supplemental jurisdiction?

Your answer _____

Part 5. What pleading should P use to assert this unfair competition claim against D?

Your answer _____

Answer to Q–1. Part 1. Yes. A compulsory counterclaim arises out of the same transaction or occurrence as the original claim. Fed.R.Civ.P. 13(a). One auto accident is one transaction or occurrence. This compulsory counterclaim must be asserted or lost.

Part 2. Yes. Since it arises out of the same transaction or occurrence, this compulsory counterclaim is part of the same case or controversy under Article III, as required by § 1367(a). The counterclaim is asserted under Fed.R.Civ.P. 13(a); Rule 13 is not referenced in § 1367(b). Because § 1367(a) applies, and § 1367(b) does not, the counterclaim qualifies for supplemental jurisdiction.

Supplemental jurisdiction may be unnecessary. Since the original claim was for negligence, we must assume the basis for federal jurisdiction is diversity. When the parties are diverse for the claim, they must also be diverse for the counterclaim. Supplemental jurisdiction would be needed only should the amount of the counterclaim fall short of the jurisdictional amount required by § 1332.

Answer to Q–2. Part 1. No. The claim is for an auto accident. The counterclaim is for an antitrust violation arising from activities factually unrelated to the auto accident. That means the two claims arise from different transactions or occurrences, so it is not a compulsory counterclaim. Defendant may assert this as a permissive counterclaim. Fed.R.Civ.P. 13(b).

Part 2. No. Since the permissive counterclaim does not arise from the same transaction or occurrence, it cannot be part of the same case or controversy under Article III as required by § 1367(a).

In this question, the counterclaim does not require supplemental jurisdiction. An antitrust violation is a federal question. It comes into federal court under § 1331.

Part 3. Yes, this is a compulsory counterclaim. Once defendant asserts the antitrust counterclaim, P must assert this state tort law unfair competition claim as a counterclaim to the counterclaim since it arises out of the same transaction or occurrence as the antitrust claim.

When pleading the original complaint, P could have joined this claim as a separate count. P and D are of diverse citizenship (or they could not be in federal court on the auto accident claim), and Fed.R.Civ.P. 18(a) allows P to assert "as many claims, legal, equitable, or maritime, as the party has against an opposing party." P chose not to join the claim at that time, but now that D has pleaded the antitrust claim, P must assert the unfair competition claim as a compulsory counterclaim or lose it.

Part 4. As the answer to Part 3 notes, plaintiff could have joined this claim in the original complaint, so supplemental jurisdiction is not needed. Assume, however, that the court decides P and D are not diverse. Then the question is whether P's state law counterclaim to D's federal question counterclaim is covered by supplemental jurisdiction. The answer is yes. Both arise from the same transaction or occurrence, which means the same case or controversy under Article III. That satisfies § 1367(a). The counterclaim is pleaded under Fed.R.Civ.P. 13(a), which is not listed in § 1367(b).

Part 5. Plaintiff should assert this compulsory counterclaim in the reply. "There shall be a complaint and an answer; a reply to a counterclaim denominated as such * * *." Fed.R.Civ.P. 7(a).

*

Q–3. Part 1. P sues D for negligence in an auto accident. D wishes to counterclaim against both P and third party X for negligence in the same auto accident. Can D do this in a compulsory counterclaim?

Your answer _____

Part 2. Assume P is a citizen of New York, D is a citizen of New Jersey, and X is a citizen of New Jersey. Does the counterclaim against both P and X qualify for supplemental jurisdiction?

Your answer _____

Q–4. P sells D an expensive piece of merchandise. D falls behind in payments, and P sues. D answers. Some months later, D discovers the merchandise is defective. Has D lost this compulsory counterclaim by failing to plead it in the answer?

Your answer _____

Q–5. P, a citizen of California, purchases merchandise from D, a large retail store in California. When P fails to make payments, D engages in vigorous collection efforts. P sues D in federal court for a violation of the Fair Debt Collection Practices Act. Is D's counterclaim for the balance due on the account a compulsory counterclaim so that it qualifies for supplemental jurisdiction?

Your answer _____

Answer to Q–3. Part 1. Yes. D can assert the compulsory counterclaim against P, and join an additional defending party to the counterclaim under Fed.R.Civ.P. 13(g): "Persons other than those made parties to the original action may be made parties to a counterclaim or cross-claim in accordance with the provisions of Rules 19 and 20." Rule 20, governing permissive joinder of parties allows joinder when the claim against the added party arises out of the same transaction or occurrence and involves a common question of law or fact. Those requirements are met.

Part 2. Yes. The compulsory counterclaim falls within § 1367(a) as part of the same case or controversy under Article III. The statute also provides "supplemental jurisdiction shall include claims that involve the joinder or intervention of additional parties."

The supplemental jurisdiction so provided by § 1357(a) is not destroyed by § 1367(b). In one view, the joinder of X is pursuant to Rule 13(g), which is not mentioned at all in § 1367(b). In another view, the joinder of X is pursuant to Rule 20, but that does not change the result because the statute refers to "claims by plaintiffs against persons made parties under Rule * * * 20 * * *." This is a claim by a defendant, not a plaintiff, so the statute by its terms does not apply.

Answer to Q–4. No. Fed.R.Civ.P. 13(a) provides several escape valves from the compulsory counterclaim rule. The one that applies here is that defendant is required to plead "any claim which at the time of serving the pleading the pleader has." Since D was unaware of the defects at the time of answering, the claim for defects is not a compulsory counterclaim. Other escape valves include that the potential counterclaim requires parties beyond the jurisdiction of the court and that the potential counterclaim is already the subject of another action.

Answer to Q–5. Maybe. Our answer is yes. Rule 13(a) defines a compulsory counterclaim as arising "out of the transaction or occurrence." There is only one set of facts between these two parties: purchase, nonpayment, and collection efforts. The two parties entered one contract. These events are all tied closely together in time and space, and form a convenient trial unit. A layperson would expect all matters arising from the purchase and payment to be tried together. They form a common nucleus of operative fact. These are all alternative ways of expressing that this is a single transaction or occurrence. As such, it constitutes one constitutional case or controversy under Article III. That means supplemental jurisdiction under § 1367(a).

Some federal courts answer no. These courts note that the law and facts of the collection efforts are different from the law and facts of the underlying debt. More importantly, they recognize that allowing the merchant to assert a compulsory counterclaim for the debt might discourage purchasers from suing initially to enforce the federal Fair Debt Collection Practices Act. Viewed in that perspective, the collection efforts are not part of the same transaction or occurrence as the purchase, and thus the counterclaim is not compulsory or supplemental. The merchant will have to sue in a separate action in state court. See the cases at 6 CHARLES A. WRIGHT, ARTHUR R. MILLER & MARY KAY KANE, FEDERAL PRACTICE AND PROCEDURE: CIVIL 2D § 1410 n. 64 (Supp. 2004).

The problem with the latter view is it ignores Rule 13(a). These two parties have engaged in only one set of interrelated dealings. That is one transaction or occurrence. The fact that the rule allows the merchant to counterclaim in federal court in this situation should be irrelevant.

B. Cross-claims

Q–6. Part 1. P, a citizen of Florida, sues D1, a citizen of Texas, and D2, a citizen of Texas, in federal court under § 1332 for breach of contract. Damages claimed are $200,000. Can D1 file a counterclaim arising from the same contract against D2 for $100,000?

Your answer _____

Part 2. Can D2 file a cross-claim arising from the same contract against D1 for $100,000?

Your answer _____

Part 3. Would such a cross-claim qualify for supplemental jurisdiction?

Your answer _____

Part 4. Can D1 then file a counterclaim against D2 for $100,000?

Your answer _____

Part 5. Would the counterclaim qualify for supplemental jurisdiction?

Your answer _____

Answer to Q–6. Part 1. No. A counterclaim is asserted against an opposing party. Fed.R.Civ.P. 13(a), (b). D1 and D2 are not opposing parties as they are both on the same side of the "v."

Part 2. Yes. A cross-claim is asserted against a co-party. Fed.R.Civ.P. 13(g). D2 and D1, being on the same side of the "v," are co-parties. Since the cross-claim arises from the same contract as the original claim, it clearly satisfies the requirement that it arise from the same transaction or occurrence.

Part 3. Yes. Since both D2 and D1 are citizens of Texas, the cross-claim does not independently satisfy the diversity requirement. Supplemental jurisdiction will be necessary.

The short answer is that a cross-claim always qualifies for supplemental jurisdiction. The longer answer is that the cross-claim, since it arises out of the same contract, is part of the same transaction or occurrence, and that requirement is is essentially synonymous with being part of the same case or controversy under Article III as required by § 1367(a). And Rule 13(g) is not one of the joinder rules eliminated from the operation of § 1367(a) by provision of § 1367(b). Since § 1367(a) applies, and § 1367(b) does not, supplemental jurisdiction exists.

Part 4. Yes. Once a defendant asserts a cross-claim against another defendant, the two become opposing parties, and the proper device for the second defendant to assert a claim back against the cross-claiming defendant is a counterclaim. Since all of these claims arise from the same contract, this would be a compulsory counterclaim.

Part 5. Yes. Since both D1 and D2 are citizens of Texas, the counterclaim does not meet the diversity requirement itself. Supplemental jurisdiction will be necessary.

The short answer is that a compulsory counterclaim always qualifies for supplemental jurisdiction. The longer answer is that the counterclaim, since it arises out of the same contract, is part of the same transaction or occurrence, which makes it so related to "claims in the action within such original jurisdiction that they form part of the same case or controversy under Article III." So § 1367(a) applies, and Rule 13(a) is not one of the joinder rules eliminated by § 1367(b).

Q–7. Part 1. P former employee, a citizen of Illinois, sues both D1 former employer, a corporation incorporated and operating solely within Illinois, and D2 former supervisor, a citizen of Illinois, for a violation of Title VII in firing her. Can D2 cross-claim against D1 for indemnity to be paid in the event P succeeds in the lawsuit?

Your answer _____

Part 2. Would such a cross-claim qualify for supplemental jurisdiction?

Your answer _____

Q–8. P, a citizen of Arizona, sues D1, a citizen of California, and D2, a citizen of California, for negligence in an auto accident occurring in California. P claims $100,000. Will a cross-claim by D1 against D2 for contribution of $50,000 qualify for supplemental jurisdiction?

Your answer _____

Q–9. P sues D1 and D2 for conspiracy to violate the federal antitrust laws. Can D1 file a cross-claim against D2 for breach of an unrelated contract?

Your answer _____

Q–10. Part 1. P, a citizen of Kentucky, sues D1, a citizen of Ohio, and D2, a citizen of Ohio, for breach of contract. D1 files a cross-claim against D2 for breach of the same contract. Can D1 at the same time join an unrelated tort claim against D2?

Your answer _____

Part 2. Would the unrelated tort claim qualify for supplemental jurisdiction?

Your answer _____

Answer to Q–7. Part 1. Yes. This cross-claim against a co-party arises out of the same transaction or occurrence as the original claim. The cross-claim need not be mature at the time of pleading: "Such cross-claim may include a claim that the party against whom it is asserted is or may be liable to the cross-claimant for all or part of a claim asserted in the action against the cross-claimant." Fed.R.Civ.P. 13(g).

Part 2. Yes. The cross-claim does not satisfy federal jurisdiction itself because it presents a state law question and the parties are not diverse.

Because the cross-claim is for possible indemnity in the event P wins her claim, the cross-claim arises from the same transaction or occurrence as the original claim and so is part of the same case or controversy under Article III. That satisfies § 1367(a). Since the original federal jurisdiction was based on a federal question under § 1331, the second paragraph of the supplemental jurisdiction statute need not be studied: § 1367(b) applies only when diversity is the sole basis for federal jurisdiction. Supplemental jurisdiction exists.

Answer to Q–8. Yes. The cross-claim does not satisfy federal jurisdiction itself because it presents a state law question and the jurisdictional amount is not sufficient.

Because the cross-claim is for possible contribution in the event P wins the claim, the cross-claim arises from the same transaction or occurrence as the original claim and so is part of the same case or controversy under Article III. That satisfies § 1367(a). Since the cross-claim is joined under Rule 13(g), which is not enumerated, § 1367(b) does not apply.

Answer to Q–9. No. Fed.R.Civ.P. 13(g) requires that a cross-claim arise out of the same transaction or occurrence. A factually unrelated claim by definition does not.

Answer to Q–10. Part 1. Yes. Once D1 asserts a proper cross-claim against D2, he can join any other claims he has against that party. Fed.R.Civ.P. 18.

Part 2. No. Diversity is absent between D1 and D2, so supplemental jurisdiction is required to bring the cross-claim and the additionally joined claim into federal court. The cross-claim qualifies for supplemental jurisdiction. *See* Answer 6. Part 3, *supra.* The unrelated claim, even though Rule 18 allows it to be joined, must find its own way into federal court. Because the added claim does not arise out of the same transaction or occurrence, it does not satisfy the requirement of § 1367(a) that it be part of the same case or controversy under Article III. No supplemental jurisdiction.

C. Third-party claims

Q–11. P commences an action against D for negligence arising from an auto accident. P serves the complaint on D on June 20. D answers with a denial on July 1. D serves a third-party complaint on 3D on July 18. Will the court strike the third-party complaint on motion of either P or 3D?

Your answer _____

Q–12. P commences an action against D for negligence arising from a three-car auto accident. D serves a third-party complaint on 3D, the driver of the third car. The third-party complaint asserts D was not negligent and 3D was negligent. Will the court strike the third-party complaint on motion of either P or 3D?

Your answer _____

Q–13. Part 1. P, a citizen of Washington, sues D, a citizen of Oregon, for $250,000 for breach of contract. Can D implead 3D, a citizen of Washington, for complete indemnity on liability on the contract?

Your answer _____

Part 2. Can 3D assert a claim against P for $125,000 for breach of the same contract?

Your answer _____

Part 3. Can P assert a claim against 3D for $125,000 for breach of the same contract?

Your answer _____

Q–14. Part 1. P, a citizen of Michigan, sues D, a citizen of Ohio, for an auto accident. D asserts a permissive counterclaim against P for breach of an unrelated contract. Assume the jurisdictional amounts in both claims are adequate. Can P implead X, a citizen of Ohio, for complete indemnity on any liability on the contract?

Your answer _____

Part 2. Can D assert a claim directly against X for breach of the same contract, and will the federal court have supplemental jurisdiction over that claim?

Your answer _____

Answer to Q–11. Yes. Rule 14 allows defendant ten days after service of the answer to serve a third-party complaint without leave of court. Since more than ten days have passed, defendant will have to obtain leave of court. This early in the litigation, the court is highly likely to grant leave to assert the impleader, so an answer of no (on reasoning that the impleader is not timely but that the court will likely grant leave instead of granting the motion to strike) is acceptable.

Answer to Q–12. Yes. A third-party claim must assert derivative liability: "is or may be liable to the third-party plaintiff for all or part of the plaintiff's claim against the third-party plaintiff." Fed. R.Civ.P. 14(a). This is not a claim of derivative liability; it is a defense that another, alternative defendant is liable directly to the plaintiff. It is not a proper use of third-party practice.

Answer to Q–13. Part 1. Yes. This is a proper use of third-party practice, since the liability would be derivative. With regard to federal jurisdiction, the original claim satisfied diversity jurisdiction (Washington v. Oregon for $250,000), and the third-party claim independently satisfied diversity jurisdiction (Oregon v. Washington for $250,000), so supplemental jurisdiction need not be considered.

Part 2. Yes. This claim by the third-party defendant directly against the plaintiff is allowed by Fed.R.Civ.P. 14(a) since it arises from the same transaction or occurrence–here the same contract–as the original claim. With regard to federal jurisdiction, the claim does not independently satisfy diversity (Washington v. Washington), so we must consider supplemental jurisdiction. Under § 1367(a), the derivative claim is part of the same transaction or occurrence, so it is part of the same case or controversy under Article III; under § 1367(b), this is not a claim by a *plaintiff* against a person made party under Rule 14. Consequently, supplemental jurisdiction exists.

Part 3. No. This claim by the plaintiff directly against the third-party defendant is allowed by Fed.R.Civ.P. 14(a) since it arises from the same transaction or occurrence–here the same contract–as the original claim. With regard to federal jurisdiction, however, the claim does not independently satisfy diversity (Washington v. Washington), so we must consider supplemental jurisdiction. Even though the claim is part of the same case or controversy under Article III for § 1367(a), this is a claim by a plaintiff against a person made party under Rule 14, which is disallowed by § 1367(b). Consequently, supplemental jurisdiction does not exist.

Answer to Q–14. Part 1. Yes. The permissive counterclaim satisfies federal jurisdiction independently (Ohio v. Michigan for sufficient amount). At that point, the original plaintiff, as "defending party," may assert a third-party claim. Fed.R.Civ.P. 14(a). The third-party claim independently satisfies federal jurisdictional requirements (Michigan v. Ohio for complete indemnity), so supplemental jurisdiction is not needed.

Part 2. Yes and yes. The claim by the original defendant D, as "plaintiff" in the Rule 14 claim directly against X, is allowed by Fed.R.Civ.P. 14(a). With regard to federal jurisdiction, the claim does not independently satisfy diversity (Michigan v. Michigan), so we must consider supplemental jurisdiction. The third-party claim is part of the same transaction or occurrence as the counterclaim, which is in federal court on its own independent jurisdictional basis, so it satisfies § 1367(a). Under 1367(b), this is not a claim by a *plaintiff* against a person made party under Rule 14. Consequently, supplemental jurisdiction exists. Even though this claim by "defendant" directly against X is equivalent to a claim by an original plaintiff directly against a third-party defendant, the plain language of § 1367(b) does not cover it. Glitch in the statute or intended, this third-party claim is in federal court.

D. Joinder of Parties

Q–15. A fire negligently started by D1 destroys P's house. Several months later, D2, D1's insurance company, refuses to pay the claim without any good faith basis for refusal. Can P permissively join both D1 and D2 as defendants in a single lawsuit?

Your answer _____

Q–16. Part 1. P1 is a pedestrian on the sidewalk. A car driven by D runs a stop sign and broadsides a car driven by P2. P2's car skids onto the sidewalk and injures P1. Can P1 and P2 permissively join together to sue D in a single lawsuit?

Your answer _____

Part 2. Assume P1 and P2 have not yet sued D. More than a year later, P1 still has not recovered from the accident injuries. She consults D2, a physician, and is treated negligently. Can P1 and P2 permissively join together as plaintiffs to sue in a single lawsuit and permissively join both D and D2 as defendants?

Your answer _____

Q–17. P, a citizen of Louisiana, undergoes an operation in which a plate and screw device is implanted into his back. The device breaks. P sues D device manufacturer, a citizen of Pennsylvania, in federal court. P sues D surgeon, a citizen of Louisiana, in a separate suit in state court. D manufacturer moves to dismiss the federal suit for failure to join a Rule 19 party. Should the motion to dismiss be granted?

Your answer _____

Q–18. P, a citizen of Virginia, enters a contract with D1, a citizen of North Carolina, and at the same time enters a related contract with D2, a citizen of Virginia. Both contracts refer to each other, and interpretation of one will require interpretation of the other. Both defendants fail to perform. P sues D1 for breach of contract. D1 moves to dismiss for failure to join a Rule 19 party (D2 cannot be joined since diversity would be destroyed). Should the motion be granted?

Your answer _____

Answer to Q–15. Yes. The first requirement for permissive joinder of defendants, that the claims against both arise from the same transaction or occurrence, or series of transactions or occurrences, is satisfied. Even though the claim against D1 and the claim against D2 are separated in time by several months, will involve little overlap in evidence, and are on different theories of recovery, the important fact is that there was only one fire. Everything arose from that single event. That is properly considered a single transaction or occurrence, and without question both claims are from a related series of transactions or occurrences.

The second requirement, that at least one common question arise, is easily met. Some of the common questions are D1's negligence in the fire, the amount of P's damages, etc.

Answer to Q–16. Part 1. Yes. The first requirement for permissive joinder of plaintiffs, that the claims of both arise from the same transaction or occurrence, is satisfied. There was only one accident. The second requirement of a single common question is easily met. Issues of D's negligence (breach of duty, causation) will arise with regard to both plaintiffs.

Part 2. Yes. Both P1 and P2 can permissively join as plaintiffs for the reasons given in the answer to Part 1. Plaintiffs can permissively join both D and D2 as defendants for the same reasons given in the answer to Q–15. Even though the medical malpractice occurred more than a year after the accident, it clearly arose from the events of the accident and therefore is part of the same (series of) transaction(s). P1 would not have been in the physician's office but for the accident injuries. The extent of P's injuries is one apparent common question.

Answer to Q–17. No. Joint tortfeasors are never Rule 19/indispensable parties. The common law has always given plaintiff the option to sue one or more at his option, and the unlucky chosen defendant cannot force joinder of, or demand dismissal for failure to join, the other(s). Temple v. Synthes Corp., 498 U.S. 5, 111 S.Ct. 315, 112 L.Ed.2d 263 (1990).

Answer to Q–18. Maybe. We hope you recognized this is a trick question. The proper answer is that no answer can be given until we grind our way through the considerations of Federal Rule 19(a) and 19(b). A categorical answer to this question, based only on the information so far at hand, would be to place a conclusory label on D2, which is exactly what Fed.R.Civ.P. 19 was rewritten in 1966 to avoid.

Q–19. Part 1. P, a citizen of Florida, is employed by D Corporation, incorporated in Delaware with principal place of business in Georgia. D supervisor, a citizen of Florida, fires D "because we don't want anyone of your religion working for us." Can P join both defendants in a single suit in federal court alleging two counts: 1) violation of Title VII of the Civil Rights Act of 1964, and 2) breach of the contract of employment?

Your answer _____

Part 2. Will the federal court have supplemental jurisdiction under § 1367 over D supervisor?

Your answer _____

Q–20. Part 1. P1, P2, and P3, all citizens of Pennsylvania, join together to open a small business and rent a property from D in New Jersey. The business does not succeed, and Ps believe the failure is because D fraudulently represented the nature of the property. P1 loses $100,000, P2 loses $50,000, and P3 loses $5,000. Can the three plaintiffs join together to sue D?

Your answer _____

Part 2. Will the court have supplemental jurisdiction over P2 and P3?

Your answer _____

Part 3. D counterclaims against P1 for rent of $5000 still due on the property. Will the court have supplemental jurisdiction over cross-claims by P1 against the other two plaintiffs for contribution?

Your answer _____

Answer to Q–19. Part 1. Yes. Plaintiff was fired once. The claims against both defendants arise from the same transaction or occurrence. Common questions not only exist, but also they likely predominate.

Part 2. Yes. Supplemental jurisdiction exists under § 1367(a) because this is a single set of facts arising from P's termination: it is one case or controversy under Article III. The analysis need not continue to § 1367(b) because that subsection applies only when the sole basis of jurisdiction is diversity. Here, a federal question–alleged violation of Title VII, a federal statute–is presented.

Answer to Q–20. Part 1. Yes. This is permissive joinder of plaintiffs. All three plaintiffs were involved in the same business deal for the same property. This is the same transaction or occurrence. Common questions involving all four include whether a fraudulent representation was made, whether defendant acted with scienter, and the like.

Part 2. Maybe. The answer to this question is the same as was discussed above in II.E.3. Diversity exists between P1 and D. The amounts claimed by P2 and P3 are insufficient. We first look to § 1367(a) and determine that all parties were involved in one constitutional case or controversy (only one business deal involving one property). Then we look at § 1367(b): "The district courts shall not have supplemental jurisdiction under subsection (a) over claims by plaintiffs against persons made parties under Rule * * * 20 * * *." This is a claim *by* persons made parties under Rule 20, not a claim *against* persons made parties under Rule 20, so the plain language of § 1367(b) does not cover this situation. How should a court respond to this apparent drafting error? Some federal courts read the statute as it is written and allow supplemental jurisdiction even though the rather clear intent was not to allow supplemental jurisdiction in such a situation.

Part 3. Maybe. The federal court certainly has supplemental jurisdiction over the compulsory counterclaim. The question is whether it has supplemental jurisdiction over P1's cross-claims against P2 and P3. The cross-claims for contribution arose from the single business deal, so § 1367(a) provides jurisdiction. While the other plaintiffs are in the position of defending parties to the cross-claims, they are still "plaintiffs" in the lawsuit. The relevant sentence of § 1367(b) again is "The district courts shall not have supplemental jurisdiction under subsection (a) over claims by plaintiffs against persons made parties under Rule * * * 20 * * *." Since the other three plaintiffs were originally made parties under Rule 20, the plain language reading of the statute is no supplemental jurisdiction. Another glitch.

E. Intervention

Q–21. When a man is killed in an auto accident, his two children as next of kin bring a wrongful death action against the other driver for negligence. Upon learning of the action, a woman who claims she is the illegitimate daughter of the deceased seeks to intervene as a plaintiff to share in any recovery. Should this nonparty be allowed to intervene of right?

Your answer _____

Q–22. Part 1. A corporation wishes to open a drug treatment facility in a vacant building that formerly was a neighborhood school. To do so, it must obtain a conditional use permit from the city. Under pressure from a neighborhood association comprised of neighboring property owners, the city council turns down the permit. The corporation sues the city to require it to issue the permit. Will the neighborhood association be allowed to intervene as a defendant of right?

Your answer _____

Part 2. Will the neighborhood association be allowed to intervene permissively as a defendant?

Your answer _____

Part 3. Assume the association does not seek to intervene. When the trial court orders the city to issue the conditional use permit and the city council decides not to appeal, will the association be allowed to intervene of right to pursue the appeal?

Your answer _____

Q–23. P, a citizen of Tennessee, sues D, a corporation incorporated in Nevada with principal place of business in Kentucky, for pollution of a body of water on which P is a landowner. The basis of federal jurisdiction is diversity. I, a citizen of Kentucky, who owns land that borders on the same body of water, petitions to intervene of right, or in the alternative permissively, as a plaintiff. Assuming Fed.R.Civ.P. 24 allows either type of intervention, will the court have supplemental jurisdiction?

Your answer _____

Answer to Q–21. Yes. The intervenor has an interest in the damages for wrongful death that may be recovered. The intervenor's interest may be impaired: the two existing plaintiffs may obtain a recovery that exhausts defendant's resources. The intervenor's interest is not adequately represented: the two plaintiffs have no interest in cutting her in for a share and the defendant has no interest in providing any share to cut. So long as the petition for intervention is timely, it should be granted.

Answer to Q–22. Part 1. No. The interests of the neighborhood association are adequately represented by the city, which is defending the action. Even though the members of the association have property interests that may be impaired, they cannot intervene of right.

Part 2. Maybe. The sole requirement that the association's defense have a question of law or fact in common with the existing parties is easily met. At that point, the court will consider other factors including delay of the proceedings, control of the litigation, and value of the association's participation.

Part 3. Maybe. Since the association is no longer adequately represented, it would have a right to intervene, so long as it has petitioned for intervention in a timely fashion. Plaintiff will argue intervention following final judgment in the trial court is not timely. The association will argue it acted promptly as soon as it had a right to intervene. While the majority opinion would be that the association may intervene of right [*see* n. 26, *supra*], the court in this particular case decided the petition to intervene was untimely. Omegon, Inc. v. City of Minnetonka, 346 N.W.2d 684 (Minn.App. 1984).

Answer to Q–23. No. Even assuming arguendo that the proposed intervention satisfies § 1367(a) since it involves the same pollution of the same body of water, § 1367(b) disallows supplemental jurisdiction in diversity cases for both intervening plaintiffs (as here) and intervening defendants.

F. Interpleader

Q–24. An insurance company, incorporated and with principal place of business in Ohio, issues a policy of life insurance with the face value of $50,000. The insured dies. The daughter of the insured, a citizen of California, sues in state court to recover the proceeds. The widow of the insured, a citizen of California, informs the insurance company she also intends to claim the proceeds. Will the insurance company be able to interplead the daughter and widow in federal court?

Your answer _____

Q–25. Part 1. P, a citizen of Illinois, advertises a baseball autographed by Babe Ruth on an internet auction website. P agrees to sell the ball to A, a citizen of Illinois, for $10,000. After the auction is closed, D, a citizen of Illinois, offers P $20,000 for the ball, and P accepts. P then receives a letter from the New York Yankees baseball club informing him that the ball was stolen from a memorabilia display owned by the club. Will P be able to bring an action against the three claimants for federal statutory interpleader?

Your answer _____

Part 2. Will P be able to bring an action against the three claimants for interpleader under the rule?

Your answer _____

Q–26. Part 1. A bank incorporated and with principal place of business in New Mexico receives a deposit for $250,000 from a depositor in Texas. The depositor dies. The depositor's wife, a citizen of Texas, claims the account. Depositor's two children, both citizens of Texas, claim the account. Depositor's business partner, a citizen of Texas, claims the account. Will the bank be able to bring an action against the four claimants for federal statutory interpleader?

Your answer _____

Part 2. Will the bank be able to bring an action against the four claimants for interpleader under the rule?

Your answer _____

Answer to Q–24. No. Neither type of interpleader—statutory or under the rule—is available on these facts. Statutory interpleader requires minimal diversity of claimants; both claimants are from California. The citizenship of the insurance company is irrelevant since it is not claiming the stake. Diversity for interpleader under the rule is satisfied since the insurance company is a citizen of Ohio and both claimants are citizens of California, but the jurisdictional amount is insufficient. The insurance company will have to interplead the claimants in state court.

Answer to Q–25. Part 1. Yes. Minimal diversity amongst the claimants exists (Illinois and New York). The amount in controversy is $500 or more. P may lay venue in either Illinois or New York, where the claimants reside. Process is available nationwide, so if P commences the action in Illinois, process may be served on the Yankees ball club in New York.

Part 2. No. Diversity jurisdiction does not exist. Plaintiff and two defendants/claimants are citizens of Illinois. Also, the amount in controversy does not exceed $75,000.

Answer to Q–26. Part 1. No. Even though § 1335 requires only minimal diversity, it requires diversity amongst the claimants, not between the stakeholder and the claimants. All claimants here are citizens of Texas. Statutory interpleader is not available.

Part 2. Yes. Complete diversity exists between the plaintiff bank and all defendant claimants. The amount in controversy exceeds $75,000. The venue statute (§ 1391(a)) allows the bank to lay venue in Texas (where all defendants reside) or New Mexico (where a substantial part of the property is located). Should the bank commence the action in federal court in New Mexico, personal jurisdiction over the Texas defendants may be a problem.

IV. COMPUTER EXERCISES

You are now ready for further work on joinder in the computer-assisted exercises available through CALI. As this edition is written, you have four exercises on joinder from which to choose. All four exercises are self-contained.

A. CALI CIV 07: An Exercise in Civil Procedure

This exercise, authored by William P. Kratzke,[28] has work on sufficiency of pleadings as well as joinder devices: counterclaims, impleader, joinder of parties, and intervention. The exercise also considers related issues of jurisdiction as these issues arise under Fed.R.Civ.P. 8, 9, 13, 14, 19 and 24. Students are presented with a hypothetical followed by six problems in which the issues are presented.

B. CALI CIV 11: A Review of Joinder Concepts

This exercise, authored by David Welkowitz,[29] is intended to allow students to review joinder of claims and parties under the Federal Rules. The exercise uses a construction project litigation as the basis for the questions. The litigation grows gradually, adding claims and parties along the way. At each step, the student is asked questions about the propriety of joining the claim and/or the party.

C. CALI CIV 18: Joinder of Claims and Parties

This exercise, authored by David Welkowitz, is designed to be used in different ways. Students may use it as a tutorial to accompany assigned readings, as a supplement to reinforce concepts discussed in class, or as a review before exams. The program is interactive, requiring the student to respond to various questions and hypotheticals to learn the principles embodied in the rules. It does not assume any specific knowledge of the joinder rules—it is designed to teach the rules from scratch.

The program uses hypertext links between various parts of the program. These links offer students options in navigating through the program so they are not forced to follow a particular order. The

---

28. Cecil C. Humphries Professor of Law, University of Memphis School of Law.

29. Professor of Law, Whittier Law School.

user is the master of the organization. All of the rules and statutes that are needed are available as part of the program and may be viewed at any time by selecting an on-screen button.

The program includes units on a variety of joinder topics: claim joinder (Rule 18); permissive party joinder (Rule 20); counterclaims; cross-claims; third-party claims (Rule 14); compulsory joinder of parties (Rule 19); and intervention (Rule 24). It also contains an extensive unit devoted to the subject matter jurisdiction problems raised by these rules. Finally, there is a review unit to allow the user to apply the principles learned in the lesson.

D. CALI CIV 21: An Interpleader Primer

This exercise, authored by David Welkowitz, briefly describes the concept of interpleader and some of the historical limitations on the remedy, but its focus is on interpleader under the federal statute and Rule 22. The lesson introduces the various procedural issues involved—such as subject matter jurisdiction, personal jurisdiction, and venue—and highlights the differences between statutory and rule interpleader on these subjects. The lesson also contains a segment on the problem presented in enjoining other pending actions. The lesson requires the student to use the relevant statutes and rules, which are included in the lesson.

*

EXERCISE SEVEN

Discovery

I. DISCOVERY UNDER THE FEDERAL RULES

A. Philosophy

Prior to the effective date of the Federal Rules of Civil Procedure in 1938, common law and code procedures generally assigned pleadings the tasks of giving notice of the nature of the case, narrowing issues for trial, weeding out groundless claims, and revealing the facts of the case. *See* Exercise Three I.A–B. Beyond the pleadings, the attorney had few or no formal devices for investigation of the opponent's case. Effective advocacy relied on keeping the opponent in the dark about the details of the case and items of evidence until the attorney could spring surprises at trial. This system has been called the "sporting theory of justice."[1]

The drafters of the Federal Rules intended to narrow the function of the pleadings to notice-giving only, and to allow the discovery devices to handle the other work of shaping the case for trial. Consequently, discovery today under the Federal Rules has three purposes:

(1) To narrow the issues, in order that at the trial it may be necessary to produce evidence only on a residue of matters that are found to be actually disputed and controverted.

(2) To obtain evidence for use at the trial.

(3) To secure information about the existence of evidence that may be used at the trial and to ascertain how and from whom it may be procured, as for instance, the existence,

---

1. Tiedman v. American Pigment Corp., 253 F.2d 803, 808 (4th Cir.1958).

custody, and location of pertinent documents or the names and addresses of persons having knowledge of relevant facts.[2]

In order to promote the general goal of the Federal Rules of trial and decision of cases on the merits, the discovery devices are designed to reduce the ability to keep the opponent in the dark and to spring surprises at trial. Of course, discovery is self-starting and self-propelled. [except certain disclosures are automatically required, as discussed in I.C. Required Disclosures, *infra*.] Some attorneys do not engage in extensive discovery in some cases, and some may not ask the correct discovery questions, so surprises still occur at trial, but the adoption of the discovery devices has given the careful, thorough attorney the ability to minimize or even eliminate such tactics by the opponent.

The philosophy of discovery of the Federal Rules has earned high praise:

> The pre-trial deposition-discovery mechanism established by Rules 26 to 37 is one of the most significant innovations of the Federal Rules of Civil Procedure. Under the prior federal practice, the pre-trial functions of notice-giving, issue-formulation and fact-revelation were performed primarily and inadequately by the pleadings. Inquiry into the issues and the facts before trial was narrowly confined and was often cumbersome in method. The new rules, however, restrict the pleadings to the task of general notice-giving and invest the deposition-discovery process with a vital role in the preparation for trial. The various instruments of discovery now serve (1) as a device, along with the pre-trial hearing under Rule 16, to narrow and clarify the basic issues between the parties, and (2) as a device for ascertaining the facts, or information as to the existence or whereabouts of facts, relative to those issues. Thus civil trials in the federal courts no longer need be carried on in the dark. The way is now clear, consistent with recognized privileges, for the parties to obtain the fullest possible knowledge of the issues and facts before trial.[3]

While the discovery system of the Federal Rules remains popular, some critics have always existed. In the past three decades, the critics have primarily pointed to the spiraling costs of litigation. The heavy costs of discovery can lead to the abuse of discovery to prevent the pursuit of meritorious claims,[4] to force

2. 8 CHARLES A. WRIGHT, ARTHUR R. MILLER & RICHARD L. MARCUS, FEDERAL PRACTICE AND PROCEDURE: CIVIL 2D § 2001, at 41 (1994).

3. Hickman v. Taylor, 329 U.S. 495, 500–501, 67 S.Ct. 385, 388–389, 91 L.Ed. 451, 457 (1947).

4. "Delay and excessive expense now characterize a large percentage of all civil litigation. The problems arise in significant part, as every judge and litigator knows,

nuisance settlements of nonmeritorious claims,[5] or to delay the processing and termination of litigation through the courts.[6] In general, say the critics, discovery as now practiced burdens society with unnecessary, nonproductive expense.

This perception of abuses resulted in amendments to the discovery rules in 1970, 1980, 1983, 1993, and 2000. Some of these changes were designed to give federal judges additional control over discovery, especially in complex cases, through pretrial conferences and discovery orders. The 1993 amendments for the first time required initial disclosure of information without any discovery request. [*see* I.C. Required Disclosures, *infra*]. The 2000 amendments narrowed the scope of discovery [*see* I.B. Scope of Discovery, *infra*].

By and large, however, despite these criticisms and adjustments, the basic philosophy of discovery under the Federal Rules has not been substantially altered since 1938. The rules are intended to allow free and open discovery so that each side can become completely informed about the opponent's case to the end of informed settlement or decision on the merits.

B. Scope of Discovery

The broad scope of discovery is set forth in Federal Rule 26(b)(1):

> Parties may obtain discovery regarding any matter, not privileged, that is relevant to the claim or defense of any party, including the existence, description, nature, custody, condition and location of any books, documents, or other tangible things and the identity and location of persons having knowledge of any discoverable matter. For good cause, the court may order discovery of any matter relevant to the subject matter involved in the action. Relevant information need not be admissible at the trial if the discovery appears reasonably calculated to lead

from abuse of the discovery procedures available under the Rules." Dissent from Order Amending Civil Rules, 446 U.S. 997, 999 (1980) (Powell, J., joined by Stewart, J., and Rehnquist, J.).

5. "But to the extent that [discovery] permits a plaintiff with a largely groundless claim to simply take up the time of a number of other people, with the right to do so representing an *in terrorem* increment of the settlement value, rather than a reasonably founded hope that the process will reveal relevant evidence, it is a social cost rather than a benefit." Blue Chip Stamps v. Manor Drug Stores, 421 U.S. 723, 741, 95 S.Ct. 1917, 1928, 44 L.Ed.2d 539, 552 (1975).

6. Several sources are collected in 8 CHARLES A. WRIGHT, ARTHUR R. MILLER & RICHARD L. MARCUS, FEDERAL PRACTICE AND PROCEDURE: CIVIL 2D § 2001 (1994).

to the discovery of admissible evidence. All discovery is subject to the limitations imposed by Rule 26(b)(2)(i), (ii), and (iii).

Note the rule restricts the scope of discovery to unprivileged matters that are relevant to the claim or defense of any party. Prior to amendment in 2000, the rule allowed discovery of matters relevant "to the subject matter involved in the pending action." This broader scope of discovery is now available only on order of the court for good cause shown. This amendment too responded to concerns of overly broad discovery and possible abuse.[7]

On the one hand, the rule specifically eliminates some possible objections to discovery. The attorney may discover material either to explore the opponent's case or to support the attorney's own case. The names of persons having knowledge—typically, witnesses to the occurrence in question—must be revealed. An opponent cannot object that the material to be discovered would be inadmissible at trial, e.g., hearsay, if the information will likely lead to admissible evidence.[8]

On the other hand, the scope of discovery is not unlimited. Federal Rule 26 places several limits on discovery. Rule 26(b)(1) provides matters that are privileged or irrelevant are not discoverable. Rule 26(b)(2) gives the court broad authority to alter the rules and to limit discovery that is cumulative, burdensome, or too expensive. Rule 26(b)(3) gives protection to "work product." Rule 26(b)(4) governs discovery from experts. Rule 26(c), dealing with protective orders, also contains general limits designed to keep discovery from becoming burdensome or oppressive.

1. Privilege

Privileged matter is outside the scope of discovery. The law of evidence provides privileges, and the law of the state where the

---

7. The amendment is designed to involve the court more actively in regulating the breadth of sweeping or contentious discovery. * * * The dividing line between information relevant to the claims and defenses and that relevant only to the subject matter of the action cannot be defined with precision. * * * The rule change signals * * * to the parties that they have no entitlement to discovery to develop new claims or defenses that are not already identified in the pleadings. FED.R.CIV.P. 26(b)(1) advisory committee's note.

8. The sentence of FED.R.CIV.P. 26(b)(1) so providing was edited in 2000 to "clarify that information must be relevant to be discoverable even though inadmissible, and that discovery of such material is permitted if reasonably calculated to lead to the discovery of admissible evidence." FED.R.CIV.P. 26(b)(1) advisory committee's note. In other words, the information sought that is not admissible must still be relevant within the meaning of the rule. Clearly, this amendment is intended to narrow the information so discoverable.

federal court sits must be consulted to determine privileges the state law recognizes, at least in federal court cases founded on diversity of citizenship.[9] Commonly accepted privileges include attorney-client, husband-wife, clergy-penitent, doctor-patient, governmental secrets, and informers. Less common privileges include psychotherapist-patient, accountant-client, and journalist-source. Some few states recognize other privileges, including dentist-patient, chiropractor-patient, nurse-patient, social worker-client, and others.

A common occurrence in a deposition is that an attorney will object to a question and then tell the witness to answer. Such an objection, perhaps to the form of the question or to material that will be inadmissible at trial, is then on the record. Should the deposition be utilized at trial, the judge can then rule on the objection. When a question calls for privileged material, the attorney may properly object and instruct the witness not to answer, for the material sought is beyond the scope of discovery.

2. Relevancy

Irrelevant material is outside the scope of discovery. Again the law of evidence supplies our guide:

> "Relevant evidence" means evidence having any tendency to make the existence of any fact that is of consequence to the determination of the action more probable or less probable than it would be without the evidence.[10]

The definition of relevant evidence in the federal rule combines two common law evidence concepts: materiality and relevancy.

Materiality is the portion of the rule that says "any fact that is of consequence to the determination of the action." In other words, the fact to be proved must be raised in the case by the pleadings. For example, assume in a tort case, plaintiff's attorney by interrogatory asks defendant to reveal the location and amount of its bank accounts. Certainly, the answer sought has nothing to do with the issues of liability or compensatory damages. Whether a defendant may be able to pay a judgment is not "of consequence" to whether the defendant is liable for damages. Accordingly, the fact is "immaterial" under the common law, and therefore "irrelevant" under Federal Rule 401. The result depends on whether the pleadings have raised an issue of punitive damages. With no such issue, the question is irrelevant and outside the scope of discovery.

9. FED.R.EVID. 501. *See* CHARLES A. WRIGHT & MARY KAY KANE, THE LAW OF FEDERAL COURTS § 93 (6th ed. 2002).

10. FED.R.EVID. 401.

With a demand for punitive damages made in the pleadings, the plaintiff will be entitled at trial to inform the jury of the amount of defendant's wealth so they will know how much money will be required to punish defendant adequately. The size of defendant's bank account would be relevant and so within the scope of discovery.

Relevance is the portion of the rule that refers to "more probable or less probable than it would be without the evidence." In other words, the evidence has a tendency in logic to prove what it is offered to prove. For example, in a fender-bender case, plaintiff attempts to prove that defendant was negligent in failure to keep a proper lookout by offering evidence that defendant three days prior to the accident had made a purchase from a pornographic book store. That evidence tends to prove defendant made the purchase but the purchase in no way relates to the accident; after hearing the evidence, the jury will not have its assessment of the probabilities of whether defendant kept proper lookout changed a whit. A similar result follows when a party attempts to prove the lessor caused damage to leased property by showing the lessor has a lot of money and previously obtained a lucrative government contract.[11]

Such examples are rare, however. In general, consistent with the policy of a broad scope of discovery, the courts have interpreted relevance generously, "to encompass any matter that bears on, or that reasonably could lead to other matter that could bear on, any issue that is or may be in the case."[12] Of course, this statement was made prior to the 2000 amendment to Federal Rule 26(b) narrowing the scope of discovery by restricting it to matters relevant to the parties' claims or defenses [see I.B. Scope of Discovery, supra], but the amendment does not change the definition of relevance.

One other question of relevance is specifically answered by Rule 26(a)(1)(D): the existence and contents of any insurance agreement that may possibly cover damages awarded in the action must be revealed–as a required initial disclosure.

3. Trial Preparation: Materials

An immunity from discovery of litigation materials "prepared or formed by an adverse party's counsel in the course of his legal

---

11. City of Cleveland v. Peter Kiewit Sons' Co., 624 F.2d 749 (6th Cir.1980).

12. Oppenheimer Fund, Inc. v. Sanders, 437 U.S. 340, 351, 98 S.Ct. 2380, 2389, 57 L.Ed. 253, 265 (1978).

duties" was created by the Supreme Court in *Hickman v. Taylor*.[13] This "work product" is not subject to discovery absent a showing by the adversary that "production of those facts is essential to the preparation of one's case."[14] Oral statements are even more difficult to obtain, since they embody even more of the lawyer's thought processes. The purposes of the work product doctrine, as envisioned by the Court, were to prevent a free ride on the opponent's investigation and to protect the adversary system.

Federal Rule 26(b)(3) now codifies the work product immunity:

> Subject to the provisions of subdivision (b)(4) of this rule, a party may obtain discovery of documents and tangible things otherwise discoverable under subdivision (b)(1) of this rule and prepared in anticipation of litigation or for trial by or for another party or by or for that other party's representative (including the other party's attorney, consultant, surety, indemnitor, insurer, or agent) only upon a showing that the party seeking discovery has substantial need of the materials in the preparation of the party's case and that the party is unable without undue hardship to obtain the substantial equivalent of the materials by other means. In ordering discovery of such materials when the required showing has been made, the court shall protect against disclosure of the mental impressions, conclusions, opinions, or legal theories of an attorney or other representative of a party concerning the litigation.
>
> A party may obtain without the required showing a statement concerning the action or its subject matter previously made by that party. Upon request, a person not a party may obtain without the required showing a statement concerning the action or its subject matter previously made by that person.
> * * *

Several points might be highlighted about the rule. First, protection is afforded only for material prepared in anticipation of litigation; materials created not in anticipation of litigation are not protected. Second, the materials need not be produced by an attorney; any representative of the party is covered so long as that person prepared the materials in anticipation of litigation. Third, this qualified immunity can be overcome by a showing of "substantial need" for the materials; the party seeking discovery and showing such need will be able to discover the materials. Fourth, the mental impressions of the attorney are protected, and as a practical matter are absolutely immune. Fifth, a person who gave a

13. 329 U.S. 495, 510, 67 S.Ct. 385, 393, 91 L.Ed. 451, 462 (1947).

14. *Id.* at 511, 67 S.Ct. at 394, 91 L.Ed. at 462.

statement in anticipation of litigation can obtain as of right a copy of that statement. Finally, the first sentence of the rule subordinates it to the following provision governing discovery of trial preparation materials involving experts; expert witnesses and their reports discoverable under Rule 26(b)(4) cannot be resisted as trial preparation materials under Rule 26(b)(3).

4. Trial Preparation: Experts

Properly stated, there is no additional limit on the scope of discovery for expert witnesses, but the Federal Rules do place special limits on the methods that may be used to discover expert testimony. Rule 26(b)(4) differentiates between experts who the party expects to call to testify at trial and experts who were retained for the litigation but are not expected to testify. The latter type of expert's opinion is discoverable only "upon a showing of exceptional circumstances under which it is impracticable for the party seeking discovery to obtain facts or opinions on the same subject by other means."[15]

The opinion of an expert to be called at trial is more readily available. Prior to 1993, the opinion of a trial expert could be obtained only by interrogatory to the opposing party, possibly supplemented by other discovery as agreed to by stipulation or as ordered by the court. After the 1993 amendments, the name and a report of the expert are part of the initial disclosures required to be made to the opponent without request.[16] Subsequent to receipt of the report, the opponent may take the expert's deposition. Rule 26(b)(4)(A).

Of course, as with other areas of discovery, the parties are allowed to stipulate to modify procedures governing or limiting discovery.[17]

5. Protective Orders

The court has power to make a protective order to limit discovery when "justice requires to protect a party or person from annoyance, embarrassment, oppression, or undue burden or ex-

---

15. FED.R.CIV.P. 26(b)(4)(B).

16. FED.R.CIV.P. 26(a)(2)(A) requires disclosure of the name of the expert and FED.R.CIV.P. 26(a)(2)(B) requires a written report including the expert's opinion, supporting information, exhibits, qualifications, and prior testimony. See I.C. Required Disclosures, *infra*.

17. See FED.R.CIV.P. 29.

pense. * * * '' Fed.R.Civ.P. 26(c). The Rule then suggests eight ways in which the court may limit discovery. Some of the protections ordered by courts under this rule include designating a time or place for discovery, requiring a certain method of discovery, prohibiting inquiry into certain matters, limiting the amount of discovery, and protecting the confidentiality of material discovered.[18]

C. Required Disclosures

From adoption of the Federal Rules in 1938 until 1993, discovery was always self-starting. A party could do as much discovery as the Rules allowed, or little or nothing. No party was required to reveal anything except in response to a proper discovery request. This procedure changed with the adoption of ''required disclosures'' by amendment to Rule 26 in 1993.[19] Now, Federal Rule 26(a) requires parties to disclose certain categories of information without request and by a definite timetable. The idea is that this basic information will be subject to request anyway and requiring disclosure saves time and expense both to the parties and to the court. Additional discovery proceeds by request, as it always has.

Three categories of information must be disclosed. Each has its own timing provision.

First, within 14 days after a meeting of the parties to discuss claims and defenses, possible settlement, required disclosures, and discovery necessary in the litigation [Federal Rule 26(f)], each party must disclose

—name, address, and telephone of persons who are likely to have discoverable information the disclosing party may use to support its claim or defense (except by impeachment);

—documents the disclosing party may use to support its claim or defense (except by impeachment);

—a computation of damages claimed; and

18. *See generally* CHARLES A. WRIGHT & MARY KAY KANE, THE LAW OF FEDERAL COURTS § 83 (6th ed. 2002).

19. The 1993 amendment to FED.R.CIV.P. 26(a) introduced required disclosures to federal practice. The amendment was controversial, and in recognition of that controversy, the amended rule allowed individual districts to opt out of the initial disclosure requirements by local rule. Several districts did so. Following several years of experience, in 2000 the Supreme Court amended the rule again to eliminate the opt out possibility. The initial disclosures indeed became ''required disclosures'' in all federal districts.

—insurance agreements.[20]

Second, within the time specified by the court, each party must disclose the name and a report of each expert to be called to testify at trial.[21]

Third, at least 30 days before trial, each party must disclose the name, address, and telephone number of each witness who may be called; the designation of any witness whose testimony is to be presented by deposition; and an identification of each document or other exhibit that it may offer.[22]

D. Discovery Devices

Any or all of the discovery devices may be employed by the attorney in any litigation. The careful attorney will develop a discovery strategy early in the litigation; decisions must be made as to which devices are appropriate, what information is necessary, and what sequence of discovery should be used.

The most popular discovery device is the *oral deposition.*[23] A witness is called before a court reporter, who administers an oath. The attorney noticing the deposition then takes the testimony of the witness; the attorney opposing the deposition may then also examine. The deposition allows discovery of new information and identifies controverted facts. The deposition of a party may narrow issues by obtaining admissions. A deposition may be taken from any person, and is not limited to parties.

The huge advantage of the deposition is flexibility. The attorney taking the testimony can follow up with questions about new information or areas where the witness seems hesitant. The deposition also allows the attorney to evaluate both the opponent's witness and the opposing attorney before trial. Should the deponent become unavailable at the time of trial, the deposition may be read into the trial record as prior testimony.[24] The primary disadvantage of the deposition is cost, which includes both the expense of the court reporter and the fees of the attorneys taking the deposition.

20. FED.R.CIV.P. 26(a)(1)(A)-(D). Certain categories of proceedings, such as habeas corpus petitions and student loan collections, are exempted from the required disclosures by FED.R.CIV.P. 26(a)(1)(E).

21. FED.R.CIV.P. 26(a)(2). *See* I.B.4 Trial Preparation: Experts, *supra.*

22. FED.R.CIV.P. 26(a)(3).

23. FED.R.CIV.P. 27–28, 30.

24. *See* FED.R.CIV.P 32; FED.R.EVID. 804(1).

A little-used device is the *deposition upon written questions.*[25] Again, the deponent is called before a court reporter and sworn, but then the reporter reads a list of questions previously submitted by the attorney and records the answers. A great deal of expense is saved since the attorney does not attend the deposition, but the loss of flexibility in inability to ask follow-up questions makes this discovery device unpopular.

Interrogatories are written questions submitted to the opposing party for answers under oath.[26] Interrogatories may be sent only to parties. While the attorney writes the interrogatories, they are still relatively inexpensive compared to the oral deposition. Some attorneys believe that an advantage of interrogatories is more complete answers are given, since research can be done and the answers can be given after proper consideration; other attorneys believe that this is a disadvantage, since the opposing attorney can sanitize the answers before they are given. Again, there is no flexibility of follow-up questions.

A *request for production of documents* allows the attorney to inspect and copy documents and other tangible things (including computer data) in the "possession, custody or control" of another party.[27] Requirement of a showing of good cause for production was eliminated by amendment in 1970, so use of this device—as all others save the physical or mental exam—proceeds without resort to the court, in the absence of objection to discovery. Usually, inspection of documents works by agreement of the parties rather than formal request for production; in a complex case, production of documents may involve thousands of hours in inspection of a party's files.

When the mental or physical condition of a party is in controversy, the court may order a *physical or mental examination* "for good cause shown."[28] While a party who claims personal injury clearly places physical condition in controversy, examinations of a party who "has not affirmatively put into issue his own mental or physical condition are not to be automatically ordered merely because the person has been involved in an accident * * *."[29] Even so, little showing of good cause is ordinarily

25. Fed.R.Civ.P. 31.

26. *See* Fed.R.Civ.P. 33.

27. Fed.R.Civ.P. 34. Although a request for production of documents and things may be sent only to a party, documents in the possession of a nonparty may be obtained by the use of a subpoena duces tecum, under Fed.R.Civ.P. 45.

28. Fed.R.Civ.P. 35.

29. Schlagenhauf v. Holder, 379 U.S. 104, 121, 85 S.Ct. 234, 244, 13 L.Ed.2d 152, 165 (1964).

required, and in fact, such examinations are typically arranged by stipulation of the attorneys.

Requests for admission require the opposing party to admit the truth of "statements or opinions of fact or of the application of law to fact, including the genuineness of any documents."[30] This device is designed to verify information and narrow issues for trial, and to save expense of unnecessary proof at trial, not to discover new information. Requests for admissions may be thought of as a brush-clearing device, not a method of obtaining truly important admissions. Admission of a disputed fact will simply be denied.

E. Sanctions for Failure to Make Discovery

A party or person from whom discovery is sought may seek a protective order from the court against inappropriate discovery.[31] Absent a protective order, the person refusing to submit to discovery will be subject to a court order compelling discovery [Federal Rule 37(a)], followed by sanctions should the person fail to obey the order [Federal Rule 37(b)]. In other words, sanctions for failure to make discovery almost always require a two-step process.

> The general scheme of the rule is that sanctions can be imposed only for failure to comply with an order of the court. Thus, when the discovery procedure itself requires a court order, as under Rule 35, or permits a court order, as when there has been a discovery conference under Rule 26(f) or a protective order has been denied under Rule 26(c), failure to obey the order can be punished immediately by any of the sanctions listed in Rule 37(b)(2). When the discovery procedure is one set in motion by the parties themselves without court order, the party seeking discovery must first obtain an order under Rule 37(a) requiring the recalcitrant party or witness to make the discovery sought; it is only violation of this order that is punishable under Rule 37(b).[32]

Available sanctions under Rule 37(b) include treating the failure as contempt of court, striking all or parts of pleadings,

---

30. Fed.R.Civ.P. 36(a).

31. *See* Fed.R.Civ.P. 26(c). *See* I.B.5. Protective Orders, *supra*.

32. Charles A. Wright & Mary Kay Kane, The Law of Federal Courts § 90, at 642 (6th ed. 2002). Four exceptions to this two-step process exist. An immediate sanction is allowed for a willful failure to appear at a deposition or answer interrogatories or respond to a request for inspection; for an unjustified refusal to make admissions; for failure to join in framing a discovery plan upon request by another party; or for failure to make a disclosure required under Fed.R.Civ.P. 26(a). *Id.*

preventing the admission of evidence, taking designated facts as established, and awarding expenses of attorney's fees.

II.   QUESTIONS ON DISCOVERY

Instructions. The questions are on the left-hand page, and the answers are on the right-hand page. Cover the right-hand page, write your answers to the questions in the spaces provided, and compare your answers to the suggested answers on the facing page.

A. Philosophy of Discovery Under the Federal Rules

Q–1. Plaintiff is swimming across a lake when she is struck by Defendant's motorboat. Defendant sends an interrogatory to Plaintiff requesting the names of all of Plaintiff's past swimming instructors. Plaintiff objects that Defendant is "just on a fishing expedition." Upon Defendant's motion, should the court compel the discovery?

Your answer _____

Q–2. Plaintiff purchases a trailer home from Defendant manufacturer, and later discovers various defects in materials and construction. When Plaintiff sues Defendant for damages, Defendant answers and serves Plaintiff with 347 interrogatories. Is Plaintiff required to answer these interrogatories?

Your answer _____

Q–3. Part 1. During her oral deposition, Defendant reveals the existence of a letter relevant to her defense; the letter, she says, is in the possession of her customer. Defendant did not produce this letter as part of her initial disclosures under Federal Rule 26(a)(1)(B). Has Defendant violated the required disclosures requirement?

Your answer _____

Part 2. Plaintiff later makes no effort to obtain the letter through discovery. At trial, when Defendant introduces the letter, will Plaintiff's objection to the evidence be sustained because the contents are "a complete surprise?"

Your answer _____

Answer to Q–1. Yes. As the Supreme Court said in Hickman v. Taylor, 329 U.S. 495, 507, 67 S.Ct. 385, 392, 91 L.Ed. 451, 460 (1947):

> No longer can the time-honored cry of "fishing expedition" serve to preclude a party from inquiring into the facts underlying his opponent's case. Mutual knowledge of all the relevant facts gathered by both parties is essential to proper litigation. To that end, either party may compel the other to disgorge whatever facts he has in his possession.

So long as the material sought is within the scope of discovery, it must be produced. On these facts, past swimming instructors could perhaps give admissible evidence on Plaintiff's swimming ability, which may be relevant to the defense of contributory negligence.

Answer to Q–2. No. Even though the philosophy of the Federal Rules generally is to allow free and open discovery, and the mere fact that a party must respond to a large volume of discovery requests is not grounds for objection, Federal Rule 33(a) allows a party to serve no more than 25 interrogatories without leave of court. This numerical limit was inserted into Rule 33 in 1993 in response to perceived discovery abuse. In an appropriate case, the court can grant leave for additional interrogatories. Another option is the parties can stipulate under Rule 29 to modify the limitations placed on discovery.

Prior to 1993, the answer to this question would have been maybe. Federal Rule 26(c) allows a party to move for a protective order from discovery demands that amount to "oppression" or cause "undue burden or expense." Should a party be able to convince the court any discovery is beyond another party's legitimate discovery needs and is in bad faith and intended to annoy, oppress, or burden, the protective order may issue. *See* I.B.5 Protective Orders, *supra.*

Answer to Q–3. Part 1. No. Defendant has not violated her obligation to make initial disclosures because Rule 26(a)(1)(B) requires her to produce documents she may use to support her defense that are in her "possession, custody, or control." This document is in the possession of a customer, not the Defendant.

Were the facts different, and Defendant had failed to make required disclosure of a document in her possession, custody, or control, Defendant would probably not be permitted to use the document at trial as a sanction for failure to disclose it. Fed.R.Civ.P. 37(c)(1).

Part 2. No. Discovery is self-starting. A party may do no discovery, if he so chooses. On these facts, Defendant revealed the existence of the letter, but Plaintiff made no discovery attempt to obtain it. The only fault involved is Plaintiff's. Surprise has not been totally eliminated from trials.

B. Scope of Discovery

Q–4. At his oral deposition, Defendant says that he consulted with his personal attorney before sending a notice of termination of contract to Plaintiff. Defendant refuses to say what the attorney advised. Will Plaintiff be able to obtain an order compelling Defendant to reveal the information?

Your answer _____

Q–5. Defendant collides with Plaintiff at an intersection. Plaintiff sues for negligence and alleges excessive speed. Plaintiff schedules a deposition upon written questions of Witness, who has already been interviewed informally by both parties. The only information Witness has is that ten minutes before the accident, she saw Defendant speeding. Will an objection by Defendant to the deposition be sustained?

Your answer _____

Q–6. Plaintiff refuses to produce a relevant, unprivileged document on the sole ground that it would be hearsay and inadmissible at trial. Will Defendant's motion to compel discovery be granted?

Your answer _____

Q–7. Defendant refuses to produce an insurance policy covering the occurrence since it would be irrelevant to the issues of liability and damages. Will Plaintiff's motion to compel discovery be granted?

Your answer _____

Q–8. Following threats of suit by Plaintiff, Defendant hires an outside accountant to analyze its books; the accountant makes a written report to Defendant. Later, Plaintiff commences suit and requests production of the accountant's report. When asked why she wants the report, Plaintiff's attorney responds "No special reason—just being thorough." Must Defendant produce the report?

Your answer _____

Answer to Q–4. No. "Parties may obtain discovery regarding any matter, not privileged, that is relevant to the claim or defense of any party. * * *" Fed.R.Civ.P. 26(b)(1). The two specific limits on the scope of discovery are privilege and relevance. The facts seem clearly to indicate that the advice came in a private consultation between Defendant and Defendant's attorney. The attorney-client privilege would apply. The material sought is outside the scope of discovery.

Answer to Q–5. Maybe. As stated in the Answer to Q–4, irrelevant material is outside the scope of discovery. *See* I.B.2. Relevance, *supra*. The question is whether the fact that Defendant was speeding ten minutes before the accident would be of *any* probative value to a jury attempting to decide whether Defendant was speeding at the time of the accident. In other words, when the jury hears Defendant was speeding earlier, would it have its assessment of the probability that Defendant was speeding at the time of the accident changed? Courts have divided on the relevance of such testimony. *See generally* John W. Strong (ed.), *McCormick on Evidence* § 185 (5th ed. 1999).

Answer to Q–6. Yes. "Relevant information need not be admissible at the trial if the discovery appears reasonably calculated to lead to the discovery of admissible evidence." Fed.R.Civ.P. 26(b)(1). Discovery of a hearsay statement may lead to the author, whose personal testimony would be admissible.

Answer to Q–7. Yes. Fed.R.Civ.P. 26(a)(1)(D) requires mandatory initial disclosure of any insurance agreement that may help satisfy potential liability in the suit. An amendment to Rule 26 in 1970 clarified that such agreements are discoverable, and insurance policies were made part of the Rule 26(a) required initial disclosures in 1993. *See* Charles A. Wright & Mary Kay Kane, *The Law of Federal Courts* § 81, at 591 (6th ed. 2002).

Answer to Q–8. No. Since the report was made in response to threats of suit, the report was clearly "prepared in anticipation of litigation," and is protected work product (trial preparation materials). Fed.R.Civ.P. 26(b)(3). Occasionally one will hear a statement that work product protection applies only to the work of an attorney or someone working for an attorney, *i.e.*, attorney's work product, but the doctrine is not so limited and covers a variety of party's representatives: "attorney, consultant, surety, indemnitor, insurer, or agent." Fed.R.Civ.P. 26(b)(3). The question indicates no showing of substantial need to overcome the work product immunity.

Q–9. As part of its regular and routine business records, Defendant keeps a record of all checks it issues. When Plaintiff sues on an account, Defendant pleads the affirmative defense of payment. Plaintiff requests production of Defendant's check record. Defendant objects that the material is work product, and that Plaintiff has shown no need to overcome the immunity. Will Plaintiff's motion to compel discovery be granted?

Your answer _____

Q–10. Plaintiff's attorney takes the statement of Witness A, who says that Witness B had also been present at the accident scene. Defendant sends an interrogatory asking for the names and addresses of "all persons known to Plaintiff who may have witnessed the accident." May Plaintiff refuse to identify Witness B on the ground that discovery of B constitutes work product?

Your answer _____

Q–11. Witness, an acquaintance of Defendant, gives an oral statement to the attorney for Plaintiff. Upon learning that Plaintiff's attorney refuses to provide a copy of the statement to Defendant's attorney because it is work product, Defendant induces Witness to demand a copy of the statement. Must Plaintiff's attorney comply?

Your answer _____

Q–12. Defendant sends Plaintiff an interrogatory requesting the names and addresses of all witnesses Plaintiff intends to call at trial. May Plaintiff object on the grounds of work product?

Your answer _____

Answer to Q–9. Yes. The check record is regularly kept as part of the business. It was not prepared in anticipation of litigation. It is not work product. Need is irrelevant. In fact, this would be a required initial disclosure of a relevant document. Fed.R.Civ.P. 26(a)(1)(B).

Answer to Q–10. No. Work product does not protect facts learned. "There is no shield against discovery * * * of the facts that the opponent has acquired, or the persons from whom he obtained the facts * * * even though the documents themselves have a qualified immunity from discovery." Charles A. Wright & Mary Kay Kane, *The Law of Federal Courts* § 82, at 597 (6th ed. 2002). Witness B should have been revealed as a required initial disclosure. Fed.R.Civ.P. 26(a)(1)(A).

Even if Witness B were not found until after Plaintiff had made her required disclosures, Plaintiff would still be under a duty to supplement the disclosures. Fed.R.Civ.P. 26(e).

Answer to Q–11. Yes. Even though the work product immunity would protect the oral statement against discovery by Defendant, Witness may demand her own statement. "Upon request, a person not a party may obtain without the required showing a statement concerning the action or its subject matter previously made by that person." Fed.R.Civ.P. 26(b)(3). *See* I.B.3. Trial Preparation: Materials, *supra.* Should Witness then hand the statement over to Defendant, that is his business.

Answer to Q–12. Yes. A party is required to identify all witnesses to an occurrence, usually phrased as all persons who may have knowledge, but a list of trial witnesses is compiled only after the attorney has sifted through all potential witnesses and decided who will be asked to testify. This mental sifting makes the list work product. "In ordering discovery of such materials when the required showing has been made, the court shall protect against disclosure of the mental impressions, conclusions, opinions, or legal theories of an attorney or other representative of a party concerning the litigation." Fed.R.Civ.P. 26(b)(3).

This question assumes the interrogatory is sent during the discovery phase of the litigation. Later, Plaintiff is required to make mandatory disclosure of a witness list at least 30 days prior to trial. Fed.R.Civ.P. 26(a)(3)(B).

Q–13. Prior to commencing suit, Plaintiff's attorney asks Expert A and Expert B to evaluate the design of a machine. As part of his required disclosures under Rule 26(a)(2)(A), Plaintiff identifies Expert B. Defendant sends an interrogatory to Plaintiff requesting the identities of any other experts Plaintiff consulted. Is Plaintiff required to identify Expert A in answer to the interrogatory?

Your answer _____

Q–14. Plaintiff sues Doctor for malpractice, and seeks to depose another Patient of Doctor who has undergone the same procedure. Patient does not want to testify because of personal privacy. When Plaintiff subpoenas Patient for a deposition, can Patient obtain any relief from the court?

Your answer _____

Answer to Q–13. No. Experts who a party expects to present at trial must be disclosed under Fed.R.Civ.P. 26(b)(3)(A). Plaintiff did so identify Expert B. Experts a party employs in anticipation of litigation who are not expected to be called as a witness at trial need not be identified absent exceptional circumstances. Fed. R.Civ.P. 26(b)(4)(B). Defendant has shown no need at all here.

Answer to Q–14. Maybe. Patient can seek a protective order from the court "to protect a party or person from annoyance, embarrassment, oppression, or undue burden or expense." Fed. R.Civ.P. 26(c). Courts are solicitous of privacy concerns of nonparties. The court could decide to protect the party or person seeking a protective order in one or more of the ways mentioned in the rule—no one present except persons designated by the court, deposition sealed, and the like.

C. Discovery Devices

Q–15. Plaintiff sues Defendant for negligence. Plaintiff sends a set of interrogatories to Witness, asking for a complete description of the accident. Should Witness decline to answer, will Plaintiff be able to obtain an order from the court compelling discovery?

Your answer _____

Q–16. A letter relevant to the action of Plaintiff v. Defendant is in the possession of Third Party. Defendant serves a subpoena duces tecum on Third Party, instructing him to make the letter available to Defendant's attorney for inspection and copying. Must Third Party comply with the subpoena [Hint: see Fed.R.Civ.P. 45(a)]?

Your answer _____

Q–17. Plaintiff sues Defendant for personal injury damages arising from a car accident, alleging that Defendant ran a red light. Defendant, without any particular showing of good cause other than the need to verify plaintiff's injuries, moves the court for an order compelling Plaintiff to submit to a physical examination. Will the court order the discovery?

Your answer _____

Q–18. In the same action described in Q–17, Plaintiff, without any particular showing of cause, moves the court for an order compelling Defendant to submit to an *eye* examination. Will the court order the discovery?

Your answer _____

D. Sanctions for Failure to Make Discovery

Q–19. Defendant notices Plaintiff's deposition. Plaintiff appears and testifies, but refuses to answer questions on one subject. Defendant immediately goes to court and moves for sanctions, specifically requesting the court to rule that any evidence on that subject will be foreclosed at trial. Will the court grant a sanction for failure to make discovery?

Your answer _____

Answer to Q–15. No. Interrogatories may be served only on parties. Fed.R.Civ.P. 33(a). Witness is not a party. The only discovery devices that may be used against nonparties are oral depositions and depositions upon written questions.

Answer to Q–16. Yes. Fed.R.Civ.P. 45(a) reads as follows:

(1) Every subpoena shall

* * *

(C) command each person to whom it is directed to attend and give testimony or to produce and permit inspection and copying of designated books, documents or tangible things in the possession, custody or control of that person * * *.

This Rule allows use of a subpoena against Third Party to obtain the letter without accompanying testimony.

Prior to 1991, Fed.R.Civ.P. 45(a) allowed use of a subpoena only to "command each person to whom it is directed to attend and give testimony," *i.e.*, at a deposition, hearing, or trial. Use of a subpoena to obtain documents from a nonparty in the absence of testimony was improper. Some states still consider use of a subpoena for documents only to be an abuse of process.

Were Third Party a party to the action, then this request to produce documents would be appropriate under Fed.R.Civ.P. 34; a subpoena would not be necessary.

Answer to Q–17. Yes. While a physical examination may be ordered under Fed.R.Civ.P. 35 only "for good cause shown," Plaintiff has clearly placed his physical condition into issue by claiming personal injury damages, and that claim alone will furnish sufficient cause for the court to order the examination.

Answer to Q–18. No. A physical examination may be ordered for a party, but only "for good cause shown." Fed.R.Civ.P. 35. Plaintiff has made no showing at all of cause for an eye exam on these facts. The court will not order a physical examination of the parties in *every* accident case. *See* Schlagenhauf v. Holder, 379 U.S. 104, 121, 85 S.Ct. 234, 244, 13 L.Ed.2d 152, 165 (1964).

Answer to Q–19. No. Sanctions for failure to make discovery is a two step process. The party seeking discovery must first move the court for an order compelling discovery. Second, should the party resisting discovery not comply with that court order, then sanctions may be imposed. *See* I.E. Sanctions for Failure to Make Discovery, *supra.* Since the first step of an order compelling discovery has not been taken, the second step of sanctions is not available.

III. COMPUTER EXERCISES

You are now ready for further work in discovery in the computer-assisted exercises available through CALI. As this edition is written, you have three exercises on discovery from which to choose. All three are discovery games in which students compete against each other. All three are self-contained, and the facts necessary to play the discovery game are proved to you as part of the exercise.

A. CALI CIV 15: Buffalo Creek: A Game of Discovery (Initial Disclosure Version)

This game, authored by Owen Fiss and Ronald Wright, Jr.,[33] introduces students to pre-trial discovery under the Federal Rules of Civil Procedure. The discovery issues arise from the mass tort litigation begun in the aftermath of the Buffalo Creek flooding disaster of 1972. This game assumes the jurisdiction has not opted-out of the Rule 26 initial and pre-trial disclosure requirements. In addition to problems about legal entitlement to discovery, the game asks players about their obligations to disclose information without awaiting a discovery request from their opponents. In many questions, after a description of potential items for disclosure or discovery, the player in possession of the information is asked if he or she wants to disclose it. Next, the receiving player is asked if he or she wants to seek discovery of the information in questions or additional information. Attorneys must decide whether the rules require disclosure of the items in question; whether to resist discovery; and must provide reasons for failing to disclose or resisting a discovery request. The computer plays the roles of the clerk of the court (to file motions) and Judge K. K. Hall (to rule on the motions and offer observations about the players performance). Players must also consider time, the cost of discovery litigation, the cost of compliance with requests, and their reputations.

B. CALI CIV 16: Randolph County: A Game of Discovery

This game, authored by Owen Fiss, Ronald Wright, Jr., and Kimberly West–Faulcon,[34] introduces students to pre-trial discovery under the Federal Rules of Civil Procedure. Like *Buffalo Creek: A*

---

33. Sterling Professor of Law, Yale Law School; Professor of Law, Wake Forest University School of Law.

34. Sterling Professor of Law, Yale Law School; Professor of Law, Wake Forest University School of Law; Student, Yale Law School.

Game of Discovery, it assumes the jurisdiction has not opted-out of the Rule 26 initial and pre-trial disclosure requirements. The discovery issues arise in the context of a class action school desegregation case. One player represents the plaintiffs who contend the school district is failing in 1994 to comply with a 1970 school desegregation order. The other player represents the defendant school district, the school board, and its employees (including a high school principal whose remarks concerning interracial dating at a prom brought him national notoriety). Several of the questions have multiple parts. After a description of potential items for disclosure or discovery, the player in possession of the information is asked if he or she wants to disclose it. Next, the receiving player is asked if he or she wants to seek discovery of the information in question or additional information. Attorneys must decide whether the rules require disclosure of the items in question; whether to resist discovery; and must provide reasons for failing to disclose or resisting a discovery request. The computer plays the roles of the clerk of the court (to file motions) and Judge Myron Thompson (to rule on the motion and offer observations about the players performance). Players must also consider time, the cost of discovery litigation, the cost of compliance with requests, and their reputation.

C.   CALI CIV 20: Woburn: A Game of Discovery

This game, authored by Owen Fiss,[35] is designed to introduce students to the fundamentals of the discovery process. It is based on the acclaimed book "A Civil Action," by Jonathan Harr, and draws its problems from the litigation arising out of the contamination of the Aberjona aquifer in Woburn, Massachusetts. Woburn provides students with a unique opportunity to acquaint themselves with the Federal Rules of Civil Procedure regarding discovery in the context of a concrete, real-life case. Assuming the roles of plaintiffs' and defendants' attorneys, the players alternate making decisions about when and how to disclose or request discovery of certain pieces of information, as well as when to cooperate with and when to oppose their opponent's discovery efforts. The simulation is highly interactive, with the computer taking the role of Judge Skinner, who occasionally intervenes to rule on discovery motions. The thirteen problem sets included with Woburn cover a wide variety of topics, including:

Mandatory initial and supplemental disclosure requirements;

35.   Sterling Professor of Law, Yale Law School.

Proper use of various methods of discovery (subpoenas, inter-rogatories, depositions, requests for document production, medical examinations, requests for admission);

Expert witness reports;

Work product and privilege defenses;

Cost-shifting for discovery activities;

Attorney's fees awards; and

Sanctions for conduct in violation of the rules.

Woburn will teach students the details of the rules. It will also illuminate the strategic dimensions of discovery. While pursuing their discovery efforts within the context of the rules, the players are forced to think strategically about the costs of various discovery activities, time constraints, and their reputation with the judge, jury, and the legal community at large. Frivolous motions are punished by a loss of reputation; time-consuming document requests may exhaust a player's financial resources. The need to juggle these non-legal factors brings the rules to life, showing the student how particular rules affect attorneys' decision-making processes in con-crete situations. The game is to be played out of class, on the student's own schedule. At the end the students will have internal-ized the structure and dynamics of the discovery rules, and be ready to discuss the more conceptual or policy-oriented issues in class. This new, internet-based interface makes Woburn easily accessible and easy to play. On-screen reports let the players know at all times how their discovery efforts are progressing, and pictures of the actual persons involved in the trial as well as of the contamination site, court documents, and so forth, further heighten the impact of the game.

EXERCISE EIGHT

Summary Judgment

I. THE LAW OF SUMMARY JUDGMENT

A. Federal Rule 56

Since 1938, summary judgment has been governed in federal courts by Fed.R.Civ.P. 56. The key language of that rule from its beginnings until today is the following: "The judgment sought shall be rendered forthwith if * * * there is no genuine issue as to any material fact." Fed.R.Civ.P. 56(c). The important concepts here are *material fact* and *genuine issue*.

While either party can move for summary judgment, it is almost exclusively a defendant's weapon. Accordingly, the following discussion assumes defendant is moving for summary judgment.

A material issue of fact is one that would affect the result of the case. For example, in an auto accident case, the fact of whether plaintiff or defendant had the green light would be material. When, however, defendant moves for summary judgment on the basis of the statute of limitations, then the motion will be granted should the court determine the statute has expired. Any fact issues in the case—color of the traffic light, speed of the vehicles, amount of damages—are immaterial. The only issue that matters to the result is whether the statute has expired.

Similarly, a suit for breach of contract presents fact issues of offer, acceptance, consideration, and damages. None of these issues is material when defendant moves for summary judgment based on res judicata. Neither would any of the issues be material should the basis for the motion be failure of plaintiff to assert the claim as a compulsory counterclaim in defendant's earlier suit against plaintiff.

Of course, these situations are uncommon. Typically, the fact issues in the case will be material.

More common is a summary judgment motion based on the plaintiff's failure to raise a genuine issue of fact. A genuine fact issue is one that is not frivolous. Plaintiff can make many factual allegations in the complaint, but a genuine issue is one that has evidentiary support. In that sense, summary judgment is the means for defendant to test whether plaintiff has anything to back up those allegations.

Plaintiff must present facts that would be admissible in evidence at the trial. "Supporting and opposing affidavits shall be made on personal knowledge, [and] shall set forth such facts as would be admissible in evidence * * *." Fed.R.Civ.P. 56(e). The affidavits—or other materials such as depositions or interrogatory answers—must be based on personal, firsthand knowledge, not hearsay or opinion.

For example, plaintiff sues for defamation, alleging defendant called him a business cheat. Defendant moves for summary judgment and includes the affidavits of three disinterested eyewitnesses all stating that they heard the entire exchange and defendant uttered no such statement. Plaintiff responds with the affidavit of a person who was not present stating she heard from another person that defendant had uttered the words. Summary judgment will be granted. The affidavit of plaintiff's witness is based on hearsay, not personal knowledge, and will be disregarded. Without it, plaintiff has no genuine issue of fact preventing summary judgment.

Or plaintiff responds by arguing that the complaint alleges the defamation occurred. This also is unavailing, as a complaint is not based on personal knowledge. Summary judgment will be granted as plaintiff has failed to come forward with admissible evidence of the fact to demonstrate a genuine issue.

What if plaintiff puts in his own affidavit—or verifies the complaint—stating that the defendant made the statement? Despite the evidence of the three disinterested eyewitnesses versus plaintiff's interested solo statement, summary judgment should not be granted. The court will not weigh the credibility of the evidence of the two sides. The summary judgment motion seeks fact issues; it does not seek to decide them.[1]

Federal Rule 56 reads in its entirety as follows:

---

1. *See generally* Jack H. Friedenthal, Arthur R. Miller & Mary Kay Kane, Civil Procedure § 9.3 (3d ed. 1999).

(a) For Claimant. A party seeking to recover upon a claim, counterclaim, or cross-claim or to obtain a declaratory judgment may, at any time after the expiration of 20 days from the commencement of the action or after service of a motion for summary judgment by the adverse party, move with or without supporting affidavits for a summary judgment in the party's favor upon all or any part thereof.

(b) For Defending Party. A party against whom a claim, counterclaim, or cross-claim is asserted or a declaratory judgment is sought may, at any time, move with or without supporting affidavits for a summary judgment in the party's favor as to all or any part thereof.

(c) Motion and Proceedings Thereon. The motion shall be served at least 10 days before the time fixed for the hearing. The adverse party prior to the day of hearing may serve opposing affidavits. The judgment sought shall be rendered forthwith if the pleadings, depositions, answers to interrogatories, and admissions on file, together with the affidavits, if any, show that there is no genuine issue as to any material fact and that the moving party is entitled to a judgment as a matter of law. A summary judgment, interlocutory in character, may be rendered on the issue of liability alone although there is a genuine issue as to the amount of damages.

(d) Case Not Fully Adjudicated on Motion. If on motion under this rule judgment is not rendered upon the whole case or for all the relief asked and a trial is necessary, the court at the hearing of the motion, by examining the pleadings and the evidence before it and by interrogating counsel, shall if practicable ascertain what material facts exist without substantial controversy and what material facts are actually and in good faith controverted. It shall thereupon make an order specifying the facts that appear without substantial controversy, including the extent to which the amount of damages or other relief is not in controversy, and directing such further proceedings in the action as are just. Upon the trial of the action the facts so specified shall be deemed established, and the trial shall be conducted accordingly.

(e) Form of Affidavits; Further Testimony; Defense Required. Supporting and opposing affidavits shall be made on personal knowledge, shall set forth such facts as would be admissible in evidence, and shall show affirmatively that the affiant is competent to testify to the matters stated therein. Sworn or certified copies of all papers or parts thereof referred to in an affidavit shall be attached thereto or served therewith. The court may permit affidavits to be supplemented or opposed by depositions, answers to interrogatories, or further affidavits. When a motion for summary judgment is made and supported as provided in this rule, an adverse party may not rest upon the mere allegations or denials of the adverse party's pleading, but the adverse party's response, by affidavits or as otherwise provided in this rule, must set forth specific facts showing that there is a genuine issue for trial. If the adverse party does not so respond, summary judgment, if appropriate, shall be entered against the adverse party.

(f) When Affidavits Are Unavailable. Should it appear from the affidavits of a party opposing the motion that the party cannot for reasons stated present by affidavit facts essential to justify the party's opposition, the court may refuse the application for judgment or may order a continuance to permit affidavits to be obtained or depositions to be taken or discovery to be had or may make such other order as is just.

(g) Affidavits Made in Bad Faith. Should it appear to the satisfaction of the court at any time that any of the affidavits presented pursuant to this rule are presented in bad faith or solely for the purpose of delay, the court shall forthwith order the party employing them to pay to the other party the amount of the reasonable expenses which the filing of the affidavits caused the other party to incur, including reasonable attorney's fees, and any offending party or attorney may be adjudged guilty of contempt.

B. Supreme Court Interpretation of Federal Rule 56

The Supreme Court has been called on to interpret Rule 56 on many occasions. Responding to criticism that lower courts had been overly cautious in granting summary judgment motions, the Court decided three cases in 1986 that became known as the summary judgment trilogy.[2] These three opinions interpreted Rule 56 in a new light and made summary judgment easier to obtain. The most important of the three opinions is the following opinion because of the Court's discussion of what the nonmoving party must show to demonstrate a genuine issue of fact.

2. Celotex Corp. v. Catrett, 477 U.S. 317, 106 S.Ct. 2548, 91 L.Ed.2d 265 (1986); Anderson v. Liberty Lobby, Inc., 477 U.S. 242, 106 S.Ct. 2505, 91 L.Ed.2d 202 (1986); Matsushita Elec. Indus. Co. v. Zenith Radio Corp., 475 U.S. 574, 106 S.Ct. 1348, 89 L.Ed.2d 538 (1986).

ANDERSON v. LIBERTY LOBBY, INC.[3]

Supreme Court of United States, 1986.
477 U.S. 242, 106 S.Ct. 2505, 91 L.Ed.2d 202.[4]

JUSTICE WHITE delivered the opinion of the Court.

[§ 1]

In *New York Times Co. v. Sullivan,* 376 U.S. 254, 279–280, 84 S.Ct. 710, 725–726, 11 L.Ed.2d 686 (1964), we held that, in a libel[5] suit brought by a public official, the First Amendment requires the plaintiff to show that in publishing the defamatory statement the defendant acted with actual malice—"with knowledge that it was false or with reckless disregard of whether it was false or not." We held further that such actual malice must be shown with "convincing clarity." *Id.,* at 285–286, 84 S.Ct., at 728–729. See also *Gertz v. Robert Welch, Inc.,* 418 U.S. 323, 342, 94 S.Ct. 2997, 3008, 41 L.Ed.2d 789 (1974). These *New York Times* requirements we have since extended to libel suits brought by public figures[6] as well. See, *e.g., Curtis Publishing Co. v. Butts,* 388 U.S. 130, 87 S.Ct. 1975, 18 L.Ed.2d 1094 (1967).

[§ 2]

This case presents the question whether the clear-and-convincing-evidence requirement must be considered by a court ruling on a motion for summary judgment under Rule 56 of the Federal Rules of Civil Procedure in a case to which *New York Times*

3. The computer-aided exercise on summary judgment requires interpretation of this opinion in the context of motions for summary judgment on both a claim for defamation and a counterclaim for battery. In their memoranda supporting and opposing summary judgment on the claim, and also on the counterclaim, both parties rely heavily on this summary judgment decision by the Supreme Court. Please study this opinion carefully in preparation for your rulings on the motions made by the parties in the computer-aided exercise.

4. Footnotes and two dissenting opinions are omitted.

5. [Editors' note.] The elements of a defamation (libel) claim are publication, disparagement, and falsity. *See* Exercise Three. Libel, unlike many slander cases, does not require special damages; the harm to reputation is sufficient for recovery. Falsity may require proof of "actual malice," as explained in the opinion.

6. [Editors' note.] Public figures are both people who have attained important, visible positions so that they have roles in the resolution of public issues and people who have voluntarily thrust themselves forward into particular controversies. *See* Gertz v. Robert Welch, Inc., 418 U.S. 323, 94 S.Ct. 2997, 41 L.Ed.2d 789 (1974). Peter Schuler is the plaintiff in the computer-aided exercise; his status as a public figure or a private figure is not free from doubt, *see generally* W. PAGE KEETON (ED.), PROSSER AND KEETON ON THE LAW OF TORTS § 113 (5th ed. 1985), but for purposes of this exercise, you should assume that Schuler is a public figure.

applies. The United States Court of Appeals for the District of Columbia Circuit held that that requirement need not be considered at the summary judgment stage. 241 U.S.App.D.C. 246, 746 F.2d 1563 (1984). We granted certiorari, 471 U.S. 1134, 105 S.Ct. 2672, 86 L.Ed.2d 691 (1985), because that holding was in conflict with decisions of several other Courts of Appeals, which had held that the *New York Times* requirement of clear and convincing evidence must be considered on a motion for summary judgment. We now reverse.

[§ 3]

Respondent Liberty Lobby, Inc., is a not-for-profit corporation and self-described "citizens' lobby." Respondent Willis Carto is its founder and treasurer. In October 1981, The Investigator magazine published two articles: "The Private World of Willis Carto" and "Yockey: Profile of an American Hitler." These articles were introduced by a third, shorter article entitled "America's Neo–Nazi Underground: Did *Mein Kampf* Spawn Yockey's *Imperium,* a Book Revived by Carto's Liberty Lobby?" These articles portrayed the respondents as neo-Nazi, anti-Semitic, racist, and Fascist.

[§ 4]

Respondents filed this diversity libel action in the United States District Court for the District of Columbia, alleging that some 28 statements and 2 illustrations in the 3 articles were false and derogatory. Named as defendants in the action were petitioner Jack Anderson, the publisher of The Investigator, petitioner Bill Adkins, president and chief executive officer of the Investigator Publishing Co., and petitioner Investigator Publishing Co. itself.

[§ 5]

Following discovery, petitioners moved for summary judgment pursuant to Rule 56. In their motion, petitioners asserted that because the respondents are public figures they were required to prove their case under the standards set forth in *New York Times.* Petitioners also asserted that summary judgment was proper because actual malice was absent as a matter of law. In support of this latter assertion, petitioners submitted the affidavit of Charles Bermant, an employee of petitioners and the author of the two longer articles. In this affidavit, Bermant stated that he had spent a substantial amount of time researching and writing the articles and that his facts were obtained from a wide variety of sources. He also stated that he had at all times believed and still believed that the facts contained in the articles were truthful and accurate. Attached to this affidavit was an appendix in which Bermant detailed the sources for each of the statements alleged by the respondents to be libelous.

[§ 6]

Respondents opposed the motion for summary judgment, asserting that there were numerous inaccuracies in the articles and claiming that an issue of actual malice was presented by virtue of the fact that in preparing the articles Bermant had relied on several sources that the respondents asserted were patently unreliable. Generally, the respondents charged that the petitioners had failed adequately to verify their information before publishing. The respondents also presented evidence that William McGaw, an editor of The Investigator, had told petitioner Adkins before publication that the articles were "terrible" and "ridiculous."

* * *

[§ 7]

Our inquiry is whether the Court of Appeals erred in holding that the heightened evidentiary requirements that apply to proof of actual malice in this *New York Times* case need not be considered for the purposes of a motion for summary judgment. Rule 56(c) of the Federal Rules of Civil Procedure provides that summary judgment "shall be rendered forthwith if the pleadings, depositions, answers to interrogatories, and admissions on file, together with the affidavits, if any, show that there is no genuine issue as to any material fact and that the moving party is entitled to a judgment as a matter of law." By its very terms, this standard provides that the mere existence of *some* alleged factual dispute between the parties will not defeat an otherwise properly supported motion for summary judgment; the requirement is that there be no *genuine* issue of *material* fact.

[§ 8]

As to materiality, the substantive law will identify which facts are material. Only disputes over facts that might affect the outcome of the suit under the governing law will properly preclude the entry of summary judgment. Factual disputes that are irrelevant or unnecessary will not be counted. See generally 10A C. Wright, A. Miller & M. Kane, Federal Practice and Procedure § 2725, pp. 93–95 (1983). This materiality inquiry is independent of and separate from the question of the incorporation of the evidentiary standard into the summary judgment determination. That is, while the materiality determination rests on the substantive law, it is the substantive law's identification of which facts are critical and which facts are irrelevant that governs. Any proof or evidentiary requirements imposed by the substantive law are not germane to this inquiry, since materiality is only a criterion for categorizing factual disputes in their relation to the legal elements of the claim and not a criterion for evaluating the evidentiary underpinnings of those disputes.

[§ 9]

More important for present purposes, summary judgment will not lie if the dispute about a material fact is "genuine," that is, if the evidence is such that a reasonable jury could return a verdict for the nonmoving party. In *First National Bank of Arizona v. Cities Service Co.,* 391 U.S. 253, 88 S.Ct. 1575, 20 L.Ed.2d 569 (1968), we affirmed a grant of summary judgment for an antitrust defendant where the issue was whether there was a genuine factual dispute as to the existence of a conspiracy. We noted Rule 56(e)'s provision that a party opposing a properly supported motion for summary judgment " 'may not rest upon the mere allegations or denials of his pleading, but . . . must set forth specific facts showing that there is a genuine issue for trial.' " We observed further that

"[i]t is true that the issue of material fact required by Rule 56(c) to be present to entitle a party to proceed to trial is not required to be resolved conclusively in favor of the party asserting its existence; rather, all that is required is that sufficient evidence supporting the claimed factual dispute be shown to require a jury or judge to resolve the parties' differing versions of the truth at trial." 391 U.S., at 288–289, 88 S.Ct., at 1592.

We went on to hold that, in the face of the defendant's properly supported motion for summary judgment, the plaintiff could not rest on his allegations of a conspiracy to get to a jury without "any significant probative evidence tending to support the complaint." *Id.,* at 290, 88 S.Ct., at 1593.

[§ 10]

Again, in *Adickes v. S.H. Kress & Co.,* 398 U.S. 144, 90 S.Ct. 1598, 26 L.Ed.2d 142 (1970), the Court emphasized that the availability of summary judgment turned on whether a proper jury question was presented. There, one of the issues was whether there was a conspiracy between private persons and law enforcement officers. The District Court granted summary judgment for the defendants, stating that there was no evidence from which reasonably minded jurors might draw an inference of conspiracy. We reversed, pointing out that the moving parties' submissions had not foreclosed the possibility of the existence of certain facts from which "it would be open to a jury . . . to infer from the circumstances" that there had been a meeting of the minds. *Id.,* at 158–159, 90 S.Ct., at 1608, 1609.

[§ 11]

Our prior decisions may not have uniformly recited the same language in describing genuine factual issues under Rule 56, but it is clear enough from our recent cases that at the summary judgment stage the judge's function is not himself to weigh the evidence and determine the truth of the matter but to determine whether there is a genuine issue for trial. As *Adickes, supra,* and *Cities Service, supra,* indicate, there is no issue for trial unless there is sufficient evidence favoring the nonmoving party for a jury to return a verdict for that party. *Cities Service,* 391 U.S., at 288–289, 88 S.Ct., at 1592. If the evidence is merely colorable, *Dombrowski v. Eastland,* 387 U.S. 82, 87 S.Ct. 1425, 18 L.Ed.2d 577 (1967) (*per curiam*), or is not significantly probative, *Cities Service, supra,* at 290, 88 S.Ct., at 1592, summary judgment may be granted.

[§ 12]

That this is the proper focus of the inquiry is strongly suggested by the Rule itself. Rule 56(e) provides that, when a properly supported motion for summary judgment is made,[7] the adverse party "must set forth specific facts showing that there is a genuine issue for trial." And, as we noted above, Rule 56(c) provides that the trial judge shall then grant summary judgment if there is no genuine issue as to any material fact and if the moving party is entitled to judgment as a matter of law. There is no requirement that the trial judge make findings of fact. The inquiry performed is the threshold inquiry of determining whether there is the need for a trial—whether, in other words, there are any genuine factual issues that properly can be resolved only by a finder of fact because they may reasonably be resolved in favor of either party.

[§ 13]

Petitioners suggest, and we agree, that this standard mirrors the standard for a directed verdict under Federal Rule of Civil Procedure 50(a), which is that the trial judge must direct a verdict if, under the governing law, there can be but one reasonable conclusion as to the verdict. *Brady v. Southern R. Co.,* 320 U.S.

---

7. [Footnote by the Court.] Our analysis here does not address the question of the initial burden of production of evidence placed by Rule 56 on the party moving for summary judgment. See *Celotex Corp. v. Catrett,* 477 U.S. 317, 106 S.Ct. 2548, 91 L.Ed.2d 265 (1986). Respondents have not raised this issue here, and for the purposes of our discussion we assume that the moving party has met initially the requisite evidentiary burden.

476, 479–480, 64 S.Ct. 232, 234, 88 L.Ed. 239 (1943). If reasonable minds could differ as to the import of the evidence, however, a verdict should not be directed. *Wilkerson v. McCarthy,* 336 U.S. 53, 62, 69 S.Ct. 413, 417, 93 L.Ed. 497 (1949). . . .

[§ 14]

The Court has said that summary judgment should be granted where the evidence is such that it "would require a directed verdict for the moving party." *Sartor v. Arkansas Gas Corp.,* 321 U.S. 620, 624, 64 S.Ct. 724, 727, 88 L.Ed. 967 (1944). And we have noted that the "genuine issue" summary judgment standard is "very close" to the "reasonable jury" directed verdict standard: "The primary difference between the two motions is procedural; summary judgment motions are usually made before trial and decided on documentary evidence, while directed verdict motions are made at trial and decided on the evidence that has been admitted." *Bill Johnson's Restaurants, Inc. v. NLRB,* 461 U.S. 731, 745, n. 11, 103 S.Ct. 2161, 2171, n. 11, 76 L.Ed.2d 277 (1983). In essence, though, the inquiry under each is the same: whether the evidence presents a sufficient disagreement to require submission to a jury or whether it is so one-sided that one party must prevail as a matter of law.

[§ 15]

Progressing to the specific issue in this case, we are convinced that the inquiry involved in a ruling on a motion for summary judgment or for a directed verdict necessarily implicates the substantive evidentiary standard of proof that would apply at the trial on the merits. If the defendant in a run-of-the-mill civil case moves for summary judgment or for a directed verdict based on the lack of proof of a material fact, the judge must ask himself not whether he thinks the evidence unmistakably favors one side or the other but whether a fair-minded jury could return a verdict for the plaintiff on the evidence presented. The mere existence of a scintilla of evidence in support of the plaintiff's position will be insufficient; there must be evidence on which the jury could reasonably find for the plaintiff. The judge's inquiry, therefore, unavoidably asks whether reasonable jurors could find by a preponderance of the evidence that the plaintiff is entitled to a verdict—"whether there is [evidence] upon which a jury can properly proceed to find a verdict for the party producing it, upon whom the *onus* of proof is imposed." *Munson, supra,* 14 Wall., at 448.

[§ 16]

. . . [W]here the First Amendment mandates a "clear and convincing" standard, the trial judge in disposing of a directed verdict motion should consider whether a reasonable factfinder could conclude, for example, that the plaintiff had shown actual malice with convincing clarity.

* * *

[§ 17]

Just as the "convincing clarity" requirement is relevant in ruling on a motion for directed verdict, it is relevant in ruling on a motion for summary judgment. When determining if a genuine factual issue as to actual malice exists in a libel suit brought by a public figure, a trial judge must bear in mind the actual quantum and quality of proof necessary to support liability under *New York Times*. For example, there is no genuine issue if the evidence presented in the opposing affidavits is of insufficient caliber or quantity to allow a rational finder of fact to find actual malice by clear and convincing evidence.

[§ 18]

Our holding that the clear-and-convincing standard of proof should be taken into account in ruling on summary judgment motions does not denigrate the role of the jury. It by no means authorizes trial on affidavits. Credibility determinations, the weighing of the evidence, and the drawing of legitimate inferences from the facts are jury functions, not those of a judge, whether he is ruling on a motion for summary judgment or for a directed verdict. The evidence of the non-movant is to be believed, and all justifiable inferences are to be drawn in his favor. *Adickes*, 398 U.S., at 158–159, 90 S.Ct., at 1608–1609. Neither do we suggest that the trial courts should act other than with caution in granting summary judgment or that the trial court may not deny summary judgment in a case where there is reason to believe that the better course would be to proceed to a full trial. *Kennedy v. Silas Mason Co.*, 334 U.S. 249, 68 S.Ct. 1031, 92 L.Ed. 1347 (1948).

[§ 19]

In sum, we conclude that the determination of whether a given factual dispute requires submission to a jury must be guided by the substantive evidentiary standards that apply to the case. This is true at both the directed verdict and summary judgment stages. Consequently, where the *New York Times* "clear and convincing" evidence requirement applies, the trial judge's summary judgment

237

inquiry as to whether a genuine issue exists will be whether the evidence presented is such that a jury applying that evidentiary standard could reasonably find for either the plaintiff or the defendant. Thus, where the factual dispute concerns actual malice, clearly a material issue in a *New York Times* case, the appropriate summary judgment question will be whether the evidence in the record could support a reasonable jury finding either that the plaintiff has shown actual malice by clear and convincing evidence or that the plaintiff has not.

* * *

[§ 20]

Because the Court of Appeals did not apply the correct standard in reviewing the District Court's grant of summary judgment, we vacate its decision and remand the case for further proceedings consistent with this opinion.

It is so ordered.

II. COMPUTER EXERCISE: CALI CIV 13

The computer-aided exercise, CALI CIV 13: Summary Judgment, is based on a case involving a claim for defamation and a counterclaim for battery. The elements of defamation can be found in Exercise Three III.B. Please re-read them now. The elements of battery are reproduced here in section II.A below. After studying the elements of both torts, and the facts of the case in II.B. below, answer the questions posed in II.C. below, and then go to the computer to test your answers.

A. The Law of Battery

The elements of the tort of battery[8] can be found in RE-STATEMENT (SECOND) OF TORTS §§ 13, 18 (1965):

§ 13. Battery: Harmful Contact

An actor is subject to liability to another for battery if

---

8. Should you wish additional understanding of battery, work through the CALI computer-aided exercises Battery Basics and Battery Puzzlers found in the torts section.

(a) he acts intending to cause a harmful or offensive contact with the person of the other or a third person, or an imminent apprehension of such a contact, and

(b) a harmful contact with the person of the other directly or indirectly results.

§ 18. Battery: Offensive Contact

(1) An actor is subject to liability to another for battery if

(a) he acts intending to cause a harmful or offensive contact with the person of the other or a third person, or an imminent apprehension of such a contact, and

(b) an offensive contact with the person of the other directly or indirectly results.

(2) An act which is not done with the intention stated in Subsection (1,a) does not make the actor liable to the other for a mere offensive contact with the other's person although the act involves an unreasonable risk of inflicting it and, therefore, would be negligent or reckless if the risk threatened bodily harm.

B.   The Facts of the Case

You are the federal district judge in the District of Wisdom. Your special term calendar for today shows a hearing on two motions for summary judgment in the case of Peter Schuler v. David Dour. [Note that this exercise, while self-contained, is a continuation of the facts in Exercise Three.] Defendant Dour has moved for summary judgment on plaintiff's claim of defamation; plaintiff Schuler has moved for summary judgment on defendant's counterclaim for battery. Your law clerk has prepared the following summary of the contents of the case file.

1.   The complaint. Plaintiff Peter Schuler is a student at Dakota State College. His student activism has made him a "name" on campus, resulting in his recent election as student body president. Since his election, Schuler has become even more active, and the most recent demonstration resulted in his photograph on page one of the local newspaper together with a brief interview. Two days later, a letter to the editor in the newspaper from David Dour questioned why anyone would follow Schuler, "who is a known user of crack cocaine."

Schuler alleges Dour knew the statement was false or he acted in reckless disregard of whether it was false. He says Dour has been out to get him ever since he was reinstated as a student at

239

Dakota State. Schuler had been the subject of a disciplinary hearing, and Dour had made the crack allegation at that time, but when Schuler filed a defamation suit, all parties eventually agreed to drop the whole matter. [*See* Exercise Three.]

2. The Answer and Counterclaim. Defendant David Dour is a professor at Dakota State College. He admits writing the letter to the editor, but denies all other allegations in the complaint, including that he knew the allegation of crack use was false or that he acted in reckless disregard of whether it was false. He alleges that he relied on "multiple reliable sources" in making the statement.

For a counterclaim, Dour alleges that Schuler came into his seminar classroom in a rage about the letter. Schuler battered Dour by pushing him out the first floor window, causing severe cuts and bruises and a broken pelvis.

3. The Reply. Schuler admits entering the doorway of the seminar room, denies touching Dour who was across the room, and alleges he is without information or belief as to Dour's injuries.

4. Medical Report. Dr. Anne Hickman, who examined Schuler at the discovery demand of Dour, reports that no traces of cocaine were found in Schuler. Any cocaine use in the past several months would have been revealed.

5. Oral Deposition of Schuler. Schuler denies ever using crack or any other form of cocaine. He denies ever using any drugs. He believes Dour "well knew" the crack allegation was false because he had made it before at the disciplinary proceedings, then quickly withdrew it when Schuler filed the first lawsuit. Schuler admits stepping into the seminar room, but denies ever touching or even approaching Dour, and says Dour appeared to fall out the window on his own.

6. Oral Deposition of Dour. Dour admits he has never personally seen Schuler use crack, but maintains he did not hold actual malice because he based the accusation on "reliable sources." He named the sources as three students at Dakota State: Jane Abbott, John Bauer, and Cynthia Croswell. Despite vigorous cross examination, Dour held fast to his story that he thought the report true. He says that he even tried to reconfirm the statement with the three students, but was unable to reach them in the short time before he sent off the letter to the editor, because he "had to strike while the iron was hot."

As to his claim of battery, Dour says he was sitting in the windowwell, teaching his seminar, when Schuler stormed into the room. "The next thing I knew, I was on the ground outside with a broken pelvis. Schuler must have pushed me."

7. Oral Deposition of Jane Abbott. Abbott states that shortly before the disciplinary hearing, she glanced through a window and saw a person using crack. She was taking a class from Professor Dour at the time, and informed him she had seen Schuler using crack. Dour told her he would take care of the matter. At the start of the next semester, Abbott had a chance encounter with Schuler that made her realize he had not been the person she saw through the window. She tried to call Dour once or twice, and left her name, but he never returned her calls. She has not talked to Dour since her class with him ended.

8. Affidavits of John Bauer and Cynthia Croswell. Both Bauer and Croswell aver that they are students of Professor Dour's and were sympathetic to his previous difficulties with Schuler in the disciplinary hearing, word of which had leaked across campus. Both Bauer and Croswell state that after the hearing, they told Dour he was doing the right thing, trying to rid the campus of a "known drug user."

9. Affidavits of Dave Duncan and Emily Early. Both Duncan and Early were students in Dour's seminar class. They aver that Schuler stomped into the doorway, but never entered the room. Dour was apparently so startled that he fell backwards out the window.

10. Plaintiff Schuler's Motion and Supporting Memorandum in Favor of Summary Judgment on the Counterclaim for Battery and Memorandum Opposing Summary Judgment on the Claim for Defamation.

11. Defendant Dour's Motion and Supporting Memorandum in Favor of Summary Judgment on the Claim for Defamation and Memorandum Opposing Summary Judgment on the Counterclaim for Battery.

C. Questions

Please answer "yes," "no," or "maybe" to the following questions. If you believe substantial arguments exist on both sides of the question, you should respond "maybe." Do not, however, base a "maybe" answer on conceivable but frivolous legal arguments. [Note the question numbers correspond to those in the computer exercise.]

Q–1. Should summary judgment be granted to plaintiff Peter Schuler on defendant David Dour's counterclaim for battery?

Your answer: _____

Q–2a. If you answered "no," what genuine issue of material fact cannot be determined on the motion?

Your answer: _____

Q–3a. If you answered "yes" or "maybe," what issue can be resolved (or may arguably be resolved) as not a genuine issue of material fact, allowing judgment to be ordered?

Your answer: _____

Q–11. Should summary judgment be granted to defendant David Dour on plaintiff Peter Schuler's claim for defamation?

Your answer: _____

Q–12a. If you answered "no," what genuine issue of material fact cannot be determined on the motion?

Your answer: _____

Q–12b. If you answered "yes," what issue can be resolved as not a genuine issue of material fact, allowing summary judgment to be ordered?

Your answer: _____

Q–12c. If you answered "maybe," what issue arguably can be resolved as not a genuine issue of material fact, allowing summary judgment to be ordered?

Your answer: _____

————————

You are now ready to go to the computer terminal. Take this exercise with you.

EXERCISE NINE

Judgment as a Matter of Law

I. JUDGMENT AS A MATTER OF LAW

A. Controlling the Jury

The judgment as a matter of law is one of many devices available to the judge to control the freedom of the jury.[1] It is probably the most important. Before discussing this device, we sketch briefly some policy arguments for and against restricting jury freedom.

Two principal arguments favor restricting jury freedom. First, without a method to take cases away from the jury, the court would be unable to dispose of frivolous cases prior to trial. For example, a person sues her neighbor, claiming the neighbor was rude to her. If the jury were totally free to decide issues of law and fact, the plaintiff would be entitled to a jury trial on the issue of whether being rude to one's neighbor is actionable. Or take a case in which the facts alleged in the complaint state a claim upon which relief can be granted, but no significant evidence supports the claim. For example, a person believes he is being poisoned by a neighbor, and so alleges in the complaint. The only evidence the plaintiff can produce is testimony that his neighbor said churlish things about him. Obviously, there ought to be some way of preventing such cases from going to the jury. The normal jury would not even want to hear them.

1. Many other devices available during and after trial, including rulings on evidence and the motion for new trial, also control jury freedom. This exercise deals only with judgment as a matter of law and its closely-related kin, the binding instruction.

A second reason for restricting jury freedom is to prevent jury lawlessness. Were a jury allowed to decide cases on an ad hoc basis, the law would be both uncertain and inconsistent. Parties in like positions would not be treated alike, and the uncertainty would encourage litigation. A jury might decide to award damages because it was prejudiced against the defendant, even though no rule of law supported its decision. A sympathetic jury might decide to award damages to an injured person even though no evidence connects defendant to the injury. The judgment as a matter of law, and the lesser power to grant a new trial when the verdict is against the weight of the evidence, provide a degree of control by the trial court, which itself is subject to control by a multi-judge appellate court.

Arrayed against these arguments are those favoring jury freedom:

1.   The jury possesses a collective wealth of common sense that allows it effectively to evaluate the testimony of ordinary witnesses.

2.   The jury's collective memory may be superior to the memory of a single judge. The jurors, working together, may be able to do a better job of piecing together the testimony.

3.   Juries are less susceptible to corruption or other forms of improper influence than are judges. The jury is an ad hoc body summoned for only a few cases, and can perform its duties without feeling the tug of conflicting personal loyalties.

4.   The jury, because it is an ad hoc body, may have more courage than the judge. Even when not elected, the judge may be subject to political influence, or at least the force of public opinion. In a controversial case, the judge may try to reach a compromise instead of giving complete victory to a controversial litigant. The jury may be more willing to take controversial stances.

5.   Many factual disputes in lawsuits are not really susceptible to rational determination. By delegating decision of these factual disputes to a multi-person body that is perceived as non-political and neutral, the judicial system may produce decisions that are more satisfying to the litigants than would be the case if a single judge made these difficult decisions.

These arguments in favor of jury freedom are stronger when applied to some aspects of the jury's job than others. When the jury makes a decision about the credibility of a witness, i.e., when it decides whether the witness is testifying falsely or mistakenly, the jury's collective competence may be superior to that of the trial judge. Common sense and collective memory may give the jury greater power to search out inconsistencies in testimony or to understand ordinary witnesses. Also, the bad judge—the one who is subject to improper influence or who does not have the courage to reach a proper decision—is less subject to appellate review on credibility decisions than on the other decisions that a trial judge must make. This limit on appellate control stems from the fact that credibility decisions are often based upon the appearance and demeanor of the witness at trial—whether the witness hesitated when giving testimony, whether the witness appeared evasive, and so forth. An appellate court cannot recapture the demeanor of a witness on the basis of the "cold record." Therefore, credibility decisions are normally left to the fact-finder at trial. When this is done, a choice must be made about giving the power to make these credibility decisions either to the trial judge or to the jury. Many would favor giving the power to the jury.

In contrast, when the decision at trial involves an issue of law, or an issue of whether certain inferences can be drawn from certain facts, the "cold record" is quite adequate for purposes of appellate review. Therefore, the arbitrary, corrupt, or incompetent trial judge can be controlled by the appellate court; less reason exists for sending these issues to the jury. Moreover, the trial judge is often better qualified to decide these issues than is the jury.

B. Judgment as a Matter of Law

1. Directed Verdict and JNOV

For hundreds of years, courts and lawyers used the devices of *directed verdict* and *JNOV* (judgment n.o.v. or judgment *non obstante veredicto*). The only substantial difference between these two devices was the timing of the motion. The motion for directed verdict was made after the opponent had rested her case, or at the close of all the evidence. In either event, the motion was made before the case was given to the jury. The motion for judgment n.o.v. was a motion for directed verdict delayed until after the jury had returned its verdict. Hence, the party was asking the court to order entry of judgment in its favor notwithstanding the jury's verdict in favor of the opponent.

The terminology, though not the timing or purpose of the motions, changed for the federal courts in 1991. By amendment to Fed.R.Civ.P. 50, the directed verdict and JNOV motions are now the same motion: a motion for *judgment as a matter of law*. The idea is that the JNOV is actually a reserved motion for directed verdict. The common name was adopted to recognize that fact and also to recognize that the directed verdict and the JNOV are really the same motion made at different stages of the proceeding.[2] In federal courts today, any motion for directed verdict or for JNOV will be treated as a motion for judgment as a matter of law.

We refer to the judgment as a matter of law, but of course the older cases, including the three reproduced later in this exercise, refer to directed verdict and JNOV. Many states also continue to use the terminology of directed verdict and JNOV. One can expect lawyers to continue to use the terms, even in federal courts, for some time to come.

The timing of the motion for judgment as a matter of law gives the trial court the option of ruling either before or after the jury's verdict. A wise judge who is unsure about whether the motion should be granted prior to submission of the case to the jury may decide to wait until after the jury has returned its verdict. The jury may moot the issue by returning a verdict in favor of the proponent of the motion. Even when the jury returns a verdict against the proponent, the proponent will almost certainly move again for judgment as a matter of law later. Then the trial judge can grant the motion.

The decision to wait may save time and money. If the appellate court decides that the trial judge was wrong in granting the motion after the verdict, it can reinstate the jury verdict instead of remanding for a new trial. That saves the litigants and the court system the cost of another trial. When the trial judge grants the motion prior to submission to the jury, and the appellate court decides the trial judge was wrong, the only likely option is to grant an entire new trial.

On the other hand, judges must decide motions properly. In a case when the jury should not be allowed to return a verdict in favor of one of the parties, granting the motion prior to submission to the jury saves the jury from going through the useless charade of returning a verdict that will soon be nullified.

The standard for granting a judgment as a matter of law [Fed.R.Civ.P. 50(a)] before the case goes to the jury or a "renewed" judgment as a matter of law [Fed.R.Civ.P. 50(b)] after the jury verdict is returned is necessarily the same, at least in theory. In practice, however, some judges require a more impressive showing

---

2. In federal practice, a motion for directed verdict had to be made at the close of all the evidence in order to preserve one's right to make the motion for judgment n.o.v. This requirement is preserved after the amendment: a motion for judgment as a matter of law must be made at the close of all the evidence in order for a party to renew the motion after the verdict is returned (old JNOV). This requirement is rooted in the history of the right to jury trial. *See* CHARLES A. WRIGHT & MARY KAY KANE, THE LAW OF FEDERAL COURTS § 95, at 685–86 (6th ed. 2002).

for a judgment as a matter of law before verdict (old directed verdict) than after verdict (old JNOV). This is so because of the differing treatments on appeal discussed above and also because the judge may be reluctant to take a case from a jury that has sat through the entire trial.

Stated generally, and therefore to some extent incompletely, the question whether a judgment as a matter of law should be granted turns upon whether the jury could reasonably return a verdict in favor of the party opposing the motion. If no reasonable jury could find for that party on the basis of the evidence that has been presented to it, i.e., reasonable minds could not differ, then the motion should be granted. As you will see later, this standard, though generally true, is in need of some qualification.

2. Binding Instructions

The judgment as a matter of law standard is of central importance in understanding another device for controlling the jury—the binding instruction. A binding instruction tells the jury that it must find a certain fact to be true; the judge decides the issue. The binding instruction differs from the ordinary instruction, which informs the jury about the law and tells the jury to apply the facts as *it* finds them.

Example:

In a slander case, defendant in the answer denies publication of a statement calling plaintiff an LSD user and raises the affirmative defense of truth. In the opening statement to the jury, defendant's lawyer states that the defense expects to prove both that the LSD statement was made privately (i.e., only to the plaintiff, so the element of publication is missing) and that the LSD statement was true.

Defendant's lawyer introduces no evidence that would support a reasonable finding the LSD statement was true. There is a genuine dispute, however, about whether the LSD statement was made publicly or privately.

In instructing the jurors, the court will tell them they can not find that the LSD statement was true, and that the only issue for their decision is whether the LSD statement was made privately. The court would issue a "binding instruction" on the issue of truth or falsity.

The binding instruction amounts to a partial judgment as a matter of law. It is issued when one of the parties would not be entitled to a favorable jury determination on a particular issue, but could still win the case because the jury might reasonably find favorably on other issues. The standard for granting a binding instruction is the same as the standard for granting a judgment as a matter of law.

Often, whether a party is entitled to a judgment or binding instruction on a certain issue will depend upon which party bears the "burden of proof" on that issue. In saying that a party bears the burden of proof, we mean that the party bears both the burden of persuasion and the initial burden of production.

3. Burdens of Production and Persuasion

While we commonly hear of the burden of proof, a more exacting analysis identifies two burdens of proof: the burden of production of evidence and the burden of persuading the jury.

A party is said to bear the *burden of production,* also called the burden of going forward with the evidence, on a particular issue if failure to offer evidence sufficient to support a jury determination on the issue will result in an adverse judgment as a matter of law against her.[3] In other words, the party with the burden of production must go forward and submit sufficient evidence so that the court can conclude that a reasonable juror *could* find more likely than not in favor of that party's position on all issues essential to her case.[4]

Obviously, the allocation of the burden of production is of great importance in deciding which party will be able to prevail on a motion for judgment as a matter of law. Where to allocate the production burden is a difficult question, and involves consideration of many possible factors.[5] At the same time, we must recognize that in the broad mine run of cases, the plaintiff, as the party attempting to change the status quo, bears the burden of production (and the burden of persuasion).

3. The party bearing the burden of production on an issue will suffer an adverse judgment if the issue is dispositive of the whole lawsuit. If it is not, e.g., it is only one of several alternative theories of recovery or defense, the party will suffer an adverse binding instruction on the issue.

4. Different courts at different times have established different tests for the sufficiency of the evidence necessary to defeat a judgment as a matter of law motion. The most popular tests are 1) the scintilla test, 2) the substantial evidence test, and 3) the greater weight of the evidence test. The most commonly used test, and the one that makes the most sense, is the one identified in the text: the party with the burden of production must submit sufficient evidence so that the court can decide a reasonable juror could find the existence of the fact more likely than not.

5. *See* Roger C. Park, David P. Leonard & Steven H. Goldberg, Evidence Law: A Student's Guide to the Law of Evidence as Applied in American Trials §§ 4.05–4.06 (2d ed. 2004).

Example:

In a slander case, plaintiff alleges, and defendant admits, that defendant called plaintiff a thief. The only issue raised by the pleadings is whether the statement was true, i.e., whether plaintiff is a thief. Neither party produces any evidence on this issue. If plaintiff bears the burden of producing evidence that he is not a thief, he will suffer an adverse judgment as a matter of law. If defendant bears the burden of producing evidence that plaintiff is a thief, she will suffer an adverse judgment as a matter of law.

The foregoing example is a case in which neither party produces *any* evidence on a dispositive issue of fact. That is the easiest case. A judgment as a matter of law will often be justified, however, even when the party with the burden of production produces some evidence relevant to the issue.

Example:

Plaintiff alleges that defendant called him a thief, and defendant denies making the statement. On the issue, plaintiff introduces only evidence that the defendant disliked him. This testimony has some tendency to suggest that the defendant would say bad things about the plaintiff. Yet it is a slender reed upon which to base a determination that she called plaintiff a thief. A jury verdict in plaintiff's favor would be nearly as arbitrary as one based on no evidence at all. The judge would be justified in granting a judgment as a matter of law because the plaintiff has not produced sufficient evidence to satisfy his burden of production.

The *burden of production* should be distinguished from the *burden of persuasion.* A party bearing the burden of production on an issue must produce sufficient evidence to create an issue for the jury. The rules about burden of production are applied by the *court* in the decision whether to send the issue to the jury. Once an issue is sent to the jury, the judge instructs the jury about the burden of persuasion, and rules about burden of persuasion are applied by the *jury* in determining which party should receive a favorable jury verdict.

Example:

The plaintiff bears the burden of persuasion on fact X. Under the relevant law, the party who bears the burden of persuasion must establish that the existence of the fact in dispute is more probable than its nonexistence, or in other words, more likely than not.[6] The court will instruct the jury about this rule. If the jury determines that the existence and nonexistence of fact X are equally probable, it should return a verdict against the plaintiff.

6. *See* ROGER C. PARK, DAVID P. LEONARD & STEVEN H. GOLDBERG, EVIDENCE LAW: A STUDENT'S GUIDE TO THE LAW OF EVIDENCE AS APPLIED IN AMERICAN TRIALS § 4.04 (2d ed. 2004).

Although the concepts of production burden and persuasion burden are distinct, the weight of the production burden depends upon the weight of the persuasion burden. For example, if a party has the burden of persuading the jury that there is "virtual certainty" that fact X is true, then to satisfy the burden of production the party would need to convince the judge that he has produced evidence sufficient to allow a reasonable jury to determine that fact X is true to a virtual certainty. Note that this is not the same thing as saying that the party must convince the *judge* that fact X is true to a virtual certainty. A judge might believe that the existence of fact X has not been established to a virtual certainty, while simultaneously believing that a reasonable jury could find its existence more likely than not.

For this exercise, you may assume that the burden of persuasion in civil actions is one of preponderance, i.e., showing that the existence of a fact is more probable than its nonexistence. Therefore, if the opponent of a judgment as a matter of law motion bears the burdens of production and persuasion, the court, in deciding whether that party came forward with sufficient evidence to satisfy the burden of production, must decide whether a reasonable jury could find the existence of the fact more probable—more likely—than not.

A party who bears the burden of persuasion and the initial burden of production is commonly said to bear the burden of proof. Usually the same party bears both burdens. In most jurisdictions, however, the burden of production can shift from one party to the other, and possibly back again, during the course of the trial. This shifting occurs when the party bearing the initial burden of production has produced evidence of such great weight that the *other* party will suffer an adverse judgment on the issue if it fails to produce evidence to the contrary.

Example:

Plaintiff sues defendant for slander, alleging that defendant called her an LSD user. The only issue for decision at trial is whether the statement was made. Plaintiff bears the burden of proof on this issue.

When plaintiff introduces evidence sufficient to permit a reasonable jury to find that the LSD statement was made, she has satisfied her burden of production and is entitled to go to the jury. Suppose plaintiff goes further, and produces evidence of such probative force that, in the absence of contrary evidence, no reasonable jury could find that the statement was *not* made. For example, plaintiff produces testimony of several unimpeached, disinterested witnesses who claim to have heard defendant make the statement. In most jurisdictions, the plaintiff would then be entitled to a judgment as a matter of law unless defendant produces some contrary evidence. In such circumstances, the burden of production has shifted to the defendant. The defendant must go forward to produce evidence sufficient to allow a reasonable juror to decide more likely than not that the statement was *not* made in order to take the case to the jury.

In the foregoing example, the plaintiff has the burden of proof, that is, the initial burden of production and the burden of persuasion. When she produces enough evidence to satisfy the burden of production, the case moves into the area of jury control. When the plaintiff produces overwhelming evidence, the burden of production shifts to the defendant, once again allowing the judge to take control. When the defendant produces evidence that contradicts plaintiff's evidence, the case will once again become a matter for the jury to decide.

While most jurisdictions permit the burden of *production* to shift, the usual rule is that the burden of *persuasion* never shifts. It remains always upon the party on whom it was originally cast. If the plaintiff bears the burden of persuasion upon an issue, then whenever the issue is sent to the jury, the jury will be instructed to find against the plaintiff if he has not satisfied the persuasion burden.[7] This instruction will be given whether or not the production burden shifted to the defendant at some point in the lawsuit.

Moreover, imposing the persuasion burden on the plaintiff affects the definition of both parties' burdens of production. In order to survive a motion for judgment as a matter of law, i.e., satisfy the burden of production, the plaintiff must produce evidence sufficient to permit a reasonable jury to find itself persuaded in her favor. In contrast, the defendant will survive a motion merely by showing that a reasonable jury could find itself *either* persuaded in his favor *or* in equipoise—that is, not persuaded by either side.

Examples:

(1) Plaintiff's decedent and defendant's decedent, driving from opposite directions, crash in the middle of the highway. Both plaintiff and defendant allege the other driver was solely at fault in crossing the center line. No evidence is submitted, since there are no witnesses and accident reconstruction is unavailable. The court will grant a judgment as a matter of law against plaintiff, the party with the burden of production, because no reasonable juror could find more likely than not in favor of plaintiff. At most, the jurors would be in equipoise as either proposition is equally likely on the evidence submitted.

7. In a few jurisdictions, the party bearing the burden of persuasion can shift it to the other side by establishing a fact that activates a presumption. *See* Unif. R.Evid. 301. The majority rule is contrary, however, and holds that even a presumption does not shift the burden of persuasion. *See* Fed.R.Evid. 301.

(2) Plaintiff farmer's cow is killed on defendant railroad's tracks. The only evidence shows that the cow was struck near both a downed fence that is the responsibility of the railroad to maintain and an open gate that is the responsibility of the farmer to keep closed. The court will grant a judgment as a matter of law against the plaintiff because no reasonable person could find more likely than not that the cow gained access to the tracks over the downed fence instead of through the open gate in this 50–50 case. The party with the burden of production must provide sufficient evidence so that a reasonable juror could assess the probabilities at least 51–49 in his favor.

4. Evidence Considered for Judgment as a Matter of Law

We have said that the issue for the court on a motion for judgment as a matter of law is whether the jury could reasonably return a verdict for the party opposing the motion. This statement is a useful simplification of the standard. In most jurisdictions, however, it is not precisely correct unless qualified, because the governing law imposes limits upon the evidence that the court may consider in determining whether a finding for the opponent would be reasonable.

No one questions the trial judge's authority to grant judgment when no evidence has been produced on a material issue, or when so little evidence has been produced by the party bearing the burden of proof that even considering only the evidence in his favor and believing all of it, no reasonable jury could find in his favor. Moreover, there seems to be general agreement that a judge should grant judgment when the only evidence in favor of the party with the burden of proof is incredible on its face—that is, it is incredible even in the absence of impeachment[8] of the testifying witnesses or contradiction[9] by other witnesses. For example, the jury cannot be allowed to base a verdict upon testimony by a

8. Impeachment refers to evidence that throws doubt upon the credibility of the witness by showing bias, bad character, prior inconsistent statements, etc. Often, this type of evidence is relevant only because the witness testifies at trial. For example, in a personal injury action between A and B, evidence that X is a convicted perjurer is relevant only if X testifies or if an out-of-court statement by X is admitted into evidence.

9. Contradiction is evidence that is inconsistent with the account given by the witness. For example, the witness testifies that defendant ran a red light; a contradicting witness testifies that the light was green.

The contradicting witness's testimony has impeachment value. For example, the jury might believe the second witness, decide therefore that the first witness is a liar, and disregard all of the first witness's testimony, including testimony that relates to matters other than the red light. The contradicting witness's testimony goes beyond impeaching the first witness, however. It is relevant to an issue in the lawsuit and would be admissible even if the first witness had not testified.

witness that he inhabits two bodies or that she saw the event by the light of the sun rising in the west.[10]

The typical situation is that the opponent of the motion has produced testimony that is not inherently incredible. In deciding whether to grant judgment, what evidence should the trial judge be allowed to consider? The judicial answers to this question can, if some variations are overlooked, be placed into three categories.

a. The Favorable–Evidence–Only Test

In determining whether a jury could reasonably find for the opponent of a judgment as a matter of law motion, the court should consider only the evidence favorable to the opponent, completely ignoring any unfavorable evidence.

This test gives the jury power to believe or disbelieve any witness (subject, of course, to the qualification that the jury may not believe a witness whose testimony is incredible on its face). For example, the jury may believe the testimony of a convicted perjurer even if it is contradicted by the testimony of 20 bishops. The testimony of the 20 bishops must be ignored by a judge ruling on the judgment as a matter of law motion because it is unfavorable to the opponent of the motion. Moreover, the jury may disbelieve the testimony of any witness, even if the witness has not been impeached or contradicted. Therefore, under this test, a court could not grant judgment in favor of a party bearing the burden of proof, since the jury might disbelieve all of that party's witnesses and find itself unpersuaded.

This test gives the jury a great deal of power, yet does not completely destroy the function of the judgment as a matter of law. The court can still grant judgment on grounds that, even believing all the favorable testimony and ignoring all other testimony, a jury could not reasonably determine that the party with the burden of proof had established a case by a preponderance of the evidence.

Example:

Decedent is found dead under conditions of apparent suicide. Decedent's widow brings a civil action against the defendant, claiming that the defendant killed her husband. She produces the testimony of W that a month before decedent's death, W saw decedent defeat defendant in a fistfight. Defendant produces 20 witnesses who were present at the

---

10. This is not to say that the court can disregard evidence it disbelieves. Standard law is that a judgment as a matter of law motion must be decided by the court without weighing credibility and granting all reasonable inferences to the party opposing the motion. A witness who testifies to facts not inherently incredible must be given full weight. Even a convicted perjurer's testimony may not be discounted.

time of the alleged fight. The 20 witnesses all testify that no fight occurred.

In determining whether to grant a directed verdict under the favorable-evidence-only test, the court must accept W's testimony that the fight took place. There is nothing inherently incredible about a fistfight, and the testimony of the 20 opposing witnesses must be ignored. The judge should still grant judgment for the defendant, however, because the jury could not reasonably infer that defendant committed murder merely on the basis of testimony that defendant had an earlier fistfight with decedent.

Another way of describing the favorable-evidence-only test is to say that the jury has the power to believe or disbelieve the direct evidence testimony of any witness, but it must be reasonable in drawing inferences from circumstantial evidence.[11]

b. The Qualified Favorable–Evidence Test

In deciding whether the jury could reasonably return a verdict in favor of the opponent of a judgment as a matter of law motion, the court should consider only (a) evidence favorable to the opponent, and (b) evidence unfavorable to the opponent that is not contradicted by direct evidence and that cannot reasonably be disbelieved. All other evidence must be disregarded.

This test still allows the jury to *believe* any testimony that is not inherently incredible; however, this test deprives the jury of the power to *disbelieve* whomever it pleases. The testimony of the convicted perjurer can still be accepted, even though contradicted by 20 bishops. The jury cannot disbelieve testimony that is not directly contradicted if it would be unreasonable to do so. Thus, this test permits granting judgment in favor of the party bearing the burden of proof.

11. Direct evidence supports a fact to be proved without any intervening inferences. In the above example, W's testimony about the fistfight is *direct evidence* that the fight took place, since W claims to have been an eyewitness. If the fact issue were whether the fistfight occurred, then the court would have no power to direct a verdict—the plaintiff's case would be supported by direct evidence that is not inherently incredible.

Circumstantial evidence is evidence that directly proves one fact, which fact then supports an *inference* that the fact to be proved is true. In the example given, W's testimony about the fistfight is *direct evidence* that the fight took place and *circumstantial evidence* that defendant murdered decedent. It does lend some support to the inference of murder by supplying a motive. If accompanied by other evidence of murder, it might be sufficiently probative to support circumstantially an inference of murder. Standing alone, however, it is not sufficient to support the inference.

Example:

P alleges in his complaint that D called him a murderer. D answers, denying that she made the statement and admitting all other allegations in the complaint. P has the burden of proof on whether the statement was made. P produces as witnesses 20 bishops who testify that they heard D make the statement. Their testimony is uncontradicted, unimpeached, and disinterested. D does not cross-examine the bishops and she rests without producing any evidence. P is entitled to judgment as a matter of law under the qualified favorable-evidence test.

Note that the qualified favorable-evidence test still gives the jury power to resolve contradictions in direct evidence. Thus, if D had taken the stand and denied making the statement, she would have been entitled to go to the jury despite the contrary testimony of 20 bishops.

Testimony can be contradicted either by direct evidence or by circumstantial evidence. If D takes the stand and denies making the statement, she has contradicted the bishops with direct evidence. Both the bishops and the defendant have testified about a fact that they claim to have perceived with their senses. In the following example, direct evidence is contradicted by circumstantial evidence.

Example:

Plaintiff and defendant have a collision in a traffic intersection. Twenty bishops testify that they were watching the traffic light in the intersection and it was red in plaintiff's direction. Their testimony is disinterested and unimpeached.

Plaintiff testifies that he was waiting for the light to change when he saw two cars in front of him start through the intersection. Plaintiff inferred that the light had changed from red to green and followed them, but does not claim that he actually saw the light change.

If believed, plaintiff's testimony supports a reasonable inference that the light had changed. Plaintiff has not, however, produced direct testimony that contradicts the bishops' testimony; plaintiff has contradicted the bishops with circumstantial evidence.

In the foregoing example, a belief in plaintiff's testimony is not logically inconsistent with belief in the bishops' testimony. Therefore, granting judgment would not deprive the jury of the power to believe the testimony of any witness; it would only deprive the jury of the power to disbelieve the bishops' testimony. Under the qualified favorable-evidence test, the trial judge would have power to grant judgment for defendant.

c. The All-the-Evidence Test

In deciding whether the jury could reasonably return a verdict in favor of the opponent of a judgment as a matter of law motion, the court should consider all the evidence, favorable or unfavorable, for both parties.

This test gives the trial judge power to resolve conflicts in direct testimony and to determine whether the jury could reasonably believe or disbelieve witnesses.

Example:

The only issue raised by the pleadings is whether defendant called plaintiff a murderer. Defendant has admitted all the other allegations of plaintiff's complaint. Twenty bishops testify that they heard defendant make the statement. Defendant denies making the statement. Under the all-the-evidence test, the trial judge could properly grant judgment as a matter of law against the defendant because the evidence is overwhelming and the jury could not reasonably believe her testimony over that of the 20 bishops.

The all-the-evidence test does not place the trial judge in the position of a juror. The judge is supposed to defer to the jury and grant judgment only when a jury verdict for the opposing party would be unreasonable.

Example:

The only issue raised by the pleadings is whether defendant called plaintiff a murderer. Defendant admitted all the other allegations of plaintiff's complaint.

Plaintiff testifies that defendant called him a murderer in the presence of third person T. Defendant denies making the statement, and T corroborates defendant's denial. The judge believes the defendant and T, yet recognizes that reasonable persons could differ about who was telling the truth. Under the all-the-evidence test, the judge should not grant judgment, since that would be weighing credibility.

The all-the-evidence test has been called the "set-aside" test, because courts adopting it have sometimes said that the judge should grant judgment if, looking at all the evidence, she would feel duty bound to set aside a verdict for the party opposing the motion for judgment as a matter of law.[12] Linking the test to setting

12. Setting aside a verdict refers to granting a new trial to the party against whom the jury has returned a verdict. *See generally* FLEMING JAMES, JR., GEOFFREY C. HAZARD, JR. & JOHN LEUBSDORF, CIVIL PROCEDURE § 7.21, at 451 n. 21 (5th ed. 2001). Granting a motion for a new trial differs from granting a motion for judgment as matter of law; the former gives the party against whom the motion is granted the opportunity to try the case a second time, while the latter does not.

Opinions enunciating the set-aside standard often do not make clear whether the standard for granting the new trial motion is the same as the standard for granting the judgment as a matter of law motion, although any court wishing to retain a principled distinction between the devices would have to grant the judgment as a matter of law motion only in particularly egregious cases when no reasonable juror

aside a contrary verdict, i.e., granting a new trial on the ground that the verdict is against the weight of the evidence, apparently allows the trial judge to resolve issues of credibility, at least to the extent of ruling that a reasonable jury could not believe a witness's testimony. Trial judges have this power when ruling on a motion for new trial, and so linking the judgment as a matter of law test gives them this power when ruling on a motion for judgment as a matter of law.

II. COMPUTER EXERCISE: CALI CIV 04

A. Introductory Note

This computer-aided exercise was written primarily to explore the three competing standards for judgment as a matter of law. The debate over the proper test to use to consider the evidence on such a motion continued in the federal courts—and state courts—for more than 50 years following the decision in Wilkerson v. McCarthy, 336 U.S. 53, 69 S.Ct. 413, 93 L.Ed. 497 (1949), reproduced at 265. The Supreme Court ended the debate for the federal courts in Reeves v. Sanderson Plumbing Prods., Inc., 530 U.S. 133, 150, 120 S.Ct. 2097, 2110, 147 L.Ed.2d 105, 121–22 (2000):

> Those decisions holding that review under Rule 50 should be limited to evidence favorable to the nonmovant appear to have their genesis in [*Wilkerson*]. * * * But subsequent decisions have clarified that [*Wilkerson*] was referring to the evidence to which the trial court should *give credence*, not to the evidence that the court should *review*. In the analogous contest of summary judgment under Rule 56, we have stated that the court must review the record "taken as a whole." [Citation omitted.] And the standard for granting summary judgment "mirrors" the standard for judgment as a matter of law, such that "the inquiry under each is the same." [Citations omitted.] It therefore follows that, in entertaining a motion for judgment as a matter of law, the court should review all of the evidence in the record.

> While the question of whether to use the favorable-evidence-only test, the qualified-favorable-evidence test, or the all-the-evidence test has been answered, the interpretations of the *Chamberlain*, *Wilkerson*, and *Simblest* opinions required in this lesson remain useful as an exercise in reading of opinions, recognition of holding and dictum, and synthesis of cases.

could find for the nonmoving party, not merely when the judge believes the verdict would be against the (great or clear) weight of the evidence.

B. Cases and Questions

Please read the following three federal cases on judgments as a matter of law (remember that these cases will refer to directed verdict and JNOV instead) and write answers to the questions before going to the computer terminal. Be prepared to give supporting reasons for your answers.

1. What arguments can be made that in the *Chamberlain* case, the Supreme Court endorsed the all-the-evidence test? Examine the *Chamberlain* opinion carefully for language supporting or refuting the proposition that the Court endorsed the all-the-evidence ("set-aside") test, and be prepared to cite sections of the opinion containing such language.

Your answer _____

2. What arguments can be made that the *Chamberlain* case is consistent with the favorable-evidence-only test or with the qualified favorable-evidence test?

Your answer _____

3. Is the *Wilkerson* case consistent with the theory that the Supreme Court follows the all-the-evidence test?

Your answer _____

4. Is the *Wilkerson* case consistent with the theory that the Supreme Court follows the favorable-evidence-only test?

Your answer _____

5. Is the *Wilkerson* case consistent with the theory that the Supreme Court follows the qualified favorable-evidence test?

Your answer _____

6. Is the *Simblest* case consistent with the theory that the Second Circuit has adopted the all-the-evidence test? The favorable-evidence-only test? The qualified favorable-evidence test?

Your answer _____

PENNSYLVANIA RAILROAD CO. v. CHAMBERLAIN

Supreme Court of the United States, 1933.
288 U.S. 333, 53 S.Ct. 391, 77 L.Ed. 819.

[§ 1]

MR. JUSTICE SUTHERLAND delivered the opinion of the Court.

This is an action brought by respondent against petitioner to recover for the death of a brakeman, alleged to have been caused

258

by petitioner's negligence. The complaint alleges that the deceased, at the time of the accident resulting in his death, was assisting in the yard work of breaking up and making up trains and in the classifying and assorting of cars operating in interstate commerce; that in pursuance of such work, while riding a cut of cars, other cars ridden by fellow employees were negligently caused to be brought into violent contact with those upon which deceased was riding, with the result that he was thrown therefrom to the railroad track and run over by a car or cars, inflicting injuries from which he died.

[§ 2]

At the conclusion of the evidence, the trial court directed the jury to find a verdict in favor of petitioner. Judgment upon a verdict so found was reversed by the court of appeals. Judge Swan dissenting. 59 F.(2d) 986.

[§ 3]

That part of the yard in which the accident occurred contained a lead track and a large number of switching tracks branching therefrom. The lead track crossed a "hump," and the work of car distribution consisted of pushing a train of cars by means of a locomotive to the top of the "hump," and then allowing the cars, in separate strings to descend by gravity, under the control of hand brakes, to their respective destinations in the various branch tracks. Deceased had charge of a string of two gondola cars, which he was piloting to track 14. Immediately ahead of him was a string of seven cars, and behind him a string of nine cars, both also destined for track 14. Soon after the cars ridden by deceased had passed to track 14, his body was found on that track some distance beyond the switch. He had evidently fallen onto the track and been run over by a car or cars.

[§ 4]

The case for respondent rests wholly upon the claim that the fall of deceased was caused by a violent collision of the string of nine cars with the string ridden by deceased. Three employees, riding the nine-car string, testified positively that no such collision occurred. They were corroborated by every other employee in a position to see, all testifying that there was no contact between the nine-car string and that of the deceased. The testimony of these witnesses, if believed, establishes beyond doubt that there was no collision between these two strings of cars, and that the nine-car string contributed in no way to the accident. The only witness who testified for the respondent was one Bainbridge; and it is upon his testimony alone that respondent's right to recover is sought to be upheld. His testimony is concisely stated, in its most favorable light for respondent, in the prevailing opinion below by Judge Learned Hand, as follows [p. 986]:

[§ 5]

"The plaintiff's only witness to the event, one Bainbridge, then employed by the road, stood close to the yardmaster's office, near the 'hump.' He professed to have paid little attention to what went on, but he did see the deceased riding at the rear of his cars, whose speed when they passed him he took to be about eight or ten miles. Shortly thereafter a second string passed which was shunted into another track and this was followed by the nine, which, according to the plaintiff's theory, collided with the deceased's. After the nine cars had passed at a somewhat greater speed than the deceased's, Bainbridge paid no more attention to either string for a while, but looked again when the deceased, who was still standing in his place, had passed the switch and onto the assorting track where he was bound. At that time his speed had been checked to about three miles, but the speed of the following nine cars had increased. They were just passing the switch, about four or five cars behind the deceased. Bainbridge looked away again and soon heard what he described as a 'loud crash,' not however an unusual event in a switching yard. Apparently this did not cause him at once to turn, but he did so shortly thereafter, and saw the two strings together, still moving, and the deceased no longer in sight. Later still his attention was attracted by shouts and he went to the spot and saw the deceased between the rails. Until he left to go to the accident, he had stood fifty feet to the north of the track where the accident happened, and about nine hundred feet from where the body was found."

[§ 6]

The court, although regarding Bainbridge's testimony as not only "somewhat suspicious in itself, but its contradiction . . . so manifold as to leave little doubt," held, nevertheless, that the question was one of fact depending upon the credibility of the witnesses, and that it was for the jury to determine, as between the one witness and the many, where the truth lay. The dissenting opinion of Judge Swan proceeds upon the theory that Bainbridge did not testify that in fact a collision had taken place, but inferred it because he heard a crash, and because thereafter the two strings of cars appeared to him to be moving together. It is correctly pointed out in that opinion, however, that the crash might have come from elsewhere in the busy yard and that Bainbridge was in no position to see whether the two strings of cars were actually together; that Bainbridge repeatedly said he was paying no particular attention; and that his position was such, being 900 feet from the place where the body was found and less than 50 feet from the side of the track in question, that he necessarily saw the strings of cars at such an acute angle that it would be physically impossible even for an attentive observer to tell whether the forward end of the nine-car cut was actually in contact with the rear end of the two-car cut. The dissenting opinion further points out that all the witnesses who were in a position to see testified that there was no collision; that respondent's evidence was wholly circumstantial, and the inferences which might otherwise be drawn from it were shown to be utterly erroneous unless all of petitioner's witnesses were willful perjurers. "This is not a case," the opinion proceeds, "where direct testimony to an essential fact is contradicted by direct testimony of other witnesses, though even there is it conceded a judgment as a matter of law might be proper in some circumstances. Here, when all the testimony was in, the circumstantial evidence in support of negligence was thought by the trial judge to be so insubstantial and insufficient that it did not justify submission to the jury."

[§ 7]

We thus summarize and quote from the prevailing and dissenting opinions, because they present the divergent views to be considered in reaching a correct determination of the question involved. It, of course, is true, generally, that where there is a direct conflict of testimony upon a matter of fact, the question must be left to the jury to determine without regard to the number of witnesses upon either side. But here there really is no conflict in the testimony as to the facts. The witnesses for petitioner flatly testified that there was no collision between the nine-car and the two-car strings. Bainbridge did not say there was such a collision. What he said was that he heard a "loud crash," which did not cause him at once to turn, but that shortly thereafter he did turn and saw the two strings of cars moving together with the deceased no longer in sight; that there was nothing unusual about the crash of cars—it happened every day; that there was nothing about this crash to attract his attention except that it was extra loud; that he paid no attention to it; that it was not sufficient to attract his attention. The record shows that there was a continuous movement of cars over and down the "hump," which were distributed among a large number of branch tracks within the yard, and that any two strings of these cars moving upon the same track might have come together and caused the crash which Bainbridge heard. There is no direct evidence that *in fact* the crash was occasioned by a collision of the two strings in question; and it is perfectly clear that no such fact was brought to Bainbridge's attention as a perception of the physical sense of sight or of hearing. At most there was an inference to that effect drawn from observed facts which gave equal support to the opposite inference that the crash was occasioned by the coming together of other strings of cars entirely away from the scene of the accident, or of the two-car string ridden by deceased and the seven-car string immediately ahead of it.

[§ 8]

We, therefore, have a case belonging to that class of cases where proven facts give equal support to each of two inconsistent inferences; in which event, neither of them being established, judgment, as a matter of law, must go against the party upon whom rests the necessity of sustaining one of these inferences as against the other, before he is entitled to recover.

[§ 9]

The rule is succinctly stated in *Smith v. First National Bank in Westfield*, 99 Mass. 605, 611–612, 97 Am.Dec. 59, quoted in the *Des Moines National Bank* case, *supra*:

"There being several inferences deducible from the facts which appear, and equally consistent with all those facts, the plaintiff has not maintained the proposition upon which alone he would be entitled to recover. There is strictly no evidence to warrant a jury in finding that the loss was occasioned by negligence and not by theft. When the evidence tends equally to sustain either of two inconsistent propositions, neither of them can be said to have been established by legitimate proof. A verdict in favor of the party bound to maintain one of those propositions against the other is necessarily wrong."

[§ 10]

That Bainbridge concluded from what he himself observed that the crash was due to a collision between the two strings of cars in question is sufficiently indicated by his statements. But this, of course, proves nothing, since it is not allowable for a witness to resolve the doubt as to which of two equally justifiable inferences shall be adopted by drawing a conclusion, which, if accepted, will result in a purely gratuitous award in favor of the party who has failed to sustain the burden of proof cast upon him by the law.

[§ 11]

And the desired inference is precluded for the further reason that respondent's right of recovery depends upon the existence of a particular fact which must be inferred from proven facts, and this is

not permissible in the face of the positive and otherwise uncontradicted testimony of unimpeached witnesses consistent with the facts
actually proved, from which testimony it affirmatively appears that
the fact sought to be inferred did not exist. This conclusion results
from a consideration of many decisions.... A rebuttable inference
of fact, as said by the court in the *Wabash Railroad* case, "must
necessarily yield to credible evidence of the actual occurrence."
And, as stated by the court in *George v. Mo. Pac. R.R. Co., supra,*
"It is well settled that where plaintiff's case is based upon an
inference or inferences, that the case must fail upon proof of
undisputed facts inconsistent with such inferences." Compare *Fresh
v. Gilson,* 16 Pet. 327, 330, 331, 10 L.Ed. 982. In *Southern Ry.
Co. v. Walters, supra,* the negligence charged was failure to stop a
train and flag a crossing before proceeding over it. The court
concluded that the only support for the charge was an inference
sought to be drawn from certain facts proved. In rejecting the
inference, this court said [p. 194]:

[§ 12]

"It is argued that it may be inferred from the speed of the train
when some of the witnesses observed it crossing other streets as
well as Bond Avenue, and from a guess of the engineer as to the
time required to get up such speed after a full stop, that none could
have been made at Bond Avenue. But the argument amounts to
mere speculation in view of the limited scope of the witnesses'
observation, the down grade of the railway tracks at the point, and
the time element involved. (Compare *Chicago, M. & St. P.R. Co.
v. Coogan,* 271 U.S. 472, 46 S.Ct. 564, 70 L.Ed. 1041.) Five
witnesses for defendant [employees] testified that a full stop was
made and the crossing flagged, and that no one was hit by the rear
of the tender, which was the front of the train.

[§ 13]

"An examination of the record requires the conclusion that the
evidence on the issue whether the train was stopped before
crossing Bond Avenue was so insubstantial and insufficient that it
did not justify a submission of that issue to the jury."

[§ 14]

Not only is Bainbridge's testimony considered as a whole
suspicious, insubstantial and insufficient, but his statement that
when he turned shortly after hearing the crash the two strings were
moving together is simply incredible if he meant thereby to be
understood as saying that he saw the two in contact; and if he
meant by the words "moving together" simply that they were

moving at the same time in the same direction but not in contact, the statement becomes immaterial. As we have already seen he was paying slight and only occasional attention to what was going on. The cars were eight or nine hundred feet from where he stood and moving almost directly away from him, his angle of vision being only 3°33' from a straight line. At that sharp angle and from that distance, near dusk of a misty evening (as the proof shows), the practical impossibility of the witness being able to see whether the front of the nine-car string was in contact with the back of the two-car string is apparent. And, certainly, in the light of these conditions, no verdict based upon a statement so unbelievable reasonably could be sustained as against the positive testimony to the contrary of unimpeached witnesses, all in a position to see, as this witness was not, the precise relation of the cars to one another. The fact that these witnesses were employees of the petitioner, under the circumstances here disclosed, does not impair this conclusion. *Chesapeake & Ohio Ry. v. Martin,* 283 U.S. 209, 216–220, 51 S.Ct. 453, 75 L.Ed. 983.

[§ 15]

We think, therefore, that the trial court was right in withdrawing the case from the jury. It repeatedly has been held by this court that before evidence may be left to the jury, "there is a preliminary question for the judge, not whether there is literally no evidence, but whether there is any upon which a jury can properly proceed to find a verdict for the party producing it, upon whom the onus of proof is imposed." *Pleasants v. Fant,* 22 Wall. 116, 120, 121, 22 L.Ed. 780. And where the evidence is "so overwhelmingly on one side as to leave no room to doubt what the fact is, the court should give a peremptory instruction to the jury." *Gunning v. Cooley,* 281 U.S. 90, 94, 50 S.Ct. 231, 233, 74 L.Ed. 720; *Patton v. Texas & Pacific Railway Co.,* 179 U.S. 658, 660, 21 S.Ct. 275, 45 L.Ed. 361. The rule is settled for the federal courts, and for many of the state courts, that whenever in the trial of a civil case the evidence is clearly such that if a verdict were rendered for one of the parties the other would be entitled to a new trial, it is the duty of the judge to direct the jury to find according to the views of the court. Such a practice, this court has said, not only saves time and expense, but "gives scientific certainty to the law in its application to the facts and promotes the ends of justice." *Bowditch v. Boston,* 101 U.S. 16, 18, 25 L.Ed. 980; *Barrett v. Virginian Ry. Co.,* 250 U.S. 473, 476, 39 S.Ct. 540, 63 L.Ed. 1092, and cases cited; *Herbert v. Butler,* 97 U.S. 319, 320, 24 L.Ed. 958. The scintilla rule has been definitely and repeatedly rejected so far as the federal courts are concerned. *Schuylkill & D. Improvement & R. Company v. Munson,* 14 Wall. 442, 448, 20 L.Ed. 867; *Commissioners of Marion*

County v. Clark, 94 U.S. 278, 284, 24 L.Ed. 59; *Small Co. v. Lamborn & Co.,* 267 U.S. 248, 254, 45 S.Ct. 300, 69 L.Ed. 597; *Gunning v. Cooley, supra; Ewing v. Goode, supra,* at pp. 443–444.

[§ 16]

Leaving out of consideration, then, the inference relied upon, the case for respondent is left without any substantial support in the evidence, and a verdict in her favor would have rested upon mere speculation and conjecture. This, of course, is inadmissible. *C.M. & St. P. Ry. v. Coogan,* 271 U.S. 472, 478, 46 S.Ct. 564, 70 L.Ed. 1041; *Gulf, etc., R.R. v. Wells,* 275 U.S. 455, 459, 48 S.Ct. 151, 72 L.Ed. 370; *New York Central R. Co. v. Ambrose, supra; Stevens v. The White City, supra.*

[§ 17]

The judgment of the Circuit Court of Appeals is reversed and that of the District Court is affirmed.

MR. JUSTICE STONE and MR. JUSTICE CARDOZO concur in the result.

WILKERSON v. McCARTHY

Supreme Court of the United States, 1949.
336 U.S. 53, 69 S.Ct. 413, 93 L.Ed. 497.

[§ 1]

MR. JUSTICE BLACK delivered the opinion of the Court.

The petitioner, a railroad switchman, was injured while performing duties as an employee of respondents in their railroad coach yard at Denver, Colorado. He brought this action for damages under the Federal Employers' Liability Act.[13]

[§ 2]

The complaint alleged that in the performance of his duties in the railroad yard it became necessary for him to walk over a wheel-pit on a narrow boardway, and that due to negligence of respondents, petitioner fell into the pit and suffered grievous personal injuries. The complaint further alleged that respondents had failed

13. Authors' note—The FELA provides a federal remedy enforceable in either federal or state court. In either forum, the issue of whether a party has met the burden of production is governed by federal law. Plaintiff has the burden of production on the issue of negligence. Contributory negligence diminishes the amount recovered, but does not bar recovery.

to furnish him a safe place to work in several detailed particulars, namely, that the pit boardway (1) was not firmly set, (2) was not securely attached, and (3) although only about 20 inches wide, the boardway had been permitted to become greasy, oily, and slippery, thereby causing petitioner to lose his balance, slip, and fall into the pit.

[§ 3]

The respondents in their answer to this complaint admitted the existence of the pit and petitioner's injuries as a result of falling into it. They denied, however, that the injury resulted from the railroad's negligence, charging that plaintiff's own negligence was the sole proximate cause of his injuries. On motion of the railroad the trial judge directed the jury to return a verdict in its favor. The Supreme Court of Utah affirmed, one judge dissenting.

[§ 4]

The opinion of the Utah Supreme Court strongly indicated, as the dissenting judge pointed out, that its finding of an absence of negligence on the part of the railroad rested on that court's independent resolution of conflicting testimony. This Court has previously held in many cases that where jury trials are required, courts must submit the issues of negligence to a jury if evidence might justify a finding either way on those issues. See, e.g., *Lavender v. Kurn,* 327 U.S. 645, 652, 653, 66 S.Ct. 740, 743, 744, 90 L.Ed. 916; *Bailey v. Central Vermont Ry.,* 319 U.S. 350, 354, 63 S.Ct. 1062, 1064, 1065, 87 L.Ed. 1444; *Tiller v. Atlantic Coast Line R. Co.,* 318 U.S. 54, 68, 63 S.Ct. 444, 451, 452, 87 L.Ed. 610, 143 A.L.R. 967; and see *Brady v. Southern R. Co.,* 320 U.S. 476, 479, 64 S.Ct. 232, 234, 88 L.Ed. 239. It was because of the importance of preserving for litigants in FELA cases their right to a jury trial that we granted certiorari in this case.

[§ 5]

The evidence showed the following facts without dispute:

[Petitioner fell into the railroad's pit while attempting to cross it on a "permanent board" that straddled it. For three years, all railroad employees had used the "permanent board" as a walkway. However, three months before petitioner's fall, the railroad had placed "safety chains" around the pit. Petitioner's position was that the railroad's employees customarily used the board as a walkway despite the safety chains, and that the railroad's failure to prevent this use constituted negligence. The railroad's position was that only the "pit workers" (who did not include plaintiff) used the permanent board after the safety chains were in place.]

Neither before nor after the chains were put up had the railroad ever forbidden pit workers or any other workers to walk across the pit on the "permanent board." Neither written rules nor spoken instructions had forbidden any employees to use the board. And witnesses for both sides testified that pit workers were supposed to, and did, continue to use the board as a walkway after the chains and posts were installed. The Utah Supreme Court nevertheless held that erection of the chain and post enclosure was itself the equivalent of company orders that no employees other than pit workers should walk across the permanent board when the chains were up. And the Utah Supreme Court also concluded that there was insufficient evidence to authorize a jury finding that employees generally, as well as pit workers, had continued their long-standing and open practice of crossing the pit on the permanent board between the time the chains were put up and the time petitioner was injured.

[§ 6]

It is the established rule that in passing upon whether there is sufficient evidence to submit an issue to the jury we need look only to the evidence and reasonable inferences which tend to support the case of a litigant against whom a peremptory instruction has been given. Viewing the evidence here in that way it was sufficient to show the following:

[§ 7]

Switchmen and other employees, just as pit workers, continued to use the permanent board to walk across the pit after the chains were put up as they had used it before. Petitioner and another witness employed on work around the pit, testified positively that such practice continued. It is true that witnesses for the respondents testified that after the chains were put up, only the car men in removing and applying wheels used the board "to walk from one side of the pit to the other...." Thus the conflict as to continued use of the board as a walkway after erection of the chains was whether the pit workers alone continued to use it as a walkway, or whether employees generally so used it. While this left only a very narrow conflict in the evidence, it was for the jury, not the court, to resolve the conflict.

[§ 8]

It was only as a result of its inappropriate resolution of this conflicting evidence that the State Supreme Court affirmed the action of the trial court in directing the verdict. Following its determination of fact, the Utah Supreme Court acted on the assumption that the respondents "had no knowledge, actual or constructive, that switchmen were using the plank to carry out their tasks," and the railroad had "no reason to suspect" that employees generally would so use the walkway. From this, the Court went on to say that respondents "were only required to keep the board safe for the purposes of the pit crewmen ... and not for all the employees in the yard." But the court emphasized that under different facts, maintenance of "a 22–inch board for a walkway, which is almost certain to become greasy or oily, constitutes negligence." And under the evidence in this case as to the board, grease and oil, the court added: "It must be conceded that if defendants knew or were charged with knowledge that switchmen and other workmen generally in the yard were habitually using the plank as a walkway in the manner claimed by plaintiff, then the safety enclosure might be entirely inadequate, and a jury question would have been presented on the condition of the board and the adequacy of the enclosure."

[§ 9]

We agree with this last quoted statement of the Utah court, and since there was evidence to support a jury finding that employees generally had habitually used the board as a walkway, it was error for the trial judge to grant judgment in favor of respondents.

[Concurring and dissenting opinions omitted]

SIMBLEST v. MAYNARD

United States Court of Appeals, Second Circuit, 1970.
427 F.2d 1.

Timbers, District Judge:

[§ 1]

We have before us another instance of Vermont justice—this time at the hands of a federal trial judge who, correctly applying the law, set aside a $17,125 plaintiff's verdict and entered judgment n.o.v. for defendant, Rule 50(b), Fed.R.Civ.P., in a diversity negligence action arising out of an intersection collision between a passenger vehicle driven by plaintiff and a fire engine driven by defendant in Burlington, Vermont, during the electric power blackout which left most of New England in darkness on the night of November 9, 1965. We affirm.

I.

[§ 2]

Plaintiff, a citizen and resident of New Hampshire, was 66 years of age at the time of the accident. He was a distributor of reference books and had been in Burlington on business for three days prior to the accident. He was an experienced driver, having driven an average of some 54,000 miles per year since 1922. He was thoroughly familiar with the intersection in question. His eyesight was excellent and his hearing was very good.

[§ 3]

Defendant, a citizen of Vermont, had resided in Burlington for 44 years. He had been a full time fireman with the Burlington Fire Department for 17 years. He was assigned to and regularly drove the 500 gallon pumper which he was driving at the time of the accident. He was thoroughly familiar with the intersection in question.

[§ 4]

The accident occurred at the intersection of Main Street (U.S. Route 2), which runs generally east and west, and South Willard Street (U.S. Routes 2 and 7), which runs generally north and south. The neighborhood is partly business, partly residential. At approximately the center of the intersection there was an overhead electrical traffic control signal designed to exhibit the usual red and green lights.

[§ 5]

At the time of the accident, approximately 5:27 P.M., it was dark, traffic was light and the weather was clear. Plaintiff was driving his 1964 Chrysler station wagon in a westerly direction on Main Street, approaching the intersection. Defendant was driving the fire engine, in response to a fire alarm, in a southerly direction on South Willard Street, also approaching the intersection.

[§ 6]

Plaintiff testified that the traffic light was green in his favor as he approached and entered the intersection; but that when he had driven part way through the intersection the power failure extinguished all lights within his range of view, including the traffic light. All other witnesses, for both plaintiff and defendant, testified that the power failure occurred at least 10 to 15 minutes prior to the accident; and there was no evidence, except plaintiff's testimony, that the traffic light was operating at the time of the accident.

[§ 7]

Plaintiff also testified that his speed was 12 to 15 miles per hour as he approached the intersection. He did not look to his right *before* he entered the intersection;[14] after looking to his left, to the front and to the rear (presumably through a rear view mirror), he looked to his right for the first time *when he was one-half to three-quarters of the way through the intersection* and then for the first time saw the fire engine within 12 feet of him. He testified that he did not hear the fire engine's siren or see the flashing lights or any other lights on the fire engine.

[§ 8]

Plaintiff further testified that his view to the north (his right) as he entered the intersection was obstructed by various objects, including traffic signs, trees on Main Street and a Chamber of Commerce information booth on Main Street east of the intersection. All of the evidence, including the photographs of the intersection, demonstrates that, despite some obstruction of plaintiff's view to the north, he could have seen the approaching fire engine if he had looked between the obstructions and if he had looked to the north after he passed the information booth. One of plaintiff's own

14. Court's footnote—Plaintiff has stated in his brief in this Court that "as he approached the intersection, he *did* look to his right" (Appellant's Brief. 5): and he emphasizes "the only direct evidence on this point . . . from the plaintiff who testified as follows:

" 'Q. You did look to the right? A. Oh yes, sir. I sure did.' " (Appellant's Brief. 12–13)

We find this testimony, lifted out of context, unfortunately to have created a mistaken impression on a critical issue in the case.

Plaintiff's complete direct testimony as to when he looked to his right, and in the sequence given, is as follows:

"Direct Examination (By Mr. Grussing)

Q. Now, tell us, Mr. Simblest, in your own words, just what occurred when you entered that intersection. A. Well, I will repeat. I had the 'green' light with me, proceeded through, was talf (sic) to ¾ through the street, looked to my right, and within 12 feet of me, here is a big, massive fire truck. . . . (Tr. 17)

Q. Did you, as you approached this intersection, did you look to your right at all to see what was coming out of the intersection? A. Coming into an intersection with people ready to go across, with fairly decent eyesight I could see from the left to the right to the front, and I had already watched in the rear before they got to that angle.

Q. You did look to the right? A. Oh, yes, sir. I sure did.

Q. Were you able, or did you see this truck approaching?

A. Within '12' feet. It was too late.

Q. The first time you saw it, it was within 12 feet of you?

A. That is right." (Tr. 19).

witnesses, Kathleen Burgess, testified that "maybe five to ten seconds previous to when he was struck he might have seen the fire truck," referring to the interval of time after plaintiff passed the information booth until the collision.

[§ 9]

Defendant testified that, accompanied by Captain Fortin in the front seat, he drove the fire engine from the Mansfield Avenue Fire Station, seven and one-half blocks away from the scene of the accident, in the direction of the fire on Maple Street. While driving in a southerly direction on South Willard Street and approaching the intersection with Main Street, the following warning devices were in operation on the fire engine: the penetrator making a wailing sound; the usual fire siren; a flashing red light attached to the dome of the fire engine; two red lights on either side of the cab; and the usual headlights. Defendant saw plaintiff's car east of the information booth and next saw it as it entered the intersection. Defendant testified that he was traveling 20 to 25 miles per hour as he approached the intersection;[15] he slowed down, applied his brakes and turned the fire engine to his right, in a westerly direction, in an attempt to avoid the collision. He estimated that he was traveling 15 to 20 miles per hour at the time of impact. A police investigation found a 15 foot skid mark made by the fire engine but no skid marks made by plaintiff's car.

[§ 10]

The fire engine struck plaintiff's car on the right side, in the area of the fender and front door. Plaintiff's head struck the post on the left side of his car, causing him to lose consciousness for about a minute. He claims that this injury aggravated a chronic pre-existing degenerative arthritic condition of the spine.

[§ 11]

Other witnesses who virtually bracketed the intersection from different vantage points were called. Frank Valz, called by plaintiff, was looking out a window in a building on the northeast corner of the intersection; he saw the fire engine when it was a block north of the intersection; he heard its siren and saw its flashing red lights. Kathleen Burgess, another of plaintiff's witnesses (referred to above), was driving in a northerly direction on South Willard Street, just south of the intersection; seeing the fire engine when it was a block north of the intersection, she pulled over to the curb

15. Court's footnote—The maximum speed attributed to the fire engine as it approached the intersection was 30 to 35 miles per hour (testimony of Captain Fortin).

and stopped; she saw its flashing lights, but did not hear its siren. Holland Smith and Irene Longe, both called by defendant, were in the building at the southwest corner of the intersection; as the fire engine approached the intersection, they each heard its warning signals and saw its flashing lights in operation.

[§ 12]

Defendant's motions for a judgment as a matter of law at the close of plaintiff's case and at the close of all the evidence having been denied and the jury having returned a plaintiff's verdict, defendant moved to set aside the verdict and the judgment entered thereon and for entry of judgment n.o.v. in accordance with his motion for a judgment as a matter of law. Chief Judge Leddy filed a written opinion granting defendant's motion.

[§ 13]

On appeal plaintiff urges that the district court erred in granting defendant's motion for judgment n.o.v. or, in the alternative, in declining to charge the jury on the doctrine of last clear chance. We affirm both rulings of the district court.

II.

[§ 14]

In determining whether the motion for judgment n.o.v. should have been granted, a threshold question is presented as to the correct standard to be applied. This standard has been expressed in various ways. Simply stated, it is whether the evidence is such that, without weighing the credibility of the witnesses or otherwise considering the weight of the evidence, there can be but one conclusion as to the verdict that reasonable men could have reached. See, e.g., Brady v. Southern Railway Company, 320 U.S. 476, 479–80 (1943); O'Connor v. Pennsylvania Railroad Company, 308 F.2d 911, 914–15 (2 Cir.1962). See also 5 Moore's Federal Practice ¶ 50.02[1], at 2320–23 (2d Ed.1968); Wright, Law of Federal Courts § 95, at 425 (2d Ed.1970). On a motion for judgment n.o.v. the evidence must be viewed in the light most favorable to the party against whom the motion is made and he must be given the benefit of all reasonable inferences which may be drawn in his favor from that evidence. O'Connor v. Pennsylvania Railroad Company, supra, at 914–15; 5 Moore, supra, at 2325; Wright, supra, at 425.

[§ 15]

We acknowledge that it has not been settled in a diversity action whether, in considering the evidence in the light most favorable to the party against whom the motion is made, the court may consider all the evidence or only the evidence favorable to such party and the uncontradicted, unimpeached evidence unfavorable to him. Under Vermont law, all the evidence may be considered. Kremer v. Fortin, 119 Vt. 1, 117 A.2d 245 (1955) (intersection collision between fire engine and passenger car). Plaintiff here urges that under the federal standard only evidence favorable to him should have been considered, citing Wilkerson v. McCarthy, 336 U.S. 53, 57 (1949). As plaintiff reads that case, the court below should not have considered anything else, not even the uncontradicted, unimpeached evidence unfavorable to him. However, we are committed to a contrary view in a diversity case. O'Connor v. Pennsylvania Railroad Company, *supra*.

[§ 16]

The Supreme Court at least twice has declined to decide whether the state or federal standard as to the sufficiency of the evidence is controlling on such motions in diversity cases. Mercer v. Theriot, 377 U.S. 152, 156 (1964) (per curiam); Dick v. New York Life Insurance Company, 359 U.S. 437, 444–45 (1959). Our Court likewise has declined to decide this issue in recent cases. Mull v. Ford Motor Company, 368 F.2d 713, 716 n. 4 (2 Cir.1966); Hooks v. New York Central Railroad Company, 327 F.2d 259, 261 n. 2 (2 Cir.1964); Evans v. S.J. Groves & Sons Company, 315 F.2d 335, 342 n. 2 (2 Cir.1963). See 5 Moore, *supra*, at 2347–50.[16]

[§§ 17 & 18]

Our careful review of the record in the instant case leaves us with the firm conviction that, under either the Vermont standard or the more restrictive federal standard, plaintiff was contributorily

---

16. Court's footnote—Assuming that the federal standard were controlling, plaintiff's contention that under that standard evidence introduced by the moving party may not be considered is open to question. Plaintiff relies on Wilkerson v. McCarthy, 336 U.S. 53, 57 (1949). But most Courts of Appeals have held that evidence introduced by the moving party may be considered, distinguishing *Wilkerson* on the ground that FELA cases are *sui generis*, 5 Moore, *supra*, at 2329.

See especially the comprehensive opinion of the Fifth Circuit in Boeing Company v. Shipman, 411 F.2d 365 (5 Cir.1969) (en banc), holding (1) that in diversity cases a federal rather than state standard should be applied in testing the sufficiency of the evidence in connection with motions for a directed verdict and for judgment n.o.v.; (2) that the FELA standard for testing the sufficiency of the evidence on such motions is not applicable in diversity cases; and (3) that the federal standard to be applied in diversity cases requires the court to consider "all of the evidence—not just that evidence which supports the nonmover's case—but in the light and with all reasonable inferences most favorable to the party opposed to the motion." 411 F.2d at 374.

negligent as a matter of law; and that Chief Judge Leddy correctly set aside the verdict and entered judgment for defendant n.o.v. O'Connor v. Pennsylvania Railroad Company, *supra*, at 914, Presser Royalty Company v. Chase Manhattan Bank, 272 F.2d 838, 840 (2 Cir.1959).

[§ 19]

Under the Vermont standard which permits all the evidence to be considered, Kremer v. Fortin, *supra*, plaintiff was so clearly guilty of contributory negligence that no further dilation is required.

[§ 20]

Under the more restrictive federal standard—i.e., considering only the evidence favorable to plaintiff and the uncontradicted, unimpeached evidence unfavorable to him—while a closer question is presented than under the Vermont standard, we nevertheless hold that plaintiff was guilty of contributory negligence as a matter of law.[17]

[§ 21]

In our view, applying the federal standard, the critical issue in the case is whether the fire engine was sounding a siren or displaying a red light as it approached the intersection immediately before the collision. Upon this critical issue, Chief Judge Leddy accurately and succinctly summarized the evidence as follows:

> "All witnesses to the accident, except the plaintiff, testified that the fire truck was sounding a siren or displaying a flashing red light. All of the witnesses except Miss Burgess and the plaintiff testified that the fire truck was sounding its siren and displaying a flashing red light."

[§ 22]

The reason such evidence is critical is that under Vermont law, 23 V.S.A. § 1033, upon the approach of a fire department vehicle which is sounding a siren or displaying a red light, or both, all other vehicles are required to pull over to the right lane of traffic and come to a complete stop until the emergency vehicle has passed. Since the emergency provision of this statute supersedes the general right of way statute regarding intersections controlled by traffic lights, 23 V.S.A. § 1054, the lone testimony of plaintiff that the traffic light was green in his favor as he approached and

17. Court's footnote—We emphasize that, solely for the purpose of testing the validity of plaintiff's claim under the federal standard, we assume without deciding that the federal standard is as stated. But compare, e.g., Boeing Company v. Shipman, *supra* note [16], at 373–75.

entered the intersection is of no moment. And since the emergency provision of 23 V.S.A. § 1033 becomes operative if *either* the siren is sounding *or* a red light is displayed on an approaching fire engine, we focus upon plaintiff's own testimony that he did not see the fire engine's flashing light, all other witnesses having testified that the red light was flashing.

[§ 23]

As stated above, plaintiff testified that he first saw the fire engine when he was one-half to three-quarters of the way through the intersection and when the fire engine was within 12 feet of his car. At the speed at which the fire engine was traveling, plaintiff had approximately one-third of a second in which to observe the fire engine prior to the collision. Accepting plaintiff's testimony that his eyesight was excellent, and assuming that the fire engine's flashing red light was revolving as rapidly as 60 revolutions per minute, plaintiff's one-third of a second observation does not support an inference that the light was not operating, much less does it constitute competent direct evidence to that effect. Opportunity to observe is a necessary ingredient of the competency of eyewitness evidence. Plaintiff's opportunity to observe, accepting his own testimony, simply was too short for his testimony on the operation of the light to be of any probative value whatsoever.[18]

[§ 24]

Plaintiff's testimony that he did not see the fire engine's flashing red light, in the teeth of the proven physical facts, we hold is tantamount to no proof at all on that issue. O'Connor v. Pennsylvania Railroad Company, *supra,* at 915. As one commentator has put it, " . . . the question of the total absence of proof quickly merges into the question whether the proof adduced is so insignificant as to be treated as the equivalent of the absence of proof." 5 Moore, *supra,* at 2320. If plaintiff had testified that he had not looked to his right at all, he of course would have been guilty of contributory negligence as a matter of law. We hold that his testimony in fact was the equivalent of his saying that he did not look at all.

18. Court's footnote—This is the arithmetical mean (.322 seconds) between the maximum and minimum time intervals, according to the evidence, within which plaintiff could have observed the fire engine travel 12 feet. The minimum interval (.230 seconds) is based on Captain Fortin's testimony that the fire engine was traveling 35 miles per hour as it approached the intersection (*supra* note [15]); the maximum interval (.411 seconds) is based on defendant's testimony that he was traveling 20 miles per hour (*supra* pages 3 and 4).

[§ 25]

Chief Judge Leddy concluded that plaintiff was guilty of contributory negligence as a matter of law: accordingly, he set aside the verdict and entered judgment n.o.v. for defendant. We agree.

[Discussion of last clear chance doctrine omitted]

Affirmed.

———————

Having studied these three opinions and answered the questions on p. 258, you are ready to go to the computer to work through CALI CIV 04: Judgments as a Matter of Law.

EXERCISE TEN

Evidence for Civil Procedure Students

This exercise has two purposes. The first is to engage you actively in legal analysis. Hence, the exercise contains some difficult questions that require careful thought. The second is to provide a survey of the rules of evidence in order to give you a deeper understanding of subjects studied in the civil procedure course.[1] Instances in which evidence rules illuminate aspects of the civil procedure course are set forth in footnotes.

I. SOME BASIC EVIDENCE RULES

The Federal Rules of Evidence were first adopted for the federal courts in 1975, and have since provided the pattern for evidence rules in a majority of states. For purposes of this computer exercise, you need only be familiar with the sections of the Federal Rules of Evidence described in this book.

A. The Requirement of Personal Knowledge[2]

Federal Evidence Rule 602 provides

1. Of course you will study these topics in depth in your evidence course. The intent here is not to anticipate that course, but rather to provide a rudimentary understanding of evidence law as it relates to civil procedure.

2. The requirement of personal knowledge is relevant to civil procedure because, *inter alia,* it is one of the features that gives the summary judgment motion its teeth. Suppose, for example, that plaintiff hears from a trusted source that defendant called plaintiff a crack user. Plaintiff's attorney would be justified in filing a slander complaint because she has "knowledge, information, and belief, formed after an

A witness may not testify to a matter unless evidence is introduced sufficient to support a finding that the witness has personal knowledge of the matter. Evidence to prove personal knowledge may, but need not, consist of the witness' own testimony. This rule is subject to the provisions of rule 703, relating to opinion testimony by expert witnesses.

The rule prevents a lay witness from testifying about an event that could be perceived by the senses unless the witness actually perceived the event. For example, if the first question asked to a witness were, "State the color of defendant's car," the question would be objectionable because the examiner has failed to produce any evidence that the witness actually saw the defendant's car. The witness's answer might be based on guesswork or secondhand information. If the witness saw the car personally, then the examining lawyer must "lay the foundation" by having the witness so testify.[3]

The personal knowledge requirement is analytically distinct from the hearsay rule. If a witness makes an assertion about a fact that can be perceived by the senses and does not purport to base her knowledge on another's statement, then the correct objection is lack of personal knowledge. If the examiner cures the personal knowledge problem by having the witness testify that she read or heard an out-of-court statement that asserted the fact in question, then the correct objection is hearsay. For example, suppose that a witness testifies "The train arrived at 8:05." If there is no evidence that the witness was in a position to observe the train, then the testimony would be objectionable on grounds that the witness lacked personal knowledge. A hearsay objection would be inappropriate because there is no indication that the witness is basing the testimony on the statement of another. Suppose, then, that the

inquiry reasonable under the circumstances" within the meaning of Fed.R.Civ.P. 11. If drafted so that it states all of the elements of slander, the complaint will withstand a motion to dismiss for failure to state a claim. *See* Exercises Three and Four.

The summary judgment motion "pierces the pleadings" and is a stronger tool for the litigant who wants judgment without trial. Suppose, in our example, that defendant moves for summary judgment and supports his motion with affidavits from himself and other persons present averring that the alleged statement was never made. If plaintiff has had enough time for investigation and discovery, then he must produce counter-affidavits or other Fed.R.Civ.P. 56 evidence (depositions, etc.), or the action will be dismissed. Moreover, under Rule 56(e), the affidavits must be "made on personal knowledge" and set forth "facts as would be admissible in evidence." *See* Exercise Eight.

3. The witness need not actually convince the judge that she saw the car, however. Rule 602 requires only evidence sufficient to support a finding by a reasonable person that the witness has personal knowledge. Once this foundation is laid, the evidence is admissible and can be considered by the trier of fact. The trier, of course, is still free to reject or accept the witness's assertion that she saw the car.

witness is asked how she knows and responds by saying "Mr. Bailey told me that the train arrived at 8:05." The requirement of personal knowledge has now been satisfied (the witness has testified about something she perceived with her senses—Bailey's statement). In the absence of a hearsay exception, however, the testimony would be inadmissible hearsay.

B. The Hearsay Rule and Its Exceptions[4]

1. The Concept of Hearsay

The credibility of a witness depends upon the witness's memory, perception, sincerity, and narrative ability. For example, suppose a witness testifies "I saw Smith in the bar on February 1." The witness might have been intoxicated, near-sighted, or simply too far away to see clearly, so the statement might be inaccurate because of infirmities of perception. The witness might be mistaken about the date because of defects in memory. The witness might have misspoken, as by saying "bar" while meaning "car," so that poor narrative ability made the utterance misleading. Or the witness might be intentionally lying.

When a witness testifies in court, the witness is under oath, subject to cross-examination, and present for observation of demeanor by the trier of fact. These safeguards are thought to increase the likelihood that the witness will try to tell the truth and that defects in credibility will be exposed to the trier. The hearsay rule is grounded on the belief that sometimes too much credence will be given to statements made in situations in which these safeguards are absent.

Not every out-of-court statement is hearsay. Under the Federal Rules, hearsay is a statement made out of court that is offered for the purpose of proving the truth of what is asserted in the statement. *See* Fed.R.Evid. 801(c). An in-court statement (a statement made by the witness while testifying) is not hearsay, and an out-of-court statement is not hearsay if it is offered in evidence for some purpose other than proving the truth of the matter asserted in

4. Knowledge about the hearsay rule is helpful in understanding many aspects of American civil procedure. For example, Fed.R.Civ.P. 56(e) requires that affidavits supporting or opposing summary judgment set forth facts that would be admissible in evidence; often the most formidable obstacle to admission is the hearsay rule. The pertinence of the hearsay rule to other aspects of civil procedure is separately noted below. For a detailed discussion of hearsay–as well as the other rules of evidence discussed in this exercise–*see* ROGER C. PARK, DAVID P. LEONARD & STEVEN H. GOLDBERG, EVIDENCE LAW: A STUDENT'S GUIDE TO THE LAW OF EVIDENCE AS APPLIED IN AMERICAN TRIALS (2d ed. 2004).

the statement. Normally (although not invariably) statements that are offered for some purpose other than showing their truth do not depend for value upon the credibility of the out-of-court declarant; hence, nothing is lost by the absence of cross-examination under oath.

This is not the place for discussion of all of the various meanings that have been imputed to the phrase "truth of the matter asserted." Even at this early stage, however, the student should attempt to become familiar with the principal types of utterances that courts deem not to be hearsay on grounds that they are not "offered for the truth of what they assert." Most such utterances fall within the following three categories:

a. Statements Offered to Show Their Effect on the Reader or Hearer

Suppose that a defendant is charged with burglary of a neighbor's garage. To explain why he was in the garage, the defendant testifies that a child told him that an intruder was in the garage and asked him to investigate. The child's statement is not hearsay if offered solely for the purpose of showing why defendant entered the garage. The statement is not being offered to show its truth (that an intruder was in fact in the garage) but only to show its effect on the hearer. Even if the child was lying or mistaken, the statement still has value in explaining defendant's conduct. Because the statement does not depend for value on the credibility of the child declarant, the absence of an opportunity to cross-examine the declarant about the basis for the statement is of no consequence.

b. Legally Operative Language

To show that A made a contract with B, testimony is offered that A said to B "I will pay $40,000 for 100 carloads of your widgets," and that B responded with "I accept your offer." Testimony about these utterances is not hearsay. The mere fact that they were made created a legal relationship, under the objective theory of contracts, even if A or B is not credible. Consequently, the utterances are said not to be offered for their truth, but merely to show that they were made.

c. Statements Used Indirectly

Suppose A tells B that C committed a crime, and the words are offered to show that A does not like C. Under traditional analysis, A's utterance is considered not to be hearsay. When offered for the purpose of showing A's dislike for C, the truth of the statement does not matter. In fact, if the statement is false, the inference may be even stronger evidence that A dislikes C.

Utterances like the one above are often characterized as circumstantial evidence, which is another way of saying that they are not offered directly to show their truth, but indirectly to show something else.[5]

One important category of indirect utterances are those that are offered as prior inconsistent statements for the purpose of impeaching a witness. Suppose a bystander tells an investigator prior to trial that a traffic light was red, and then testifies at trial it was green. The bystander's prior statement is not hearsay when offered solely to impeach credibility. The statement, under traditional analysis, is not being offered to prove the truth of its assertion, but merely to show that the witness is not credible because she said different things at different times.

2. *Exceptions to the Hearsay Rule*

Even though a statement is hearsay, it is admissible if it falls under one of the exceptions to the hearsay rule. The Federal Rules of Evidence list twenty-nine exceptions. This computer exercise deals only with the ones set forth in these materials.

a. *Present Sense Impression Exception*

Rule 803(1) provides that hearsay is admissible if it is "A statement describing or explaining an event or condition made while the declarant was perceiving the event or condition, or immediately thereafter." Example: "Look at that car running the red light."

The Advisory Committee's Note to Rule 803(1) states "The underlying theory of [this exception] is that substantial contemporaneity of event and statement negative the likelihood of deliberate or conscious misrepresentation."

5. Direct evidence states the proposition to be proved directly. When a witness testifies "I saw defendant punch plaintiff," that is direct evidence. Circumstantial evidence requires an inference from the fact observed to the fact to be proved. When a witness testifies "I heard a smack, turned quickly, saw plaintiff going down, and saw defendant standing over him," that is circumstantial evidence that defendant punched plaintiff. Despite popular perception, circumstantial evidence can be quite powerful. Would you, for example, believe defendant punched plaintiff after hearing only the second witness statement above?

b. Excited Utterance Exception

Rule 803(2) provides an exception for "A statement relating to a startling event or condition made while the declarant was under the stress of excitement caused by the event or condition." Example: "Oh, no. The car struck the pedestrian."

The rationale of this exception is that excitement is likely to prevent deliberate fabrication.

c. Present State of Mind Exception

Rule 803(3) provides, in relevant part, that hearsay is admissible if it is "A statement of the declarant's then existing state of mind, emotion, sensation, or physical condition (such as intent, plan, motive, design, mental feeling, pain, and bodily health), but not including a statement of memory or belief to prove the fact remembered or believed * * *." Examples of the exception include such statements as "My leg hurts" offered to show that the leg hurts (but not the statement of memory "My leg hurt"), or "I am fond of John" offered to show the declarant's fondness for John, or "I am going to Crooked Creek" offered to show that declarant did later go there (but not "I went to Crooked Creek").

Although there are dangers of misrepresentation (for example, a plaintiff may exaggerate pain), the exception can be justified on grounds of necessity (determining mental or physical state without use of statements by the subject is difficult) and the absence of some of the hearsay dangers (for example, the danger that a declarant's bad memory will lead to mistake is absent in a present tense statement).

d. Dying Declaration Exception

Rule 804(b)(2) provides an exception for "[A] statement made by a declarant while believing that the declarant's death was imminent, concerning the cause or circumstances of what the declarant believed to be impending death." The exception applies to civil actions and to criminal prosecutions for homicide. Example: "Jill shot me."

The theory behind the dying declaration exception is that a person knowing he is about to die is unlikely to tell falsehoods.

e. Declaration Against Interest Exception

In relevant part, Rule 804(b)(3) provides an exception for "A statement which was at the time of its making so far contrary to the declarant's pecuniary or proprietary interest, or so far tended to subject the declarant to civil or criminal liability, or to render invalid a claim by the declarant against another, that a reasonable person in the declarant's position would not have made the statement unless believing it to be true." Example: "I owe you $1,000."

The theory is that a person is highly unlikely to make a statement against his own interest unless that statement is true.

f. Admission of a Party Opponent[6]

Rule 801(d)(2) provides that a statement by a party is not hearsay when offered against that party. For reasons not here relevant, the rulemakers decided to treat admissions as a special category of utterances that are not hearsay instead of treating them as hearsay admissible under an exception. Under the Fed.R.Evid., an admission is not hearsay even when offered to prove the truth of its assertion.

The admissions exclusion is broad and important. *Any* statement by a party clears the hearsay barrier when offered by an opposing party.[7]

g. Former Testimony Exception; Depositions

Two of the safeguards that are thought to make courtroom testimony reliable are present during the taking of a deposition. The deponent is under oath and is subject to cross-examination. Nevertheless, courtroom testimony is considered to be superior to deposition testimony. In the courtroom, the witness is available for observation by the trier of fact, and the solemnity of the courtroom may encourage the witness to tell the truth. Moreover, the cross-examination that occurs during a deposition or other former testimony may not be an adequate substitute for courtroom cross-examination. The main purpose of cross-examination during a deposition is usually the discovery of information, not the revelation of defects in the witness's credibility. For these reasons, depositions are not freely admissible when a nonparty deponent is

---

6. The admissions rule is helpful in understanding several aspects of the Federal Rules of Civil Procedure. For example, it has an important effect upon the use of interrogatory answers at trial. Rule 33(b) provides that answers to interrogatories may be used at trial "to the extent permitted by the rules of evidence." The hearsay rule poses no obstacle to use of an opposing party's answers; they are admissions of a party opponent.

7. In addition, statements by an employee will sometimes be vicariously admissible against an employer and statements by one co-conspirator will sometimes be admissible against other co-conspirators. These aspects of the admissions rule are beyond the scope of this essay.

available to testify in court, though deposition testimony does have a more favored status than ordinary out-of-court statements. Should the witness become unavailable, depositions (and certain other instances of former testimony) are generally admissible.

h. Business Records Exception

The business records exception is commonly used. It allows, for example, the introduction by a business of account books showing that a defendant is indebted to it. Without this exception, a business would have a tough time proving that a customer actually purchased its product and owes money. Third parties may also use the exception for a variety of purposes; for example, a personal injury plaintiff may use the exception to introduce hospital records pertinent to her injury.

Business records are said to be reliable for a number of reasons: the business relies upon them, people making entries have a duty to be accurate, the records are likely to be checked systematically, and regularity in keeping records makes the record-keeper develop the habit of precision.

The federal business records rule is set forth in Fed.R.Evid. 803(6), which provides a hearsay exception for

> A memorandum, report, record, or data compilation, in any form, of acts, events, conditions, opinions, or diagnoses, made at or near the time by, or from information transmitted by, a person with knowledge, if kept in the course of a regularly conducted business activity, and if it was the regular practice of that business activity to make the memorandum, report, record, or data compilation, all as shown by the testimony of the custodian or other qualified witness, unless the source of information or the method or circumstances of preparation indicate lack of trustworthiness. The term "business" as used in this paragraph includes business, institution, association, profession, occupation, and calling of every kind, whether or not conducted for profit.

i. Other Exceptions

Many other exceptions to the hearsay rule, ranging from trivial (inscriptions on tombstones) to important (public records), exist. This essay does not purport to be comprehensive, but describes only exceptions and exclusions that are particularly important or that present interesting challenges in interpretation.

C. Relevancy and Its Counterweights

Federal Evidence Rule 402 declares that irrelevant evidence is inadmissible. Under the Federal Rules, however, evidence is rarely irrelevant, because Fed.R.Evid. 401 deems evidence to be "relevant" if it has "[A]ny tendency to make the existence of any fact that is of consequence to determination of the action more probable or less probable than it would be without the evidence."

This definition of relevance is a broad one. Under it, almost every item of evidence that a rational lawyer might offer would be relevant. For example, evidence that a defendant has been in prior accidents tends slightly to support the inference that the defendant is not a careful driver and then the further inference that the accident at issue was defendant's fault. The prior accidents would therefore be relevant under the definition of Rule 401.

Such evidence is, however, normally excluded. In a civil case, the evidence would be inadmissible for two reasons. The evidence of other accidents is offered to prove defendant has a character trait of poor driving. Character evidence is not admissible in civil cases (Fed.R.Evid. 404(a)), and in any event character ordinarily may not be proved with evidence of specific acts of conduct (Fed.R.Evid. 405(b)). Even without specific rules about character evidence, however, the evidence may be inadmissible because of Rule 403, discussed below.

Another example is the result of a polygraph test. Probably the result, if obtained by a reliable operator, has enough value to satisfy Rule 401's definition of relevance. Yet the jury might give the result undue weight or be confused, and the evidence attacking or supporting the validity of the test is likely to be lengthy and tangential. One would expect the result to be excluded under Fed.R.Evid. 403, which provides that

> Although relevant, evidence may be excluded if its probative value is substantially outweighed by the danger of unfair prejudice, confusion of the issues, or misleading the jury, or by considerations of undue delay, waste of time, or needless presentation of cumulative evidence.

Rule 403 is not the only rule designed to prevent the introduction of evidence that is prejudicial or a waste of time; it is merely the most general one. The Fed.R.Evid. also set forth specific rules for certain recurring situations in which the balance of probative value and prejudicial effect tips in favor of exclusion. *See, e.g.,* Fed.R.Evid. 404–405 (character evidence), Fed.R.Evid. 411 (evidence of liability insurance). For purposes of this exercise, you need not become acquainted with any of the relevance rules except Rules 401, 402, and 403. If you think that evidence ought to be excluded under Rule 403 in the computer exercise, say so. If you are right and there is also a more specific rule excluding the evidence, then the computer will tell you.

D. The Opinion Rule

There are two aspects of the rule limiting the admission of opinion testimony by lay (non-expert) witnesses. First, the lay witness must not express an opinion about something that requires special skill, knowledge, or education—for example, a lay witness could not testify that the injury she received caused her to develop cancer. Second, lay witnesses are sometimes prevented from expressing opinions even about matters that require no special skill. For example, a lay witness would not ordinarily be permitted to testify that one of the parties in an accident "was driving negligently" and the other was not. The evidence would be excluded on grounds that the testimony in that form would not be helpful to the trier of fact. The trier, not the witness, should decide whether the driver was negligent; in making the determination the trier would be helped by specific testimony about what the driver was doing but not by the witness's conclusion of negligence.

Courts have encountered difficulty in applying a rule that purports to distinguish between "facts" and "opinions":

> That doctrine is based on the simplistic assumption that "fact" and "opinion" differ in kind and are readily distinguishable. The formula proved to be the clumsiest of tools for regulating the examination of witnesses. * * * Any conceivable statement, no matter however specific, detailed, and "factual," is in some measure the product of inference as well as observation and memory. * * * The distinction between so-called "fact" and "opinion" is not a difference between opposites or contrasting absolutes, but a mere difference in degree with no recognizable bright line boundary.[8]

The Federal Rules of Evidence adopt a pragmatic view of the opinion rule that encourages specificity while still permitting lay opinions when they will be helpful. Fed.R.Evid. 701, entitled "Opinion Testimony by Lay Witnesses," provides

> If the witness is not testifying as an expert, the witness' testimony in the form of opinions or inferences is limited to

---

8. John W. Strong (ed.), McCormick on Evidence § 11, at 45–46 (5th 1999).

those opinions or inferences which are (a) rationally based on the perception of the witness, (b) helpful to a clear understanding of the witness' testimony or the determination of a fact in issue, and (c) not based on scientific, technical, or other specialized knowledge within the scope of Rule 702.

E. Lawyer–Client Privilege

The statements in the following text describe features of the common law lawyer-client privilege as it exists in most American jurisdictions.[9] The Federal Rules of Evidence do not codify rules of privilege. Fed.R.Evid. 501 merely provides that when the source of a substantive rule of decision is state law, then state rules of privilege must be followed in federal court; otherwise, the federal courts are instructed to use "[T]he principles of the common law as they may be interpreted by the courts of the United States in the light of reason and experience."

The lawyer-client privilege prevents a lawyer from testifying about communications between lawyer and client made in confidence during the course of the professional relationship. The privilege is based upon the theory that justice will best be served if the client confides freely in the lawyer, knowing that the lawyer cannot be required to testify about what the client has said.

A communication is considered to be given in the course of a professional relationship if the client has consulted a lawyer or a lawyer's representative for the purpose of securing legal services from the lawyer. The communications are protected even if the client ultimately decides not to hire the lawyer. Moreover, the privilege covers both disclosures of the client to the lawyer (or the lawyer's representative) and advice given by the lawyer to the client.

The privilege does not apply unless the communication was "confidential." If the client intended that the lawyer make the communication public, then the communication is not privileged. Similarly, if the client made a disclosure to the lawyer in front of third persons in circumstances indicating that the communication was not intended to be confidential, the communication is not privileged.

Moreover, the privilege applies only to communications between the client and the lawyer (or the lawyer's representative).

9. *See generally* Roger C. Park, David P. Leonard & Steven H. Goldberg, Evidence Law: A Student's Guide to the Law of Evidence as Applied in American Trials §§ 8.03– 8.12 (2d ed. 2004).

Not everything that a lawyer learns while representing a client is privileged. For example, suppose that a lawyer visits the scene of an accident, observes the relative position of the automobiles, and interviews eyewitnesses. Neither the lawyer's observations nor the statements made by the eyewitnesses would be protected by the privilege.

The fact that the lawyer-client privilege would not apply to these observations and statements does not mean that the lawyer would be free to disclose them voluntarily. First, they are work product.[10] Second, the lawyer has an ethical duty not to divulge information learned in the course of the professional relationship even if it falls outside the scope of the lawyer-client privilege. Model Rule of Professional Conduct 1.6(a)(1) prohibits a lawyer from revealing a confidence or secret of a client. A "confidence" is information protected by the attorney-client privilege; a "secret" is "other information gained in the professional relationship that the client has requested be held inviolate or the disclosure of which would be embarrassing or would be likely to be detrimental to the client." Model Rule 1.6(d). A lawyer may reveal "confidences and secrets when permitted under the Rules of Professional Conduct or required by law or court order." Model Rule 1.6(b)(2).

The lawyer-client privilege is narrower than the lawyer's duty to preserve the client's secrets because society has a special interest in requiring that information be presented in courtroom testimony so that the trier can make a decision based on all the known facts. When the lawyer is not testifying in court, there is no equivalent reason for allowing the lawyer to reveal embarrassing or detrimental facts learned while working for the client.

There are several specific exceptions to the lawyer-client privilege, such as the exception permitting the lawyer to reveal communications in order to prevent a future crime, that are not within the scope of this exercise.

F. The Best Evidence Rule

Suppose that the wording of a written contract is of significance in a lawsuit. May the party relying on the contract prove its contents with oral testimony? If not, may a copy of the writing be introduced in lieu of the original?

At common law, the best evidence rule supplied the answer to these questions. Generally, it required the proponent to produce

---

10. The statements of eyewitnesses are given qualified protection from discovery as trial preparation materials as set forth in Fed.R.Civ.P. 26(b)(3). *See* Exercise Seven I.B.3. The work product doctrine and the lawyer-client privilege are distinct.

the original writing or to make an acceptable excuse for not having it. Neither oral testimony nor a copy was admissible in the absence of an excuse for not presenting the original.

One need hardly explain why the original of a writing is preferable to oral testimony about its contents. The preference for an original writing over a duplicate is more questionable. Modern methods of copying are far more accurate than the hand-copying used at the time of inception of the rule.

The Federal Rules of Evidence contain a version of the best evidence rule[11] that retains a general preference for the original while taking into account improvements in methods of copying. Fed.R.Evid. 1002 provides the basic rule of exclusion, stating that except where otherwise provided by rule or statute, "To prove the content of a writing, recording, or photograph, the original writing, recording, or photograph is required * * * ."

Federal Evidence Rule 1003 creates an exception for duplicates made by photocopy, carbon copy, or similar methods; they are admissible unless there is a genuine issue about the authenticity of the original or other circumstances make use of the duplicate unfair.

Rule 1004 deals with other situations in which the original is not required. Basically, the rule provides that the original is not required when the person offering evidence of its contents shows a good excuse for not producing the original, i.e., the original is missing or unobtainable. In these circumstances, other evidence of the contents of the original (including oral testimony about what the document said) is admissible. Nonproduction because the proponent has lost or destroyed the original in bad faith is not accepted as a good excuse. Fed.R.Evid. 1004(1). Rule 1004 also provides an exception for unimportant documents on collateral issues; neither the original nor an excuse for nonproduction is necessary when "The writing, recording, or photograph is not closely related to a controlling issue." Fed.R.Evid. 1004(4). For example, when a witness testifies that she knew that the date of the collision was November 7 because the newspaper contained a story about her mother on that day, the newspaper need not be produced.

You should guard against the tendency to overgeneralize the best evidence rule. No rule has ever invariably required the "best evidence" to be offered on every matter. For example, a lawyer

11. The federal rulemakers avoided use of the term best evidence rule. The name has been retained in this computer exercise since it is the traditional name for the rule requiring documentary originals, and it will no doubt continue in use for some time to come.

may elect to call only one witness to a collision, despite the fact that ten others were better placed to observe it; the rule simply has no application in this situation, despite the fact that the lawyer is not using the "best evidence" available. Similarly, a lawyer may elect to use hearsay testimony that is admissible under an exception in lieu of calling the actual witness. The federal best evidence rule applies only to evidence of the contents of writings, recordings, or photographs; it has nothing to do with other types of evidence.

G. Leading Questions

On direct examination, a lawyer ordinarily may not "lead" the witness by asking a question that suggests the desired answer. Thus, "Was defendant wearing a green plaid jacket?" would be improper; "What was defendant wearing?" would not. There are, however, many situations in which leading questions are permitted. These include testimony about undisputed preliminary matters ("Were you present at the April 19 board meeting?"); here, leading does no harm and speeds up the proceedings. Leading questions are also permitted if the witness appears to need some assistance. For example, if the attorney has unsuccessfully sought to elicit a fact from the witness by non-leading questions ("Was anyone else there?"), the attorney may then use a leading question ("Was Mr. Hand there?"). In this instance, the trier has had the opportunity to see that the witness cannot testify without leading, so it can discount the witness's testimony accordingly.

Leading questions are also permitted on cross-examination, except in relatively rare situations in which the witness being cross-examined is strongly partial toward the cross-examiner. Accordingly, cross-examination of a witness with questions such as "Isn't it true that the robber's face was completely covered?" would ordinarily be permitted. Indeed, good cross-examination may be all leading questions. There is little danger that the witness will be overly influenced by suggestive questions on cross, and in any event leading questions may be the only way to pin down an uncooperative witness.

Fed.R.Evid. 611(c) sets forth the general rule and its exceptions as follows:

Leading questions should not be used on the direct examination of a witness except as may be necessary to develop the witness' testimony. Ordinarily leading questions should be permitted on cross-examination. When a party calls a hostile witness, an adverse party, or a witness identified with an adverse party, interrogation may be by leading questions.

II. COMPUTER EXERCISE: CALI CIV 06

A. General Instructions

Read all of the material in this chapter before going to the computer terminal. Also, check your civil procedure casebook to see whether it has an essay on evidence. If it does, read the essay.

The computer will print out simulated trial testimony in question and answer form. You will be asked to assume the role of the trial judge and rule on objections to that testimony. Because you will sometimes need to know what answer is expected in order to rule on an objection, the computer will tell you both the attorney's question and the answer that the witness would give if permitted.[12]

If you decide to sustain an objection (i.e., exclude the evidence), push the "s" button on the computer keyboard. If you decide to overrule an objection (i.e., admit the evidence), push the "o" key on the computer keyboard. You will be asked to explain your rulings. Sometimes the computer will print out its own list of possible justifications for your ruling; more often, it will ask you to choose a justification from Display One or Display Two.[13] Display One and Display Two are reproduced at the end of this exercise. Do not refer to Display One or Display Two to answer a question

---

12. Normally, of course, the witness would not answer unless the judge overruled the objection. If necessary, the judge could hold a bench conference beyond the hearing of the jury for the purpose of finding out what answer the examining attorney was seeking.

13. The following is a sample question:

Computer:

Plaintiff's lawyer continues the direct examination of the witness as follows:

Q. After the collision, what happened?

A. The defendant got out of his car and came over to mine.

Q. Did he say anything?

A. Yes.

Q. What was it? OBJECTION

A. He said, "It wasn't my fault—the brakes went out."

Push "s" to sustain or "o" to overrule. Then push "return."

Student:

"s"

Computer:

You have ruled that the testimony is inadmissible. Why must this testimony be excluded?

Look at DISPLAY ONE, push a number key to indicate your answer, and then push "return." If you want to change your mind and want to overrule the objection, push "o".

unless the computer tells you to do so. The displays are not relevant to all of the objections, so reference to them at the wrong time can be misleading.

B. Background Facts About the Lawsuit

This case is a civil action to recover damages for personal injuries sustained when an automobile driven by plaintiff was involved in an intersection collision with an automobile driven by defendant. At a pre-trial conference, you learned that plaintiff will seek to prove defendant ran a red light, drove his car knowing its brakes were bad, drove at an excessive speed, and failed to keep a proper lookout. Defendant will deny these acts of negligence and claim that plaintiff was negligent in ignoring a police officer's warning not to enter the intersection in which the collision occurred.

C. Display One and Display Two

DISPLAY ONE

1. Irrelevant/prejudicial

2. Best evidence rule

3. Leading question

4. Opinion rule

5. Hearsay

6. Privilege

7. No personal knowledge

(Push ''o'' if you have changed your mind and want to overrule the objection.)

DISPLAY TWO

1. The statement falls under the dying declarations exception.

2. The statement falls under the declarations against interest exception.

3. The statement falls under the business records exception.

4. The statement is the admission of a party.

5. The statement falls under the present sense impression exception.

6. The statement is not offered to prove the truth of the matter asserted.

7. The statement does not involve a spoken statement.

8. The statement falls under the present state of mind exception.

9. The statement falls under the excited utterance exception.

(Push ''s'' if you have changed your mind and want to sustain the objection.)

———————

You are now ready to go to the computer to work through CALI CIV 06: Evidence for Procedure Students. Take this exercise with you so you can refer to the rules of evidence discussed and Display One and Display Two (but do not refer to the Displays on any question unless the computer instructs you to do so, since they are not relevant to several of the questions).

*

EXERCISE ELEVEN

Preclusion

I. INTRODUCTION

A. Overview

Preclusion can be one of the most analytically difficult areas of civil procedure. The basic doctrines of preclusion are relatively straightforward, but in the application of concrete situations to those doctrines lies the difficulty. One can easily say the balance of the entire claim is precluded, but what is the full extent of the claim? One can easily say that only an issue necessary to the result is precluded, but when is an issue necessary? This exercise explores these concepts.

The term preclusion is an umbrella for the related series of doctrines that deal with deciding when a court will bar litigation of a claim or issue because that claim or issue has already been decided in a previous action. This entire area of the law comes to us from common law decisions. It is not treated in the Federal Rules of Civil Procedure.

Working with the common law decisions in preclusion is made more difficult because terminology in the area is not uniform. Courts and commentators can and do disagree, for example, on the meaning of "res judicata." The majority use the term to apply only to preclusion of *entire claims*, but the Restatement (Second) of Judgments uses it more broadly to apply also to preclusion of issues. Beyond these disagreements, some courts simply misuse the terms. Accordingly, our first order of business is to explain the meaning of the many terms in this area as they are used in this exercise.

To avoid this dispute over the scope of res judicata, we will use terms of clear meaning: *claim preclusion* and *issue preclusion*. Claim preclusion bars claims; it is claim wide. Issue preclusion bars issues; it is issue wide.

Both require two lawsuits—neither applies to a direct attack on a judgment in the same proceeding. A judgment in the first lawsuit is asserted to preclude all or part of the second lawsuit. Preclusion does not operate within a single lawsuit. A motion to vacate a judgment cannot be defeated by application of preclusion.

Claim preclusion, or what most courts and commentators would call res judicata, provides that a final, valid judgment on the merits will prevent parties (and those in privity with them) from relitigating the entire claim, *i.e.*, all issues that were or should have been litigated, in a second action. Typically, a plaintiff will have split the claim, asserting only part of it in the first suit. The plaintiff may bring a second suit on an additional theory of recovery or for additional damages. Even though never litigated, these additional theories or damages are precluded. Should the plaintiff have won the first suit, the additional matters are sometimes said to have *merged* into the first judgment. Should the plaintiff have lost the first suit, the additional matters might be said to be *barred* by the first judgment. Some might therefore refer to claim preclusion as merger and bar. Claim preclusion covers the entire claim.

Issue preclusion, or what many would call collateral estoppel, provides that a final, valid judgment on the merits will prevent parties (and those in privity with them) from relitigating an issue that was actually litigated and necessary to the prior judgment should the same issue arise in a different claim. For example, A sues B for negligence. A receives a judgment after trial. B then sues A for negligence in the same incident. B will be precluded from relitigating the issue of her negligence (and will therefore lose on summary judgment in a contributory negligence state). Issue preclusion covers only individual issues.

Both of these doctrines will be developed in more detail in the following sections of this introductory essay, but first we mention two doctrines that are related, yet distinct. *Law of the case* works within a single case. It provides that once an issue is decided by an appellate court, the decision will be binding on the lower court on remand; it will also be binding through self-restraint by the appellate court should the case return on a second appeal. *Stare decisis*, or precedent, applies the result in a case to a second, factually-similar case. The doctrine is based in principles of stability and consistency, and attempts to ensure that like-situated litigants are treated alike. While preclusion doctrines require the same parties and are binding even in different jurisdictions, a precedent will be applied to different parties but will be treated as only persuasive rather than binding in different jurisdictions.

B. Policy

Preclusion is supported by policies protecting both private and public interests.

Policies protecting private litigants from being "twice vexed" by the same claim are strong. First and foremost, the prevailing party has a definite interest in the stability of the judgment. This means the party can rely on a decision, such as ownership of property, in planning for the future. Beyond this consideration, litigation is always a burden, financially and emotionally; second litigation of the same matter is an additional burden. Preventing relitigation also serves the end of halting a potential means of harassment of a person.

Public policies served by preclusion are equally or more weighty. Preclusion is a necessity so that the judgment of a court is not a mere empty gesture. The state has a definite interest in the end of litigation, not only to protect its judgments but also to conserve finite judicial resources. This promotes efficiency in a court system, and makes room for the court to hear other parties' disputes. When litigants understand that the court will apply preclusion, the litigation will have an end. Persons other than the parties will also be able to rely on judgments.

At the same time, promotion of these policies comes at a price. The second claim or issue is precluded no matter what its merit. The court may even be convinced that the first judgment was wrong. It is still preclusive. "Res judicata reflects the policy that sometimes it is more important that a judgment be stable than that it be correct."[1]

C. Affirmative Defense

Claim preclusion and issue preclusion are affirmative defenses, enumerated in Federal Rule 8(c).[2] Consequently, they must be

---

1. JOHN H. FRIEDENTHAL, MARY KAY KANE & ARTHUR R. MILLER, CIVIL PROCEDURE § 14.3, at 636 n. 6 (3d ed. 1999).

2. "Res judicata" is listed in FED.R.CIV.P. 8(c). One of your authors uses this term to refer to both claim preclusion and issue preclusion. Your other author uses res judicata to refer to claim preclusion and collateral estoppel to refer to issue preclusion. "Estoppel" is also listed in FED.R.CIV.P. 8(c).

pleaded or they will be lost. The court will not likely raise the defense on its own initiative.[3] A party might also waive its right to assert a preclusion defense by actions explicit or implicit in the first litigation.

II. THE PRECLUSION DOCTRINES

A. Claim Preclusion

Claim preclusion provides that a final, valid judgment on the merits prevents relitigation of the entire claim, including all matters that were or should have been litigated, by the same parties, plus others in privity with them. The constituent elements of claim preclusion are the following:

1) a final, valid judgment on the merits;

2) the same parties, plus others in privity with them; and

3) the entire claim, including all matters that were or should have been litigated.

We briefly examine each of these three elements in turn.

1. Final, Valid Judgment on the Merits

All courts agree that claim preclusion requires a final, valid judgment. To be valid, a judgment must have been reached by a court with proper subject matter and personal jurisdiction. The judgment is valid when the court had jurisdiction, even though the result of the case may be thought erroneous. To be final, the court must have completed "all steps in the adjudication * * * short of execution."[4] Consequently, a judgment is final, for preclusion purposes, even though it remains unexecuted. More importantly, most courts hold a judgment of a trial court final even though the losing party takes an appeal.

Disagreement among courts and commentators is encountered when the element of a final, valid judgment is expanded to include "on the merits."[5] Most would agree that the judgment must have been on the merits to support claim preclusion, although agreement with that proposition is not universal. The problem arises in

3. JOHN H. FRIEDENTHAL, MARY KAY KANE & ARTHUR R. MILLER, CIVIL PROCEDURE § 14.3, at 636 n. 10 (3d ed. 1999).

4. RESTATEMENT (SECOND) OF JUDGMENTS § 13 (1982).

5. *See generally* JOHN H. FRIEDENTHAL, MARY KAY KANE & ARTHUR R. MILLER, CIVIL PROCEDURE § 14.7, at 667–73 (3d ed. 1999).

the context of a pretrial dismissal of a claim. While a dismissal for lack of jurisdiction certainly is not on the merits, a dismissal for failure to state a claim is treated as on the merits by most courts. While almost all courts agree that a default judgment or a consent judgment can support claim preclusion, they disagree whether voluntary dismissal or involuntary dismissal for rule violation can support claim preclusion. For example, is claim preclusion supported by involuntary dismissal under Federal Rule 41(b) for failure to prosecute? Such a result would appear to have nothing to do with the merits, yet the rule itself provides otherwise.[6] Such problems have prompted some commentators to eliminate the requirement that the judgment be "on the merits."[7] Every court and commentator does agree that a judgment reached after trial, summary judgment, or judgment as a matter of law is on the merits.

2. Same Parties and Others in Privity

A judgment will not be preclusive unless the parties in the second suit are identical to, or are in privity with, the parties in the first suit. Any stranger to the first litigation cannot be bound by it. Two suits with different parties may qualify for issue preclusion, but not for claim preclusion. Little difficulty is presented in determining whether the same parties are involved; somewhat more difficulty is presented in determining privity.

The answer historically has been that people were in privity only when they acquired the same interest that had been litigated in the first suit, *i.e.*, the person was a successor in interest to a party. Typically, the person might obtain the interest by inheritance, or by assignment. Over the years, courts have extended the concept of privity into other areas. A person who actually controlled the first suit is in privity with the party, as when an insurance company provides the defense for a policyholder who is the named party. Privity will be found between legal representatives and the

---

6. Fed.R.Civ.P. 41(b) provides as follows:

For failure of the plaintiff to prosecute or to comply with these rules or any order of court, a defendant may move for dismissal of an action or of any claim against the defendant. Unless the court in its order for dismissal otherwise specifies, a dismissal under this subdivision and any dismissal not provided for in this rule, other then a dismissal for lack of jurisdiction, for improper venue, or for failure to join a party under Rule 19, operates as an adjudication upon the merits.

7. RESTATEMENT (SECOND) OF JUDGMENTS § 19, comment a (1982). The drafters of the Restatement allow a court to consider sound judicial administration and fairness in determining whether the second action should be precluded, and allow exceptions to preclusion when the first decision may be thought not on the merits.

people they represent, such as guardian and ward, trustee and beneficiary, and the like. Commercial relationships may also support a finding of privity, such as employer and employee. Some commentators even go so far as to say that privity has been so expansively interpreted that it now has become only a verbal symbol for any type of relationship that a court will use to bind a nonparty to a judgment.

One must keep in mind that, even though expanded over the years, privity remains narrow. Persons similarly situated or of like interests with parties are not in privity with them. All instances of persons in privity involve a legal relationship.

3. Same Claim Barred, Including All Issues That Were or Should Have Been Litigated

The preclusive effect covers the entire claim, including not only issues that were litigated but also all issues that should have been litigated. A plaintiff who sues on only one of two available theories of recovery will be precluded from later proceeding on the other theory. The preclusion might be called merger or bar, depending on whether plaintiff won or lost the first action. The same can be said for a plaintiff who seeks damages in the first action, and sues again for additional damages in a second action. Even though plaintiff legitimately discovers additional, unanticipated damages, he will be precluded.

Since the same claim is precluded, the question becomes when the same claim is presented, or how expansively the claim in the first suit will be defined.

Note first that we use the word "claim" instead of the phrase "cause of action." While the cause of action was important at common law, and remains of importance in the minority of American jurisdictions that are code states, it has been rendered obsolete in federal courts and the states that have patterned their rules after the Federal Rules of Civil Procedure.[8] Accordingly, we refer only to claim.

Having said that, we also note that some states choose to define claims broadly to encourage joinder and discourage multiple litigation. Other states choose to define claims rather narrowly out of concern for the perceived harshness of preclusion.

What test can be used to define the limits of a claim? Some courts look at whether the same evidence would be used in both

8. The drafters of Fed.R.Civ.P. 8(a)(2) intentionally chose not to use the phrase cause of action, instead requiring "a short and plain statement of the claim."

suits. Let us suppose that B is employed by A. A fires B and in the course of the exit interview, becomes agitated and strikes B in the face. B sues A for race discrimination in the firing and the case proceeds to judgment. In a second action, B sues A for breach of contract and battery. The breach of contract theory would be supported by the same evidence as the discrimination theory—the contract, evaluations, etc.—so would be part of the same claim. The battery would be supported by completely different evidence— the striking, etc.—so would be a different claim and preclusion would not apply.

Other courts attempt to determine whether the second action would have the effect of destroying the first judgment. Using the same hypothetical of A firing B, one would expect that neither theory would be part of the same claim: no matter what the result on the discrimination action, a later decision for or against breach of contract or for or against battery would not destroy the first judgment.

Probably the test most commonly used by courts wishing to narrow the effect of claim preclusion asks whether the same primary right was violated by the same primary wrong. This is known as the primary right-primary wrong test. In the above hypothetical of A firing B, each of the separate theories would be a primary right and a primary wrong, so neither of the other two theories would be precluded. Courts adopting this test would likely call the theories causes of action. Similarly, an auto accident might produce both personal injury and property damage to a driver. Under the right-wrong test, the right of not having personal injury inflicted matches the wrong of not inflicting personal injury on another. The property damage is a separate matching of right-wrong, and so a different claim. Or, a theory of restitution would be considered different from a theory of damages for breach of the same contract.

Today, many courts have abandoned these efforts in favor of a transactional test. This test refuses to define a claim through narrow legal theories, and instead determines the scope of a claim by the transaction, *i.e.*, the facts, presented. The transactional approach looks to what a lay person would expect to be included in a single litigation and fits perfectly into the scheme of the Federal Rules of Civil Procedure.[9] The transactional approach produces this rule:

9. Fed.R.Civ.P. 8(a)(2) requires the pleader to assert a "short and plain state-ment of the claim." The drafters of the rule understood claim in a transactional sense, not a legal right-legal wrong sense. *See* Exercise Three I.B–C.

(1) When a valid and final judgment rendered in an action extinguishes the plaintiff's claim pursuant to the rule of merger or bar * * * the claim extinguished includes all rights of the plaintiff to remedies against the defendant with respect to all or any part of the transaction, or series of connected transactions, out of which the action arose.

(2) What factual grouping constitutes a "transaction," and what groupings constitute a "series," are to be determined pragmatically, giving weight to such considerations as whether the facts are related in time, space, origin, or motivation, whether they form a convenient trial unit, and whether their treatment as a unit conforms to the parties' expectations or business understanding or usage.[10]

What matters, therefore, is what theories or damages were sufficiently factually related that they could have been brought in the first suit. Should plaintiff have omitted theories of recovery then available to her, she has split her theories and will be subject to claim preclusion. Should plaintiff have omitted elements of damages that could have been brought in the first suit, she has split her damages, and will be subject to claim preclusion.

This transactional test for a claim produces different results in the hypotheticals considered above. Consider first the firing of B by A. B was fired only once, and was punched during the course of the firing. That is one grouping of facts, only one transaction, and therefore one claim. Plaintiff B cannot split it into two actions, and claim preclusion will apply. The breach of contract and the battery theories will be barred or merged into the first judgment. Similarly, one auto accident produces one claim, including all types of damages flowing from it, so a second action on property damage would be precluded by the first judgment on personal injury. One contract produces one claim, no matter whether the theory is restitution or damages.

The same concept permeates federal practice. A federal case is defined expansively as including "a common nucleus of operative fact." United Mine Workers v. Gibbs, 383 U.S. 715, 725, 86 S.Ct. 1130, 1138, 116 L.Ed.2d 218 (1966). The language is adopted in RESTATEMENT (SECOND) OF JUDGMENTS § 24, comment b (1982). Gibbs was dealing with jurisdiction of a federal court over pendent theories of recovery (now supplemental jurisdiction) and clearly adopted the idea of a lay view of the extent of a transaction when it concluded that when the theories "are such that he would ordinarily be expected to try them all in one judicial proceeding," the court has jurisdiction. This understanding is carried forward into supplemental jurisdiction. 28 U.S.C. § 1367(a) extends federal jurisdiction over "the same case or controversy under Article III of the United States Constitution." See Exercise Six I.B.2.

10. RESTATEMENT (SECOND) OF JUDGMENTS § 24 (1982).

The transactional test gives broad scope to res judicata. It gives full effect to the policies supporting the doctrine.[11]

B. Issue Preclusion

While claim preclusion covers the entire claim, issue preclusion prevents relitigation of an individual issue. Issue preclusion provides that a final valid judgment prevents the same parties, plus others in privity with them, from relitigation in another claim of issues actually litigated and necessarily decided by that judgment, unless unfairness would result.[12] The constituent elements of issue preclusion (collateral estoppel) are the following:

1) a final, valid judgment;

2) the same parties, plus others in privity with them;[13]

3) an identical issue in the new claim;

4) the issue was actually litigated;

5) the issue was necessary to the judgment; and

6) no unfairness would result.

We briefly examine each of these six elements in turn.

1. Final, Valid Judgment on the Merits

As discussed above in II.B.1 for claim preclusion, the first requirement for issue preclusion is a final, valid judgment. The court must have had jurisdiction, and the judgment must be final except for execution or appeal.

The requirement of a judgment to support issue preclusion is both narrower and broader than for claim preclusion, however. It is narrower in that a default judgment or a consent judgment cannot support issue preclusion because neither was litigated. It is broader in that issues estopped need not involve the merits of the case. For example, plaintiff sues defendant in a distant state. Defendant

---

11. See the discussion in I.B, *supra*. Exceptions exist when claim preclusion will not prevent splitting a claim. *See* LARRY L. TEPLY & RALPH U. WHITTEN, CIVIL PROCEDURE 955–58 (3d ed. 2004) and the discussion in II.C, *infra*.

12. "When an issue of fact or law is actually litigated and determined by a valid and final judgment, and the determination is essential to the judgment, the determination is conclusive in a subsequent action between the parties, whether on the same or a different claim." RESTATEMENT (SECOND) OF JUDGMENTS § 27 (1982).

13. The requirement of mutuality has been abandoned in the federal courts and many states, as discussed in II.B.2, *infra*.

303

appears and contests personal jurisdiction. Defendant loses the jurisdictional challenge and does not fight the merits, allowing plaintiff to obtain a default judgment. Plaintiff then sues in defendant's home state to enforce the judgment. This is treated as a different claim: the first claim is on the underlying transaction, and the second is on the foreign judgment. Defendant will be precluded from relitigating the issue of personal jurisdiction because it was actually litigated and decided, even though it did not involve the merits. On the other hand, should defendant have ignored the process from the distant court, it could litigate the issue in the home state because the issue would never have been litigated.

2. Same Parties and Those in Privity

Traditionally, issue preclusion has required the same parties, or privies, in both actions; this requirement was the same as claim preclusion, discussed above in II.A.2. The reason a nonparty cannot be bound by a judgment in which it did not participate is this would violate due process. The reason is more difficult to discover when a party to the first action is to be bound by a nonparty to the first action. Certainly, the bound party had its day in court, so due process is not offended. What then prevents binding a party by a nonparty to the first action?

Historically, the doctrine of *mutuality* was thought to require the identical parties in both suits. The doctrine was based on fairness, *i.e.*, any party seeking to take advantage of a favorable result in the first case must have been at risk of an unfavorable result in the same case. Accordingly, when the first suit was between A and B, the second must also be between A and B; a second suit between A and C would not serve for issue preclusion.

The doctrine of mutuality began to break down in the states in the early 1940s. Today, although some states cling to mutuality, most states and the federal courts have abandoned mutuality in favor of ruling that issue preclusion may bind a person who was a party to the first action, even though the opposing party in that action was different from the opposing party in the second action. The person to be precluded has had a day in court. Of course, due process still prevents a nonparty to the first action from being bound. In a simple example, when the first action is between A and B, and the second action is between A and C, then A may be precluded in the second action. C, as a nonparty to the first action, may not be bound.

Nonmutual issue preclusion can work in two situations: defensive collateral estoppel and offensive collateral estoppel. The policies behind the two are quite different.

Defensive collateral estoppel would apply in this situation. A sues B for patent infringement. Following full litigation, the court adjudges the patent invalid. A then sues C for infringement of the same patent. C pleads collateral estoppel against A on the issue of the validity of the patent. C is using collateral estoppel defensively, to defeat plaintiff's claim.[14] Similarly, a plaintiff who sues the employer (master) for a car accident when the employee (servant) was driving will be collaterally estopped on the issue of the employee's negligence by an unfavorable judgment in the first action. Most courts recognize nonmutual defensive collateral estoppel.

The policies behind the doctrine are strong. Preventing relitigation of an issue litigated and decided against a plaintiff promotes stability of judgments, economy of judicial resources, and prevention of inconsistent results, and also protects the second defendant from harassment by the plaintiff.

A more questionable situation is presented in offensive collateral estoppel, a situation in which defendant loses the first action and a new plaintiff seeks to take advantage of the first judgment against defendant in a second action. The Supreme Court approved use of offensive collateral estoppel in the following situation. D was sued by P for issuing a false proxy statement; D demanded a jury trial. Before the case went to trial, the Securities and Exchange Commission sued D for issuing the same false proxy statement. The SEC action went to a court trial and D lost. P then successfully asserted that judgment as collateral estoppel in the jury action on the issue of the falsity of the proxy statement (even though defendant thereby lost the right to have a jury decide the issue).[15] Note that here the prior judgment was being used offensively by plaintiff instead of defensively by defendant. Offensive collateral estoppel is used most often in a mass tort situation. When the first plaintiff proceeds to a successful judgment, the other plaintiffs in the lawsuit pipeline can and do move for partial summary judgment on the issue of liability.

The policies for offensive collateral estoppel are quite different from defensive collateral estoppel. Rather than encouraging plaintiff to join all parties in the first suit, the incentive is for potential plaintiffs to stay out of the first suit. Should the first plaintiff be successful, another plaintiff can then file suit and assert collateral estoppel. Should the first suit be unsuccessful, another plaintiff can

14. *See* Blonder–Tongue Labs., Inc. v. University of Illinois Found., 402 U.S. 313, 91 S.Ct. 1434, 28 L.Ed.2d 788 (1971).

15. *See* Parklane Hosiery Co. v. Shore, 439 U.S. 322, 99 S.Ct. 645, 58 L.Ed.2d 552 (1979).

then file suit and start from the beginning; the second plaintiff, as a nonparty to the first suit, cannot be collaterally estopped. This different consequence raises fairness concerns.[16] Also, the policy of promoting efficiency to the court system may be undermined instead of encouraged by offensive collateral estoppel, since the incentive is to wait, see, and file additional suits instead of joining the first suit.

Despite these policy differences between nonmutual defensive collateral estoppel and nonmutual offensive collateral estoppel, many courts today allow both.

3. Different Claim; Identical Issue

The claim must be different; otherwise, claim preclusion would apply, since it covers issues that were or should have been litigated. *See* II.A.3, *supra.* A different claim with a common issue would be presented, for example, should a landlord sue on rent due for the month of October and proceed to judgment, then bring a second action for rent for the month of November. Each month is a separate claim.

In many situations, the issue will be identical without question. At other times, the court may decide that the issue is not identical despite its close similarity.[17] For example, a decision on tax treatment in one year may not be the identical issue to tax treatment in another year. Circumstances may also change. The burden of proof may be different in the two actions. Of course, when the burden of proof is more favorable to the party to be estopped, the issue may be found identical: when a defendant is convicted of murdering a relative in a criminal proceeding, that judgment can be used to collaterally estop the same person as plaintiff/beneficiary in a suit against the insurance company for the proceeds of a

---

16. One author has posited the following extreme case. A train wreck injures 50 people. All bring separate actions against the defendant railroad. Should the first plaintiff to reach trial win, then offensive collateral estoppel allows the other forty-nine plaintiffs also to win. On the other hand, should plaintiff one lose, and plaintiff two lose, and so on through plaintiff twenty-five losing, when plaintiff twenty-six wins, do plaintiffs twenty-seven through fifty win by collateral estoppel? *See* Brainerd Currie, *Mutuality of Collateral Estoppel: Limits of the Bernhard Doctrine,* 9 Stan. L. Rev. 281, 289 (1957). We believe the answer is that no collateral estoppel is possible in such a situation as soon as plaintiff number one loses; the other 49 plaintiffs must drive their own engines. At the same time, should plaintiff number one win, then the other 49 win. That result may appear unfair to defendant, but defendant has had its day in court on the issue of liability, and there is no reason to believe that the result in the other cases would be different.

17. *See generally* John H. Friedenthal, Mary Kay Kane & Arthur R. Miller, Civil Procedure § 14.10 (3d ed. 1999).

policy on the life of the deceased. Note in this example there is no mutuality of the parties, yet defensive collateral estoppel would be applied.

4. Issue Must Have Been Actually Litigated

Collateral estoppel will apply only to an issue that actually was litigated in the first action. That means, by definition, dispositions such as default judgments, consent judgments, and voluntary dismissals cannot qualify for collateral estoppel. Similarly, issues that may appear in the final judgment, but which were not the subject of contest in the action, will not support collateral estoppel. Should a defendant admit an issue in the answer, or even fail to contest it at trial, the issue would not have been litigated. On the other hand, a judgment by summary judgment or by judgment as a matter of law may qualify for collateral estoppel should the motion have been contested.

When an issue was not actually litigated, the policy of finality of judgments will be outweighed by the policies of fairness and decision on the merits. A party may not litigate an issue in the first action for various reasons, including 1) small amount in controversy, 2) inconvenient forum, or 3) poor timing for the litigation.[18]

Whether an issue was litigated may be difficult to determine. The decision may require looking at the record of the first action. Should the record be unclear, the court will probably find the issue was not litigated. This situation would arise often when the first action was determined by a general verdict. For example, A sued B for breach of contract and the defense pleaded was a denial and also a release. The general verdict was for B, the defendant. Was only the breach litigated, or was only the affirmative defense litigated, or were both litigated? Extrinsic evidence may provide the answer, but extrinsic evidence cannot contradict the record.

5. Necessary

Collateral estoppel will not be applied unless the decision on the issue in the first action was necessary, *i.e.*, essential, to the result. For example, P sues D for negligence and D pleads contributory negligence. The judgment is for D on a finding of no negligence. A further finding of contributory negligence against P is not necessary to the result and accordingly is not preclusive. This requirement is rooted in fairness, which is that a party should be

18. LARRY L. TEPLY & RALPH U. WHITTEN, CIVIL PROCEDURE 965 (3d ed. 2004).

estopped only on essential issues from the first action because the party may not have made a full effort on nonessential issues. Further, the court may not have considered such nonessential issues as closely as it did the necessary issues, and no appellate review was likely pursued.

The party who prevailed may have lost some of the issues. These issues cannot be used to estop the party in a second action because necessarily they were not essential to the outcome of the case. Recall the previous hypothetical of A suing B for breach of contract with a denial and an affirmative defense of release. Should the jury find by special verdict that the contract was valid but that B had been released, B wins. The issue of the validity of the contract cannot be the basis of preclusion against B in a second action because B prevailed in the first.

Alternative findings in the first action pose a problem. Again, in the previous hypothetical in which A sued B on a contract and B pleaded an affirmative defense of release, should A prevail on a general verdict, the judgment necessarily was against B on both the contract and the release. Both would be collaterally estopped in a second action. On the other hand, should B prevail on the general verdict, one is not clear whether the contract or the release, or both, afforded the basis for the decision. The situation may be clarified should the court have employed a special verdict; assuming the jury specially found for B on both the contract and the release, as alternative findings both may be collaterally estopped in a second action.[19]

Some of the older opinions distinguish between mediate facts and ultimate facts in whether collateral estoppel should apply. An ultimate fact was one on which the action was based, such as an element of the case; a mediate fact was a mere evidentiary one from which an ultimate fact could be inferred. Ultimate facts were appropriate for collateral estoppel; mere mediate facts were not. Assume D is driving a car that strikes P1, and a half-hour later in a second accident strikes P2. P1 sues for negligence and by special verdict the jury finds D had been drunk and was negligent. In the action by P2, no preclusive effect will be given to the finding D was drunk as that was only an evidentiary fact allowing an inference to the ultimate fact that D did not use due care. This terminology is outdated. Today's approach looks to whether a fact was necessary to the result, not to how the fact fits into the hierarchy of the inferential structure of the elements of the case.

---

19. This is the majority rule, but some courts and the Restatement disagree, on the ground that this will encourage appeals. *See* RESTATEMENT (SECOND) OF JUDGMENTS § 27 (1982).

6. Fairness

Even when all of the five above tests for collateral estoppel are met, the court may still refuse to apply the doctrine should the result appear to be unfair because of an inadequate "opportunity or incentive to obtain a full and fair adjudication in the initial action."[20] Some examples of situations in which a court has refused issue preclusion because of unfairness include inadequate representation in the first action, small amount in controversy in the first action, apparent compromise by the jury in the first action, and unforeseeability of additional action(s).

Interestingly, one assertion of unfairness might be that collaterally estopping a party in a second action would deprive it of the right to jury trial. This type of unfairness did not prevent the Supreme Court from approving use of offensive collateral estoppel.[21]

C. Exceptions to Preclusion

Situations exist in which the elements of one of the preclusion doctrines fit, yet the court will refuse to apply the doctrine. While we do not develop these situations in any depth as they are beyond the scope of this brief note, they include when preclusion would defeat a strong governmental policy, when preclusion was waived by a party in the first action, when the law has changed in the interim, and when the jurisdictional limitations of the first court prevented the full claim from being litigated. This is especially true when both the federal courts and state courts are involved.[22]

III. QUESTIONS ON PRECLUSION

Instructions. The questions are on the left-hand page, and the answers are on the right-hand page. Cover the right-hand page, write your answers to the questions in the spaces provided, and compare your answers to the suggested answers on the facing page. P represents plaintiff, and D represents defendant.

20. RESTATEMENT (SECOND) OF JUDGMENTS § 28(5)(c).

21. Parklane Hosiery Co. v. Shore, 439 U.S. 322, 99 S.Ct. 645, 58 L.Ed.2d 552 (1979).

22. *See generally* LARRY L. TEPLY & RALPH U. WHITTEN, CIVIL PROCEDURE 972–78 (3d ed. 2004).

A. Claim Preclusion

Q–1. Part 1. P sues D for damages in construction of a house, asserting theories of breach of warranty and negligence. D moves to dismiss for lack of personal jurisdiction. The motion is granted, and the case is dismissed. P later sues D using the identical complaint in another state's court. D pleads res judicata. Does claim preclusion apply?

Your answer _____

Part 2. Instead, the motion to dismiss for lack of personal jurisdiction is denied. Following jury trial, P obtains a judgment. Six months later, D moves to vacate the judgment on the ground of fraud. P pleads res judicata. Does claim preclusion apply?

Your answer _____

Part 3. The motion to dismiss for lack of personal jurisdiction is denied. Following jury trial, P obtains a judgment. D appeals. While the appeal is pending, P files a second action for damages from construction of the house, alleging a theory of strict liability. D pleads res judicata. Does claim preclusion apply?

Your answer _____

Q–2. Part 1. P, purchaser of shares of D Corp. pursuant to a prospectus issued by the corporation, sues on the ground that the prospectus contains a false statement. P obtains a final judgment of damages for $9,500; the judgment is satisfied. P2, a neighbor of P, who purchased shares of D Corp. pursuant to the same prospectus, sues on the ground that the prospectus contains the same false statement. P2 pleads the first judgment as res judicata. Does claim preclusion apply?

Your answer _____

Part 2. P3, a nephew of P, obtains the shares from P by inheritance. Dissatisfied with the amount of the judgment in the first case of P v. D Corp., and being a nonparty to that case, P3 sues D Corp. on the ground that the prospectus contained a false statement. Does res judicata apply?

Your answer _____

Answer to Q–1. Part 1. No. Claim preclusion requires a final, valid judgment. While some courts and commentators differ on whether the judgment must be on the merits, all would agree that a dismissal for lack of jurisdiction cannot support res judicata.

Part 2. No. This is a direct attack on a judgment within the same action. Res judicata can apply only in a second action.

Part 3. Yes. This is a situation in which P has split theories of recovery, and res judicata will apply. The pendency of an appeal does not affect the finality of the trial court's judgment.

This answer is based on a transactional definition of claim. See II.A.3, *supra*. A primary right-primary wrong definition would likely produce the opposite result.

Answer to Q–2. Part 1. No. Claim preclusion requires the same parties, or those in privity with those parties, in both actions. In this hypothetical, the first action is P v. D Corp. and the second action is P2 v. D Corp. The common party in both suits is D Corp. This may allow use of collateral estoppel against D Corp., in a state that has abandoned the requirement of mutuality, but claim preclusion still strictly requires parties or those in privity with them in both suits.

Similarly, the judgment against D Corp. in the first action may support stare decisis, or precedent, in the second action, but this is not res judicata.

Part 2. Yes. The nephew obtained the shares by inheritance from P. Consequently, P3 is in privity with P. Since P was a party to the first action, P's privies are also bound by res judicata. This is a situation in which P has split damages.

Q–3. P sues D in federal court for age discrimination because D terminated her employment. Following a jury trial and verdict, judgment is entered for D. P later files action against D in state court for breach of employment contract and defamation. D pleads the affirmative defense of res judicata. Does claim preclusion apply?

Your answer _____

Q–4. P sues D for punching him in the nose. P's proof on damages is not entirely satisfactory, and the jury awards only $2000. Several months later, P stumbles on additional evidence that supports a new, substantial element of damages. P sues D for the additional damages. Does res judicata apply?

Your answer _____

Answer to Q–3. Yes. Res judicata is claim wide, precluding all matters of fact and law that were or should have been litigated. P was terminated once: she has one claim, which arose in a single transaction. She must assert all her theories of recovery in the same action, instead of splitting her theories as she did in this hypothetical. Both of the state law theories could have been pleaded in separate counts in the federal action (Fed.R.Civ.P. 10(b)), and supplemental jurisdiction (28 U.S.C. § 1367) would allow the federal court to hear the state law theories as well as the federal law theory. *See* Exercise Six I.B. P's other theories are barred by the unfavorable result in the first action.

P might argue that the defamation theory is a separate transaction. If the defamation occurred at the time of termination, clearly there is a single transaction. If the defamation occurred later, as in an unfavorable job reference, P might argue the separation in time makes this a separate transaction, and so a separate claim. We would answer that this is one common nucleus of facts, and a lay person would expect all of it to be tried together. It is a single transaction, or series of transactions. Therefore, it is a single claim. *See* RESTATEMENT (SECOND) OF JUDGMENTS § 24(2) (1982), reproduced in II.A.3, *supra*.

Note that the converse court situation might save P's unpleaded theory. Should the first action have been brought in state court, with P failing to plead a federal law theory, that theory might be outside the operation of res judicata when the federal theory could not have been brought in state court. This would apply when the federal theory involved exclusive federal jurisdiction, not concurrent jurisdiction, as in this hypothetical.

This answer is based on a transactional definition of claim. See II.A.3, *supra*. A primary right-primary wrong definition would likely produce the opposite result.

Answer to Q–4. Yes. P has split his damages, as well as his nose. Claim preclusion includes all matters of fact and law that were or should have been litigated. Certainly, all elements of damages arising out of a single tort are included, and are merged into the favorable result in the first action. This answer is the same under both the transactional approach and the primary right-primary wrong approach since both cases involve injury to the person.

P may be able to obtain some relief by moving to vacate the first judgment on the ground of newly discovered evidence, but that would be a direct attack on the first judgment, and is not relevant to a discussion of res judicata.

B. Issue Preclusion

Q–5. John and Mary Homeowners signed a contract with AAA Builders to construct their dream home. When the Homeowners moved in, they discovered shoddy work in several rooms and sued AAA Builders for breach of warranty. The Homeowners obtained a judgment. Some time later, AAA Builders sold its business to BBB Builders. BBB studied the books and discovered that not all of the payments from Homeowners had been collected. BBB Builders sued Homeowners to collect the payments. Defendant Homeowners defended on the ground of shoddy work. Does collateral estoppel apply on the issue of the quality of the work?

Your answer _____

Q–6. P Corp. is in the business of selling freezers and frozen meat. It requires buyers to sign a preprinted, standard form contract. D signs a contract, but when the quality of the meat is unsatisfactory, refuses to pay. P Corp. sues on the contract, and D defends that the interest rate on the contract is usurious under state law. The jury verdict is for D and judgment is entered. P Corp. later sues D2, another buyer, on the same standard form contract. D2 pleads that the interest rate is usurious and moves for summary judgment on the grounds of collateral estoppel. Does collateral estoppel apply?

Your answer _____

Answer to Q–5. Yes. There is a final, valid judgment. The parties are the same in both actions (BBB is in privity with AAA as the purchaser of the business). The claim is different, but the issue of the quality of the work is identical, was actually litigated, and was necessary to the result in the first action. Issue preclusion/collateral estoppel will apply.

Homeowners might also be able to defend on the ground that BBB Builders's predecessor in interest AAA Builders failed to plead a compulsory counterclaim (assuming the action was brought in a federal court or a state that has compulsory counterclaims), but that is not a collateral estoppel issue.

Answer to Q–6. Yes. The hypothetical presents a different claim (P Corp. v. D2 instead of P Corp. v. D) with an identical issue (the usurious rate) that was actually litigated and necessary to the first judgment. In those states that have abandoned mutuality, collateral estoppel will be applied because the party to be estopped, P Corp., was a party to the first action and had its day in court. This is defensive collateral estoppel.

The answer would be different in states that retain the doctrine of mutuality, since the parties in the two suits are not the same, and there is no privity between the two defendants, even though they have similar interests. Also, had the first judgment gone against D, the result could not be used against D2, since D2 was not a party to the first action.

Q–7. Dumper, Inc. Is in the waste disposal business. Two lakefront property owners on Lake Wishuwerhere sue Dumper, Inc. for disposing of waste in their lake in violation of federal and state waste disposal statutes and regulations. The defense is that no dumping occurred. Following trial to the court, the judge finds that the dumping did occur and orders judgment for plaintiffs. Hearing of this result, the remaining 84 homeowners on the lake join together to file suit against Dumper, Inc. for damages for the unlawful dumping. Does collateral estoppel apply?

Your answer _____

Q–8. Part 1. Ten plaintiffs, join permissively to sue D University for gender discrimination in its promotion policies. Following extensive negotiation, the university allows a consent judgment to be entered against it. Additional plaintiffs then bring suit against the university for the same promotion policies, and move for partial summary judgment on the issue of discrimination, asserting issue preclusion. Does issue preclusion/collateral estoppel apply?

Your answer _____

Part 2. Same facts as part 1, except D University answers denying any discrimination, and the case goes to trial. D University concedes the issue following presentation of plaintiffs' case in chief. Does collateral estoppel apply?

Your answer _____

Part 3. Same facts as in part 1, except D University contests the issue throughout trial, and the jury verdict is for plaintiffs. Does collateral estoppel apply?

Your answer _____

Answer to Q–7. Yes. Dumper, Inc. defended the common issue of unlawful dumping and lost. The issue in these different claims was actually litigated and necessary to the result. No reason exists to believe that a court would reach a different result in another litigation. Accordingly, Dumper, Inc. will be collaterally estopped from denying the unlawful dumping even though no mutuality exists. This is offensive collateral estoppel.

Defendant might argue that unfairness would result because the first action involved only two homeowners and the second involves 84. This argument likely would not prevent collateral estoppel because the defendant could easily have foreseen that other owners would also seek to enforce their claims and would have had every incentive to defend the first action vigorously.

Defendant might also argue that the second group of owners should not be allowed to lie in the weeds to await the outcome of the first action and then take advantage of a favorable result. Although a few courts have hinted of requiring such potential additional plaintiffs to join or intervene in the first action, the courts have not insisted on mandatory joinder or intervention.

Answer to Q–8, parts 1–3. Collateral estoppel requires that the issue have been actually litigated. The facts in parts 1 and 2 show the issue was not fully litigated, so no collateral estoppel can apply in the second action. In part 3, the issue was fully litigated, so collateral estoppel applies.

Q–9. P sued D Cabco for personal injuries and property damage arising when one of Cabco's taxicabs collided with P's car. Cabco defended on two grounds: 1) the driver was an independent contractor instead of an agent, so no negligence could be imputed to it, and 2) the driver was not negligent. By special verdict, the jury found that the driver was an agent, but was not negligent, so judgment was entered for D Cabco. A second suit had been filed before the first action went to trial; it involves a collision between the cab of the same driver and P2. P2 now argues that collateral estoppel prevents D Cabco from denying the agency of the driver. Does collateral estoppel apply?

Your answer ⎯⎯⎯⎯⎯

Q–10. P purchased a ten-year-old used car "as is" from Dealer for $995. A week later, the radio stopped working and P paid $125. to fix it. He sued Dealer in small claims court for the $125., alleging that Dealer should have a 30–day implied warranty on every car it sells. Dealer denied any implied warranty and sent its sales manager to court without a lawyer to defend the action. P won the $125. A year later, P2 purchased a used car "as is" from Dealer for $19,995, and later sued Dealer for $12,000 for various defects in the car on a theory of 30–day implied warranty. Does collateral estoppel apply?

Your answer ⎯⎯⎯⎯⎯

Answer to Q–9. No. The issue of the agency of the cab driver was not necessary or essential to the result in the first action. D Cabco won, so issues found against it by definition cannot have been necessary to the result. Collateral estoppel cannot apply.

Answer to Q–10. Maybe. The elements of collateral estoppel are satisfied in this hypothetical: a final, valid judgment; the same party to be estopped (offensive collateral estoppel); a common issue in the two actions on different claims; issue actually litigated; issue necessary to the result. A court will, however, refuse to apply collateral estoppel when unfairness would result.

Defendant Dealer will argue that the first action involved such a small amount that it had insufficient incentive to litigate fully—it could not have foreseen the substantial consequences in later actions. Also, it was not represented by an attorney in the first action; granted, this was its own choice, but was again a function of the small amount involved.

P would argue that the small amount in the first action does not control because Dealer should have realized that the result could have consequences beyond the individual action. Even though there is disagreement, many jurisdictions recognize small claims judgments can support preclusion. Similarly, the absence of legal representation in the first action was a decision by Dealer.

Given the small amount and the absence of legal representation, fairness may prevent application of collateral estoppel in this hypothetical, but the result is not clear.

IV. COMPUTER EXERCISE: CALI CIV 17

You are now ready for further work in the preclusion doctrines in CALI CIV 17: Preclusion. The exercise is self-contained, so you will not need to take this book with you.

†